THE SOUND OF SILENCE

THE SOUND OF SILENCE

THE SELECTED TEACHINGS OF
AJAHN SUMEDHO

Preface and introduction
by Ajahn Amaro

Wisdom Publications
199 Elm Street
Somerville MA 02144 USA
www.wisdompubs.org

Library of Congress Cataloging-in-Publication Data
Sumedho, Ajahn.
  The sound of silence : the selected teachings of Ajahn Sumedho / Ajahn Sumedho ; preface
and introduction by Ajahn Amaro.
    p. cm.
  Includes index.
  ISBN 0-86171-515-2 (pbk. : alk. paper)
  1. Spiritual life—Buddhism. 2. Meditation—Buddhism. I. Title.
  BQ5675.S86 2007
  294.3'444—dc22

                              2007014699

ISBN 978-0-86171-515-2   ebook ISBN 978-0-86171-958-7
21 20 19 18
6 5 4

Cover design by Rick Snizik. Interior design by Gopa&Ted2, Inc. Set in Diacritical Bembo
11.75/16.5. Drawings by Sister Cittapālā. Photo by Ajahn Amaro.

Wisdom Publications' books are printed on acid-free paper and meet the guidelines
for permanence and durability of the Production Guidelines for Book Longevity of
the Council on Library Resources.

♻ This book was produced with environmental mindfulness.
For more information, please visit wisdompubs.org/wisdom-environment.

Printed in the United States of America

Please visit fscus.org.

Awareness is your refuge:

Awareness of the changingness of feelings,

of attitudes, of moods, of material change

and emotional change:

Stay with that, because it's a refuge that is

indestructible.

It's not something that changes.

It's a refuge you can trust in.

This refuge is not something that you create.

It's not a creation. It's not an ideal.

It's very practical and very simple, but

easily overlooked or not noticed.

When you're mindful,

you're beginning to notice,

it's like this.

Ajahn Sumedho

CONTENTS

It is spring in southern England. Hertfordshire is blooming. May blos-
soms deck the hedgerows. Fifty people, including a few nuns and monks,
multihued and peacefully intent, pace to and fro over rain-speckled grass.

Now it's evening in the long, narrow central building—long since con-
verted from a school dormitory to be the retreat center meditation hall.
Ajahn Sumedho regales the group with tales of his faux pas as a novice,
nearly forty years ago in Thailand. Heartfelt laughter billows through the
fragile windowpanes, into the cooling night.

Amid dawn mist, shawl-wrapped, silent friends share a warming mug of tea
on the benches outside the kitchen—it's almost time for the morning chant-
ing. It's a snowy winter evening, three nuns and one of their novices scurry
along the pathway to the temple, bundled up against the wind and the cold.

SUCH VIGNETTES ABOUND at Amarāvatī during the retreats
that are held there. Some of these events are structured for
the public, like the one that took place during nine days in
May 2005; others are held more for the monastic community, and
are ten times as long, such as that of the winter of 2001.

This book is a revised and expanded edition of *Intuitive*
Awareness—the original having comprised a collection of eleven

talks, given by Ajahn Sumedho, during that winter retreat of '01. In this present edition these have been combined with and embellished by sixteen further talks, drawn from the spring session of '05. (Dates of the talks are listed in the appendix.)

Each of these two sets of times and occasions has its own ambience and style, as should be expected. The intention of bringing them together in this book, however, is that they should inform and complement each other—as if in one gallery were arranged an assortment of Monet's many paintings of haystacks, progressing through their multitudinous lights and seasons, while in the neighboring gallery there hung a collection of his equally numerous waterlily compositions.

Just as a visitor to the exhibition would be treated to these two domains of the artist's explorations, so too the reader here is treated to these two modes of Ajahn Sumedho's expositions—Dhamma teachings for monastics and for the lay Buddhist community—and is invited to move back and forth easefully between these different realms.

Needless to say these two styles of teaching have a great deal in common, as in the analogy of Monet's lily and haystack paintings. However, they also differ in tone and content, and, necessarily, different elements will be meaningful and useful to different people. For example, the additional talks presented here include two on the subject of mindfulness of the body, so very helpful in assisting us to slow down and to be grounded in the present, in a world grown increasingly frenzied; they also carry an increased emphasis on the precarious nature of reliance on conceptual thought (a tendency so endemic to the secular world) in the talks "Views and Opinions" and "Thinking and Habits."

The wisdom teachings contained here are many and various; furthermore, it is the hope of the editors that, in this rich variety, there has been a broad enough range encompassed that as many dispositions as possible have been served by the insights expounded here.

The printed word is not the real thing: "awareness" (and all the other words contained here) is simply a complex of black symbolic marks fixed upon the white field of a page, it is not the quality of awareness itself. Nevertheless, what the Buddha referred to as "the miracle of instruction" (*anusāsani-pāṭihāriya*) is comprised of the fact that, when a receptive and well-primed heart hears or reads the Dhamma, a genuine transformation, a liberation, an awakening of that heart can be catalyzed. This is truly a miracle, and as the Buddha also said, of all types of miracle this one is supreme.

Therefore, may the hearts of all who have had the good fortune to encounter the wisdom contained in this small book be encouraged, prompted to awaken in this way and swiftly realize the end of all suffering.

Ajahn Amaro
Abhayagiri Monastery
California

INTRODUCTION
BY AJAHN AMARO

Twenty years ago, in 1984, the germinal monastic community of the newly opened Amarāvatī Buddhist Centre settled into a cluster of barrack-like buildings on a windy hilltop in Hertfordshire. The name of the new monastery (meaning "The Deathless Realm") was chosen both as a resonance of the ancient Buddhist city in Andhra Pradesh, in southern India, and as a counteractive force to the "Mutually Assured Destruction" of the nuclear arms race, then gleefully being pursued by Ronald Reagan, Margaret Thatcher, and the Soviet Union.

The meditation space that we used at that time was a former school gymnasium and assembly hall. The windows were cracked, patched with plastic and tape, drafty or missing completely. Gym markings crisscrossed the cold wooden floor. A large golden Buddha image sat on the old school stage, spotlit and surrounded by filmy blue curtains that we had hung to beautify the shrine and suggest the quality of infinite space.

Since 1981, when the community was largely based at Citta-viveka Monastery, in Chithurst, West Sussex, it had been our custom to set aside the midwinter months, after the New Year, to be a time of communal retreat. At that time of year the English weather does not allow much in the way of building work to go on, visitors are few and the days are short and dark—it is thus a perfect situation to use for turning the attention inward and taking time to cultivate formal meditation practice in a very thorough way.

Amarāvatī was opened in 1984 to provide living space for the burgeoning monastic community (group photos of the time show twenty or more eight precept postulants and forty nuns and monks) and a place where we could hold retreats for the public. So when this move was made it provided an even more expansive situation for the winter retreats, and for Ajahn Sumedho to continue to guide the community in his inimitably comprehensive and inspiring way.

The winters of 1984, '85, and '86 were spectacularly icy. Winds howled down from Siberia, seemingly uninterrupted by any solid object until they bit into our bones. It was not uncommon to be wearing six or seven layers of clothing through the day and then to climb into our sleeping bags at night still wearing most of them. We sat bundled in thick robes and blankets for meditation and to listen to instructional talks. The air was icy but vibrant, as there was a powerful and pervasive sense of community spirit among us.

Sometimes in those days it seemed that the main source of energy in the whole system, and certainly what our hearts were warmed and guided by, was Ajahn Sumedho's apparently limitless capacity to expound on the Dhamma, especially during the winter retreats. Naturally enough in that situation a lot of guidance was needed—the majority of us were fairly new to meditation and monastic training and we needed all the help we could get, particularly within a routine of noble silence and walking and sitting meditation all day. Thus Ajahn Sumedho gave extensive instruction, often two or three times a day. There would be "morning reflections" during the first sitting of the day before dawn, often more reflections after the breakfast of gruel and tea, sometimes questions and answers at afternoon teatime, and finally a formal Dhamma talk in the evening.

From those early icy times up until the present, in 2006, Ajahn Sumedho has continued to guide the monastic community at Amarāvatī. Every winter he has explored and expounded on the Dhamma, and frequently recordings have been made of his teachings.

Even though those days now seem long gone, and much has changed, there are some elements that have remained stable to the present day, like a constantly returning phrase or rhythm in a musical piece or, more accurately, like the defining style of a master painter that instantly tells you this is a Monet, that is a Van Gogh.

Now at Amarāvatī the site in the old Dhamma hall-gymnasium is occupied by the Temple, the new meditation hall constructed in stages through the 1990s. The orientation is slightly different—the building now faces east rather than north—and it is a soaring pyramidal structure rather than a utilitarian rectangular box. The great, light, open space within is punctuated by a broad ring of solid oak pillars; it is so silent and still it seems to stop the minds of those who visit. The floor is a blanket of warm white rock, and a barnlike lattice of thick trusses and beams laces the high ceiling and the walls. But the trees across the courtyard remain, now a little taller and fuller, and the brown weatherboarding on the remaining older buildings is edged by frost in the winter morning light, just as before.

In the same way that some elements of the buildings and the members of the community have changed and some have continued, the winter retreat teachings Ajahn Sumedho has given in recent years have similarly matured and transformed. They are still built upon a foundation of many classic elements of Buddhism—the Four Noble Truths, reflections on the arising and ceasing of the five *khandhas,* teachings on contemplation of mind *(cittānupassanā)*—but the manner of exposition of these and other key elements, as well as his development of particular skillful means *(upāya),* has evolved and expanded during these last twenty years. Thus, even though the talks gathered in this book can, in some respects, happily stand on their own, it might also be helpful to bear in mind that they exist within a context.

First of all, these talks were given to experienced monastics and a few well-seasoned laypeople. Many who were listening knew Ajahn Sumedho's favorite themes very well, and he knew that they knew them well; therefore often explanatory material was left unsaid and much knowledge was assumed. Just as a musician might play a few notes to evoke a familiar piece and know of their audience: "They can fill in the rest, they know that old theme!" Or a painter might use a trademark motif thinking: "Pop in that bowler hat again, they know all the other places it appeared." Similarly here, Ajahn Sumedho is often exploring, describing, and extemporizing on very familiar themes. So if the reader occasionally feels a lack of explanation, or if the meaning escapes, the encouragement is to let the music, the balance of tones and colors, tide you over.

Secondly, the aim of the editors in compiling this book has been explicitly to maintain the style and spirit of the spoken word. Dhamma talks have strong nonverbal elements—the mood in the room, the energetic exchanges between the speaker and the listeners, the season, the hour of the day or night, all that has gone before within the group—so it is wiser to treat a collection of talks such as this as if exploring an art gallery, or listening to a musical piece, rather than as a systematic explanation of a fixed subject. As Ajahn Sumedho himself commented, "The book is meant to be suggestions of ways to investigate conscious experience. It's not meant to be a didactic treatise on Pāli Buddhism."

So, as you make your way through these pages and you encounter "Intuitive Awareness," "The End of Suffering Is Now," "The Sound of Silence," and all the others, the suggestion is to let them be received into the heart, to allow them to resonate, and to let the intuitions and guidance that they spark ripen as they will. Just as, when we progress through an art gallery we don't think, "What's the exact information that this painting is imparting to me?"

Thirdly, ever since the time of the Buddha, his disciples have evinced a wide range of teaching styles and favorite themes when expounding the Dhamma. And this same variety is a striking characteristic of what is known today as the Thai forest tradition—the largely nonacademic, meditation-centered, rural monastic communities that model their way of practice on the discipline and lifestyle of the Buddha and his earliest monastic disciples.

Over time an individual teacher will tend to take a particular Dhamma theme or meditation technique and spend years, sometimes decades, exploring and expanding on that topic. For example, Luang Por Sim was noted for his emphasis on death contemplations; Ajahn Buddhadāsa spent several years discoursing on *idappaccayatā*—the law of conditionality; Ajahn Toon Khippapañño vigorously insists the Path should be represented as *paññā, sīla, samādhi,* and emphatically not as *sīla, samādhi, paññā;* Ajahn Fun was known for his infinite extrapolations on the word *"Buddho"*—as a concentration technique, an investigation of awareness or as a devotional practice; Luang Pu Dun was known for his teachings on *"Citta* (the heart) is Buddha"; and Ajahn Chah was fond of offering people conundrums like "If you can't go forward, you can't go back, and you can't stand still—where can you go?" or "Have you ever seen still, flowing water?"

Over time it is quite usual for such experienced teachers to develop not only their favorite themes but also to cultivate their own, often idiosyncratic usage of scriptural terms. For example, Ajahn Mahā Boowa's usage of the term "eternal citta," or Ajahn Toon's insistence on the radical difference between *dassanañāṇa* (vision and knowledge) and *ñāṇadassana* (knowledge and vision). In this light it might be useful to take a look at some of the terms Ajahn Sumedho uses frequently in this collection—particularly "the sound of silence," "intuitive awareness," and "consciousness"— which have taken on such distinctive meanings over the years.

The first of these, "the sound of silence," is described in the talk with that title. Since it is not a meditation method found in classical Theravāda handbooks, it might be helpful to provide a little background about how Ajahn Sumedho came to develop it and to refer to some of the other spiritual traditions that use it as part of a meditation practice.

It was in the winter retreat of January 1981, at Chithurst Monastery, that Ajahn Sumedho first started to teach this method to the monastic community. He said that he had begun to notice a high-pitched, ringing tone when he left Thailand in 1977 and spent his first winter in England, in the Hampstead Buddhist *Vihāra*. He pointed out that, as Thailand was such a noisy country, particularly amidst the crickets and cicadas in the forest at night (when one does most formal meditation practice), he had not noticed this inner sound before. But when he came to London, despite being a large metropolis, he found that it became very quiet late at night, especially when the air was muffled by the presence of a blanket of snow.

In the silence of those nights he began to perceive the ever-present inner sound, seemingly beginningless and endless, and he soon found that he was able to discern it throughout the day and in many circumstances, whether quiet or busy. He also realized that he had indeed noticed it once before in his life, when he had been on shore leave from the U.S. Navy in the late '50s and, during a walk in the hills, his mind had opened into a state of extreme clarity. He remembered that as a wonderfully pure and peaceful state, and he recalled that the sound had been very loud then. So those positive associations encouraged him to experiment and see if it might be a useful meditation object. It also seemed to be an ideal symbol, in the conditioned world of the senses, of those qualities of mind that transcend the sense realm: not subject to personal will, ever present but only noticed if attended to; apparently beginningless and endless, formless to some degree, and spatially unlocated.

When he first taught this method to the Sangha at Chithurst that winter, he referred to it as "the sound of silence" and the name stuck. Later, as he began to teach the method on retreats for the lay community, he began to hear about its use from people experienced in Hindu and Sikh meditation practices. In these traditions, he found out, this concentration on the inner sound was known as *nāda yoga,* or "the yoga of inner light and sound." It also turned out that books had been written on the subject, commentaries in English as well as ancient scriptural treatises, notably *The Way of Inner Vigilance* by Salim Michaël (published by Signet). In 1991, when Ajahn Sumedho taught the sound of silence as a method on a retreat at a Chinese monastery in the United States, one of the participants was moved to comment, "I think you have stumbled on the *Shūrangama samādhi.* There is a meditation on hearing that is described in that sūtra, and the practice you have been teaching us seems to match it perfectly."

Seeing that it was a practice that was very accessible to many people, and as his own explorations of it deepened over the years, Ajahn Sumedho has continued to develop it as a central method of meditation, ranking alongside such classical forms of practice as, "mindfulness of breathing" and "investigation of the body." The Buddha's encouragement for his students was to use skillful means that are effective in freeing the heart. Since this form of meditation seems to be very supportive for that, despite not being included in lists of meditation practices in the Pāli Canon or anthologies such as the *Visuddhimagga*, it seems wholly appropriate to give it its due. For surely it is the freedom of the heart that is the purpose of all the practices—and that freedom is the final arbiter of what is useful and therefore good.

A second term that Ajahn Sumedho has given particular meaning to is "intuitive awareness." As with the "sound of silence" there are many places in the talks contained here, particularly in the chapter "Intuitive Awareness" itself, where he elucidates the ways in which he is using this term. However, it might be helpful here to reflect a little on its usage, just to clarify it in relation to other ways of employing the same words.

In this book the phrase "intuitive awareness" is a translation of *sati-sampajañña*. The quality of sati-sampajañña is part of a continuum of three elements. The first element is *sati*, the raw, mindful cognizance of an object. The second element being "satisampajañña," referring to the mindful, intuitive awareness of an object within its context; the final element is *"sati-paññā"*—usually translated as "mindfulness and wisdom"—which refers to the appreciation of an object in respect to its essential nature as transitory, unsatisfactory, and not-self. Ajahn Chah used to characterize the relationship between these three elements as being like the hand, arm, and body: sati is that which picks things up, sampajañña is like the arm that enables the hand to get to the required place, paññā is the body which provides it with the life force and the directive element.

Throughout these talks Ajahn Sumedho develops the connection between the terms sati-sampajañña and intuitive awareness. In so doing he is endeavoring to clarify and expand the common renderings of sampajañña as "clear comprehension" or even "self-awareness." His chief concern is that these translations do not give a sense of the true broadness of that clarity. Thus he is experimenting with an expression that conveys a deliberately expansive quality and that includes the element of mystery; for it is important for the English wording also to imply an attunement of the heart to experiences that the thinking mind cannot understand or that, as he says, are "foggy, confused, or uncertain." The word "intuitive" is used because it perfectly conveys the mixture of a genuine apprehension of reality, yet also that the reason why things are the way they are might not be at all apparent.

The final and perhaps most significant term to look at in this light is "consciousness." The Pāli word viññāṇa is almost invariably translated into English as "consciousness." In Buddhist psychology viññāṇa generally means a discriminative consciousness that acts via one of the six sense-doors: eye, ear, nose, tongue, body, or mind. It means the act of cognizing a knowable object. However, this is not the only way that the Buddha uses the term. As Ajahn Sumedho observes, there are two places in the discourses where a substantially different set of qualities are associated with the term. The phrase that he quotes, "viññāṇaṃ anidassanaṃ anantaṃ sabbato pabhaṃ," comes in part from the Dīgha Nikāya 11.85 in the Kevaddha Sutta and, in part from the

Majjhima Nikāya 49.25. The former passage comes at the end of a colorful and lengthy teaching tale recounted by the Buddha. He tells of a monk in whose mind this question arises: "I wonder where it is that the four great elements—Earth, Water, Fire, and Wind—cease without remainder?" Being a skilled meditator, the bhikkhu in question enters a state of absorption and "the path to the gods becomes open to him." He begins by putting his question to the first gods he meets, the retinue of the Four Heavenly Kings, the guardians of the world; they demur, saying that they do not know the answer, but that the Four Kings themselves probably do: he should ask them. He does, they do not, and the search continues.

Onward and upward through successive heavens he travels, continually being met with the same reply: "We do not know, but you should try asking…" and is referred to the next higher level of the celestial hierarchy. Patiently enduring the protracted process of this cosmic chain of command, he finally arrives in the presence of the retinue of Mahā-Brahmā and puts the question to them; once again they fail to produce an answer but they assure him that the Great Brahmā Himself, should He deign to manifest, will certainly provide him with the resolution he seeks. Sure enough, before too long Mahā-Brahmā appears, but he too does not know the answer, and he chides the monk for being a disciple of the Buddha yet not going to his own teacher with such a question.

When he finally meets the Buddha and asks him, he receives this reply:

> But, monk, you should not ask your question in this way: "Where do the four great elements—Earth, Water, Fire, and Wind—cease without remainder?"

Instead, this is how the question should have been put:

"Where do earth, water, fire, and wind

And long and short, and fine and coarse,

Pure and impure no footing find?

Where is it that both *nāma* (name) and *rūpa*

(form) fade out,

Leaving no trace behind?"

And the answer is:

"In the awakened consciousness—

the invisible, the limitless, radiant

[*viññāṇaṃ anidassanaṃ anantaṃ sabbato pabhaṃ*].

There it is that earth, water, fire, and wind,

And long and short, and fine and coarse,

Pure and impure no footing find.

There it is that both nāma and rūpa fade out,

Leaving no trace behind.

When discriminative consciousness comes to

its limit,

They are held in check therein."

The term *anidassana-viññāṇa* has been translated in various other ways: "where consciousness is signless" (Walshe), "the consciousness that makes no showing" (Ñāṇamoli), and, most helpfully, by Bhikkhu Ñāṇananda in his book *Concept and Reality* (p. 59) as "non-manifestative consciousness." It is unlikely that the English language has a single term that can accurately convey the constellation of meanings that "anidassana-viññāṇa" possesses; however, it is generally this set of qualities that Ajahn Sumedho is referring to when he uses the simple term "consciousness."

As he says, "viññāṇaṃ anidassanaṃ anantaṃ sabbato pabhaṃ" is "a mouthful of words that point to this state of natural consciousness, this reality." So the reader should bear in mind that, most of the time, he is deliberately using the single word "consciousness" as a shorthand for "anidassana-viññāṇa." Naturally, he also uses the word with its customary scriptural meaning of discriminative cognizing, as well as in the sense of "rebirth consciousness" *(paṭisandhi-viññāṇa)*— for example: "When we are born into a physical birth, we have consciousness within this form." In addition, Ajahn Sumedho also occasionally uses the word in the ordinary English sense, i.e. describing the state of not being *un*conscious, being awake and aware of one's surroundings and identity.

An obvious parallel to Ajahn Sumedho's usage of the word "consciousness" is the Thai phrase *poo roo* as employed by many of the forest Ajahns. The literal translation of *poo* is "person," and *roo*, "knowing." So "poo roo" has been variously rendered as "knowing," "the one who knows," "awareness," or even "Buddha wisdom." It is also a term that can be used to convey a large spectrum of meanings from the simple act of the mind cognizing an object (as in classical definitions of viññāṇa) through varying levels of refinement (as in being the witness of phenomena arising and passing away) to the utterly unobstructed awareness of the fully awakened heart.

So "poo roo" can mean everything from simple cognition to the wisdom of a fully enlightened Buddha. And, just as with Ajahn Sumedho's employment of the word "consciousness," it is necessary with the term "poo roo" to look at the context, and to take into account the favorite expressions of the Ajahn in question, in order to discern the intended nuances of meaning—ergo, caveat lector!

Since there is such a variety of meanings contingent upon the one word "consciousness" in this book, it would thus be wise for the reader always to reflect on the circumstance in which the word is being used. In this light, it might be felt by some that it would have been more helpful not to have used "consciousness" in such a broad range of ways, that perhaps sticking to more familiar terminology might have been easier on the listeners and readers—perhaps using a word like *citta,* "heart," as defining the agent of pure awareness, instead of anidassana-viññāṇa. But this is not the way that such organic and freestyle methods of teaching usually work.

As said above, it has been the explicit aim of the editor of this book to maintain the spontaneous and informal style of Ajahn Sumedho's spoken words. All of his talks are extemporaneous, taking shape as they are expressed according to the needs of the listeners present. And part of this methodology of instruction is that it often demands that the listeners or readers expand their range of view of what the teaching and practice is, and how certain words can and should be used. Furthermore, this spontaneous and direct method of expounding the Dhamma encourages the audience to allow themselves to be changed by what they see and hear, rather than judge it according to whether or not it complies with familiar and favored patterns of thinking. Are we going to complain to Van Gogh that a church built like that would never stand up? Probably not...

So as you, reader, wend your way through these pages and explore this small gallery of Ajahn Sumedho's teachings, it is our fond hope that you find here words and images that help to awaken and free the heart. Whatever is thus meaningful and good, please take it and install it in your life, and whatever is not, please leave it and pass it by in peace.

WELCOME, READER! In order to gain the maximum benefit from this book, I would encourage you to take a few extra minutes in reading this preface and Ajahn Amaro's introduction. This book in its entirety is a contemplation, a reflection on the *"way it is."* In Ajahn Sumedho's words, this reflective approach is

> an empowerment. I am presenting things for you to investigate. I am not telling how you should think or even practice but presenting things to stimulate you, to look at things rather than just accept what I say or disagree with it.

Reflection is not something that you can do—it's what the mind inclines to when you are relaxed and open. Another way of saying this is, it's an attitude: the way you look at yourself and the world, is a choice—a choice to be who you really are, rather than what you think you may be.

Contemplation, on the other hand, is using the thinking mind to reflect. It's taking a thought consciously, letting it affect the mind and seeing what effect it has. To help with understanding this, Ajahn Sumedho reflects a lot on *self,* personality or who we think we are. Accordingly, he often follows his reflections with the phrase, "isn't it?" The way Ajahn Sumedho uses this is to give you a chance to reflect or contemplate on what he has just said. In addition, if you were to remove the "isn't it?" to make the book more readable, what you would get is a list of instructions and imperatives, which is not what he is suggesting.

This book has been kept in the manner Ajahn Sumedho speaks, so the text may not be technically flawless. It is easy to write a book on Buddhism, the ABC approach, of doing this and getting that. The scriptures say this, that teacher says that. These books have a role within the structure of any religion but what Ajahn Sumedho is supporting you in, is to *wake up* to your full potential. Although "wake up" is a simple statement, the implications on society and the complex issues that arise in the world are profound. The Theravādin monastic lifestyle is often portrayed as dry, sterile, and escaping from the complex issues of the world. Yet Ajahn Sumedho's reflections offer humor, and deep insight into the conditions that support these complexities. He suggests that in reacting to these complexities, we tend to refer back to something we have learned, through our social and cultural conditioning. This is already the past, a memory. So we get manipulated, either by our own memories or by the social, cultural, and political environment. In this process of waking up, you are asked to investigate who you are, what the world is. In this way when we come from stillness, rather than reaction, we can then serve ourselves and humanity.

One way of describing stillness and the movement of the mind, which Ajahn Sumedho assumes you know, is the analogy of the turning wheel. If you imagine a wheel of a car: the tire is where there is movement, in the center of the tire there is no movement, stillness. When we are not coming from stillness then we are on the wheel. When we are attached to something or want to get rid of something then we are again pulled out from the center on to the wheel—the endless circle of becoming/suffering.

Another word that Ajahn Sumedho uses to support this investigation into who we are, and which is not commonly used is *immanent*. This is mainly used within a religious context; it has a sense of inclusiveness within the element of transcendence. Also, Ajahn Sumedho uses the word transcendence not as referring to something *out there,* something to be attained, but as a quality that is here and now, which includes the human form.

Ajahn Sumedho has been a monk for over forty years, and this book conveys an intuitive understanding of the Buddha's teaching. The Dhamma reflections herein come from a ten-day retreat given by Ajahn Sumedho at Amarāvatī Buddhist Monastery Retreat Centre in the United Kingdom in May 2005—along with other reflections offered mostly in 2001. The retreats have a relaxed and humorous ambience.

Humor is an important part of the reflective style of Ajahn Sumedho as sometimes we can take life so seriously. By taking some of the human conditions and turning them into absurdities, we can get perspective on the way we bind ourselves to those very conditions. So, when we start to accept ourselves as we are, not as some ideal of who we think we should be, a relaxation can take place. This creates space for insight to arise. For some people this space is recognized as what Ajahn Sumedho refers to as the sound of silence, or simply a quiet or empty mind. However it manifests, this points to the unconditioned, beyond body and mind objects.

From this place of spaciousness, social and personal conditioning can be investigated or reflected upon, thus freeing the heart from the delusion of identifying with the personality. This is not a process of rejecting ourselves, of considering certain thoughts and feelings as wrong, but of learning to be a silent witness to all that arises without attaching to that experience or rejecting it. In essence it's about trust, accepting what arises in experience as "the way it is" or, as Ajahn Sumedho often likes to say, "welcoming the suffering." It is about listening, being receptive to and fully including everything.

It may seem confusing that the reflections in this volume sometimes contradict each other, one talk suggesting that "suffering should be understood" and then the next cautioning against using the word "should." But what can be noticed is the all-encompassing point behind the contradictions. This is the point to trust: awareness.

Refuge is not in a teacher or scriptures but in the heart's own purity. This point never changes, it has no views and opinions, is not affected by anything, and yet is fully alive, responsive, spontaneous, and compassionate—fully here and now.

This book has been transcribed and edited by a number of Sangha members and lay people, with additional support from Wisdom Publications. The editor would like to thank them very much for their many hours of work. Any misunderstandings or errors arising in this book rest with the editor. This book is offered as a sharing from the people who have benefited from Ajahn Sumedho's teachings, his great devotion to Dhamma, and his encouragement. As Ajahn Sumedho says in the chapter on welcoming suffering:

> I'm not interested in proving that I'm right, that my translations are the best, but just seeing how they work,

what the effect is in the here and now. I am sharing this with you as a way of encouraging you to have that right and that freedom to know yourself.

May whatever merit that arises from this book be dedicated to the benefit of all sentient beings.

Sāmaṇera Amaranātho
Amarāvatī Buddhist Monastery

IT IS IMPORTANT to keep reminding ourselves that we are recognizing a natural state of timelessness, because experience is always now, here and now. Whether you think you experience things in the past or anticipate possibilities in the future, all that—memories of the past or anticipation of the future—is happening now. And so this is the illusion of time because, in the ordinary world, time is our reality. We believe totally in, are committed to, time as reality. The aim of meditation is to keep reminding ourselves of the present. Experience is always in the present; it's here and now, what is called *paccuppanna-dhamma* (the reality of now).

The mind wanders, and you start thinking, and then it will start planning for the future or remembering the past. Awareness, then, is bringing attention to the way the mind works. The future is a thought in the mind, in the present, and the past is a memory. You can be aware of thinking, be aware of thought. We are not our thoughts; our thoughts are artificial creations. So we can think anything. It can be reasonable or totally insane or whatever, but thinking is an artifice that we tend to identify with, intimidate ourselves with, and we let our thoughts control us. So we're establishing a sense of confidence in the present, mindfulness, sati-sampajañña, here and now.

For example, we use the four postures: sitting, standing, walking, lying down. These are the movements of the body that we use throughout the day and night, normal movements. And so the body is here and now. Obviously you're experiencing your body now, and it's sitting. So now just reflect on the experience of sitting. Begin to just notice, just feel, and bring into consciousness this obvious fact that we tend not to notice, not pay attention to. And yet it is a reality of this present moment, the body. For every one of us, our body is present, here and now, whatever condition it might be in. In whatever state of health or unhealth, pleasure or pain, it is the way it is. So now for a few minutes just contemplate this. Bring attention to the experience of being with the sitting of your own body.

When I bring attention to my body, I notice the pressure of just the body sitting on the seat—that's an obvious sensation—I begin to be aware of my spine or whether I'm feeling tension in the body…the shoulders…hands and feet. They're here and now; just observe them, be a witness to the body as it's sitting. Being in the position of a witness or an observer, that's all. It's not being a critic, not passing judgment on your body at this moment, whether it's pleasurable or painful or whether you think you're sitting well or not. Trust yourself just to be the observer. The experience of sitting…just focusing on that, on the physical body. Here and now is like this. And so you're bringing into consciousness the body as experience. Now, we can sit here all morning and think about various things; we can plan for the future or remember the past. We can travel all over the world just sitting here in this shrine room. I can go to Thailand or Australia within just a few seconds—that's not what we're here for, not for traveling, but for being here.

We want to define things, have something to grasp, to get hold of, and cling to. But this isn't a matter of clinging. It's just paying attention, isn't it? So it's learning to trust this innate ability, this simple ability we all have to just be with what is, using the body as a focus. The body is a pretty solid condition compared to the mental states you have. It is more stable than your thoughts or emotions. It's heavy, and it is a sensitive form, a conscious sensitive form. When I contemplate like this, I become more aware of just the feeling—what's going on in the body. There's a sense of the belly or the chest or the heart, where the feet are, the hands…the pressures…just simple things like one hand touching the other. Or the clothes on your body, just feeling the sensation of your clothes touching your skin; ordinary sensations that we never pay attention to unless they get really painful, unless they make us pay attention. Now, we're not waiting until something forces our attention, we're paying attention—using the body as the object of awareness.

So if your mind tends to wander, that's all right, don't make a problem about anything whatsoever. When you realize you're off thinking about something, gently bring your attention back to the body, just being a witness to the experience of sitting.

The nature of the mind is to wander. Notice with thinking that you have one thought and then it stimulates, associates, with the next one—that's why it wanders. Something will come up, a thought, and then it'll wander into associations. The awareness of that: you're not a thought, you're not a thinking process. Thinking is a habit that we've developed. In order to think you have to remember; it's language, isn't it?—language and memory. So what I'm pointing to is awareness, not ideas or thoughts. It's learning to recognize and to be able to realize this awareness, here and now, because it's always with us, it's never absent. When we forget, we get caught into our views, opinions, habits. With meditation it's bringing us back to this centerpoint, the here and now, the awareness that includes. So awareness includes the body, that's why you can be aware of the body. You can be fully with the reality of this body, as experience here and now.

You can feel the temperature, whether you feel hot or cold. The body is a sensitive conscious form and we tend to react when it gets too hot or too cold. Instead of just reacting to it, bring attention to the feeling of warmth or the coolness, just being aware of it. The temperature, pressure, the activities of the body, blood, its energies, circulation, nervous system—all this is here and now. So we're observing it; we don't have to experience it in any certain way or in a terribly refined way. Just trust in the simple, natural ability of being the observer of the experience of sitting.

The attitude is to be relaxed, to have this sense of being at ease. If you're trying too hard, you're not mindful. You may have ideas about what I'm saying: you can make it into something that you have to do, and you try to do what you think I'm telling you to do. What I'm saying is more of an encouragement. What I'm trying to do on this retreat is not tell you what to do but encourage you. I'm just trying to keep pointing and encouraging you to trust your own awareness of this moment.

Another object right now is breathing. This is a physiological function of the body that happens whether we like it or not, no matter what, until we're dead. If you're not breathing right now, that means you're dead. So you can use the breath as a focus because this is happening here and now, the inhalation and exhalation. Now, you can feel the breath through the body and the nostrils. You can feel the rise and fall of the abdomen—you can feel it in your chest—as you breathe in and out. And they're different, you know. When they teach mindfulness of the breath different teachers use different places of focus.

Notice right now, where do you feel your breath best? Where can you just notice the breath? What part of your body tends to be the most obvious? Put attention onto the breathing of the body, then concentrate on that particular point. So if it's at the nostrils then just stay with the breath for an inhalation. Breathe in—sustain your attention on just that experience of inhaling and then exhaling. You're sustaining your attention on something, on what is happening now, and using that as a focus. So using the breath, the normal breathing, don't try to control anything. It's not like you have to breathe in a certain way or control your breath—just the way you're experiencing it. Just let it be that way, and use that, just the inhalation, exhalation, rising, falling... because that's happening right now. It's just what it is, it's natural, it's nature. It's just the way it is. And you're a witness to it, because you recognize you're in this position of the Buddho, or the knower, the witness.

In the Thai forest tradition they use this mantra a lot called *Buddho,* which is the name of the Buddha—Awakened Knowing. It's conscious knowing. When we took the refuges last evening, we took refuge in the Buddha. So now you're actually in the position of the witness, the knowing. It's the Buddho, knowing the way it is, the breath is like this. Now when I say the breath is like this, that's a thought, but it's also pointing, it helps to remind you to be with the breath. It's not a criticism or an analysis or a wandering thought, is it? It's not thinking about breathing; I'm just saying be with the breath, notice the breath. Buddho helps you to focus and remember to just use the breath as a focus...to begin to recognize awareness.

The breath and the posture are natural conditions. This is Dhamma, in other words. In Thai the word for nature, what is natural, what we don't create out of our own desires and delusions, is "Dhamma." The Buddha knowing the Dhamma, the truth of the way it is; the relationship of Buddha to Dhamma, rather than me, Ajahn Sumedho, trying to practice meditation. If I come from this—from me, Ajahn Sumedho, trying to practice meditation—I'm back into a personal scenario. That's not Dhamma, not natural. It's a creation, an artifice, a convention. The name "Ajahn Sumedho" is a convention, and "my meditation practice" is another conventional way of thinking. It comes from thinking, "I'm somebody that's got to practice Dhamma." We're starting right from the very center of being right now, just learning to recognize a natural state of being, before you create yourself.

So using the breath and the body: these are just ordinary natural conditions that you're experiencing at this time. That's why being aware of the body is a very grounding experience if we tend to be caught in our thinking a lot. Our culture, our society, tends to be very cerebral, and we get caught up in all our ideas and thoughts. So we can live in a totally artificial environment most of the time, one that we create, and we're creating a sense of myself and what I think and my past and my future, and my abilities or my inabilities. And these are artifices; these are creations that human beings add to the present moment. So you're recognizing awareness, realizing just the simplicity of awareness, you're not creating it; it's not something that you have to believe in or get hold of but just recognize. It's simple, very simple. It's very natural.

The breath and the body, these are focuses for when we meditate. Now the point of this is nothing more than to be able to recognize awareness, that which is aware of the breath and the body. It's just this. You can't find it as an object. Your breath is an object, isn't it? You can be aware of inhalation and exhalation, and you can be aware of the experience of sitting, of your body, the pressure of sitting on the floor, or the clothes on your body, or the heat or the cold. So this awareness, you don't create that. It's a natural state of being.

With your breath, when you know your mind is wandering, that you're thinking about something, gently go back to the point on your body where you experience the breathing, and practice just sustaining your attention on this rhythm of your breathing. So you notice the difference between an inhalation and an exhalation. Inhaling is like this. Exhaling is like this. They're different, aren't they? It's not preferring one over the other. It's just noticing, being able to sustain and rest in a kind, relaxed, and attentive way to just the breathing that your body is engaged in. Being at ease with yourself, don't make this into some kind of thing you have to do. It's very important to develop this trust in yourself, in your awareness. It's a relaxed state of being. When you try too hard, you know you're going back into the habits of "I've got to, I've got to do this": a kind of compulsion, having to make this into some kind of project that you have to get hold of and achieve. Meditation is just returning, a kind of letting go of the world, instead of trying to get something—just letting go, and then just being. Learning to be at peace and at ease with the breathing, with what's happening now, with the body.

Apārutā tesaṃ amatassa
dvārā ye sotavantā
pamuñcantu saddhaṃ

I USE THE WORD "reflection" a lot, because through the ability we have to reflect we can know freedom from birth and death, from suffering. The human mind gives us a thinking mind. We can analyze and criticize because of memory, language, and so forth. So we have concepts of good/bad, right/wrong, and the like, and it's very dualistic. If you've got right, there's going to be wrong; if you've got male, there's going to be female; the same for day/night, good/bad, big/little. So when we're caught in the momentum of thinking, then we're stuck in what we call a dualistic realm. It's a kind of linear realm where one thing goes on to the next; it's like your inhalation and exhalation. So this is pointing to the conditioned realm.

We're using the words "conditioned realm" or "the realm of phenomena." This is what we're experiencing through the senses and through the thinking mind. The body is a condition, and then we have the senses—the eyes, ears, nose, tongue, the body itself, the brain. All of these are conditions, are phenomena, and they arise and cease. The body is born, grows up, gets old, and dies. With the inhalation, you reach the end of it and then it's the exhalation. It's like when you're born you grow up to a certain peak and then you start getting old. And that's the pattern of *samsāra* or conditioned phenomena. The thinking mind is conditioned.

Now, we weren't born thinking, were we? When a baby is born it's conscious—it's experiencing consciousness within a separate form, a human form, a baby's body. But it doesn't have a concept of itself. It doesn't conceive itself as being a boy or a girl. Later on we're told, "you're a boy" or "you're a girl," and then we're told our race, nationality, ethnic group. You're not born thinking, "Oh, I'm Sri Lankan." You're told you're Sri Lankan later on. So these are pointing to conventions we artificially create onto the phenomenal experience of the body and consciousness. Language is an artificial thing. Consciousness is natural—we didn't create it. Humans don't create it. And the body is a natural condition, just like the trees and the flowers, the birds and the bees. All these are just the natural state of this sense realm that we're experiencing. And then we—in our human condition—create onto that the sense of a self: "I am, this is my body, this is mine, and I'm a male, I'm American, I'm a Buddhist monk, I'm Ajahn Sumedho, I'm a good monk or a bad monk."

I'm just pointing to the artifices—the human-made conventions that we strongly identify with. So when we're going to the breath, using the breath as a focus, we don't create the breath. It's natural, it just operates whether we think or not—whether we think it's my breath or whatever, it doesn't matter—it is what it is. And the body itself—experiencing the four postures with awareness. The body is either sitting, standing, walking, or lying down. And then you can do unusual postures, like standing on your head or swinging from a tree or something. So we're pointing to the ordinariness of this moment, not to some special, extreme condition that we might enjoy at times; just the ordinariness of breathing, the ordinariness of sitting, standing, walking, lying down.

Usually, when we get to the extraordinary, it takes more awareness. It's like if you're a rock climber—I've never done it, but I've always admired such people because for me that's a rather frightening thing to do. But that's not usually a demand made on us in our lives. It's something we choose to do and it's quite dangerous, I suppose—you have to be very much aware. When your life is in danger, when you're physically in danger, you find that you go on automatic pilot. Most of us do. When you're threatened by something and you pick that up, there is something in you, a kind of instinctual survival mechanism, that's very much aware. So you may find yourself doing quite unusual things that your sense of self would think impossible. Like a heroic act in a war, saving others, or something like that. That's usually a rare occurrence, where the conditions are of a life-threatening experience of danger, and you can respond in a way that, if you thought about it and identified with it, you probably couldn't do.

There's no particular, imminent danger around here that I'm aware of. There's no threatening possibility of danger that we have to prepare ourselves against right now—as in the case of an air raid or terrorist attack. So we come to a meditation center like Amarāvatī and it's a fairly safe place. Nothing really all that dangerous ever happens here—as yet—and so it's a Buddhist center, a Buddhist monastery. We're in a moral form. With the eight precepts that we take when we are on retreat, we can take each other for granted; we can trust each other on the behavioral level. We've all agreed to live under these precepts about action, speech, and behavior. And that also gives us the sense that we don't have to be like the squirrels here in Amarāvatī, where as soon as they get out of the tree they're in danger. So they're very alert to any sound or any movement because squirrels feel safe in trees but not on the ground. Well, obviously, if we had to live up in a tree, we wouldn't feel very safe—at least I wouldn't. On the land, on the ground here I feel quite safe. Now we can just notice what this is like—moral precepts are agreements about behavior and give our lives a kind of security.

We're not like animals in the jungle—survive is about the best they can do. We can trust each other because, from my experience, meditation retreats don't attract Mafia thugs, criminals, drug peddlers, or perverts. Such people don't usually feel attracted to places like this. So it's a fairly safe place to be. Now, creating this sense of safety is important because we do live in a dangerous realm. We know that we're very vulnerable creatures. We don't have very tough hides, we're easily injured, easily damaged physically, and we are also very sensitive creatures, so we can be hurt emotionally. If somebody makes some nasty insulting comment, we can feel our heart quiver. Just the way somebody might look at me—if they give me a hostile look.

Pointing to this realm, you're experiencing now a sensory realm—not in the context of a personal experience anymore, but the way it is. Just contemplate what your life is, as experience, from the time you're born to this present moment: it's the experience of sensitivity. Because things are impinging on your senses all the time—passing in front of your vision, or as sounds through your ears, or odors through the nose, tastes through the mouth, the tongue. The pleasure and pain, heat and cold through the body, the emotional habits—sensitivity is like this. It's not going to be the experience of just pleasure—seeing just the beautiful objects, melodious sounds, fragrant odors, wonderful tastes, and warm, pleasurable sensations on your body and skin—we're subject to whatever's happening around. We don't have that much control over what we're going to experience.

So this is what sensitivity is about. We would *like* to have only pleasure, to have just beauty around us and beautiful music and delicious food and fragrant odors, and a sense of safety and security and peace and harmony and happiness. This is what we call heaven. But this realm we're in is not heaven, is it? It's a sense realm, not an ethereal one. We've got a body that's not an ethereal form. It's not made out of ether but of the four elements: the earth element, fire, water, wind. The body is like this—it's coarse, made of these coarse elements, and it's sensitive. So using the body and the senses as a focus, we can reflect on sensitivity. You can be aware of pleasure and pain; you can be aware of your emotional state in the present. This awareness, then, is what the Buddha is pointing to as our refuge. Because awareness allows us to discern where wisdom can operate in our lives, rather than habitual reactions.

When we're merely conditioned by experience, we tend to react to what's happening. If we're experiencing happiness we want more. We tend to grasp at happiness, trying to have as much as we can get. We would like security, to have lots of money and surround ourselves with beautiful things. We'd like a stable society, a well-run country, a well-run government, a good economy, to have security, safety. That would make us feel good, give us a pleasant feeling all the time. But this realm—its very nature is change, and it's insecure. You can't have just inhalations, you've also got to exhale. You can't stay at the peak moment of your perfect form, when you are most beautiful, most healthy, most youthful. Many people try! And they're never very successful.

Old age, sickness, death are natural also—and this is just the way things are in this realm, in this phenomenal realm that we're experiencing, this sense realm. So what I'm doing is reflecting on life, on the nature of this body, on the experience through the senses, on what sensitivity is. I can see how on a personal level I'm conditioned; my personality is conditioned. I would like harmony and peace. I'd like to live in a Sangha of monks and nuns where there are never any difficulties, sharing our lives, marching to *nibbāna*. A place where problems never arise, with no misunderstandings...that's the ideal of a heavenly monastery. They have monasteries like that probably up in heaven. But here on earth they're like this.

So we do our best. We all agree there are moral precepts and we agree to live in this way; there are agreed ways of behaving that make life more simple. At least we're not endlessly negotiating rights and demands, personal privileges, and so forth. Even though it's a hierarchical structure based on seniority, it's also based on compassion. Even in a monastery at its very best—with all the best monks and nuns that you could possibly ever imagine—there are still the contingencies, the surprising events, the things you don't like, things you don't want, the snake in the garden, the worm in the apple, the fly in the ointment. We'd like just apples with no worms, and gardens with no poisonous snakes—but that's idealizing, isn't it? That's wanting something that's not the way life is. So it's getting to know experience as human individuals, now. Being sensitive is like this.

Now when I say "like this," it's reflecting on the reality of this moment: the body's like this; the mind, the mood that I'm experiencing, the mental state is like this. I'm not telling you whether my mental state is good or bad—I don't know how to describe the mood I'm in right now—it is what it is. All I can say is that I'm in a pretty good mood right now. If I were in a rotten mood you'd be hearing something slightly different, wouldn't you? Now, one of the epithets for the Buddha is *lokavidū*—knower of the world. Don't leave that up to some kind of abstract Buddha up there—I mean, you're taking refuge in Buddha. Our refuge in Buddha, then, is the Buddho—knowing the world as the world. And so this is reflecting on it, and not judging the world as bad. We're not against the world—we're not trying to destroy the world. We're not annihilationists or condemning phenomena. Sometimes Buddhists can sound like they're condemning everything: "It's all impermanent, not self, it just leads to suffering." You meet Buddhists like that—they just grasp at the conventional forms of Buddhism, and then operate from grasping at things like *(speaks in a very gloomy voice)*: "life is suffering and it all ends in death"—*(continues very morosely)* "And there's no God, there's no self!"—That is not reflecting on the nature of the world, is it? Because the world is a changing experience.

The nature of phenomena is to change—arising, ceasing, being born, and dying—that movement of what we call *aniccā*, or impermanence. So we begin to use this concept of aniccā—not projecting that onto experience. We're not saying that "everything is impermanent" as some kind of position we take. This reference to aniccā is to just notice change. Notice the movement of your breath. Nothing wrong with the breath moving, is there? It's not a judgment, but just paying attention to the reality of change that we're experiencing through the senses.

When you recognize the mood you're in—notice that you can't sustain a mood—when you really look at it, it's changing. It moves in different ways, arises and ceases. All sensory experiences—what we see, hear, smell, taste, and touch, thought itself, emotion, all conditioned phenomena—are impermanent. This is not a teaching or a statement to grasp, not a basis to operate from. It's a teaching to explore, so as to really be the knower of impermanence. Now, what is it that can know impermanence? Is a condition able to know another condition? It's by using awareness—because that's not a condition we create, is it? Just paying attention, staying alert here and now, allows us to reflect, to notice the way it is, to observe.

So the Buddho—or Buddha—is the knower, is the knowing. We call it Buddha, but I'm not saying, "Oh, *I'm* a Buddha!" because then it's getting back into me as a person again. We're not trying to convince ourselves that we've got a little Buddha inside us, or anything like that. We're not trying to conceive anything about Buddha; we're being that knowing, being that awareness. And that's why, on this retreat, we reinforce that knowing—that sense of confidence in knowing in this direct way. Because that's what is most difficult for most of us. We're so convinced, so bound to our thoughts, views, opinions, and identities, we never get any perspective on them. We just judge them. We make value judgments about ourselves, about the world that we live in—how it should or shouldn't be, how *I* should or shouldn't be. "I shouldn't think bad thoughts. I should only have loving, kind thoughts, I'm a senior monk, so I should only have compassionate and kind thoughts, I should never have negative, selfish, or childish thoughts or emotions!" That's the critical mind, isn't it? The sense of myself, identifying with the age of the body: "I'm a senior monk, I'm an old man, I'm senior" and "I should be..." or "I shouldn't be...." But within that is the awareness that this is a creation—I create myself in this way. So by reflecting, by observing yourself, you begin to notice the difference between awareness—which you don't create, which is not self—and the ways you create yourself. Now, how do I create myself as a person? I have to start thinking: "I'm Ajahn Sumedho." If I'm just aware, then there's no "Ajahn Sumedho" in my mind.

Sometimes the perception "I'm Ajahn Sumedho" arises. But usually I don't think like that very much. I don't need to go around thinking "I'm Ajahn Sumedho" all the time. So if I'm not thinking about myself then I think, "I am a senior monk," and I start getting caught up in remembering the past, thinking about mistakes I've made. I tend to judge thoughts as bad or good—that all comes from the critical mind, doesn't it? That's the critical faculty. Thinking is a critical faculty. Now, I'm not condemning thinking—it's a very useful function to have. But as an identity it's a failure. You're not at all what you think, you know—what you think you are is not what you are. And yet we tend to believe what we think we are. So we carry around with us these limited perceptions we hold about ourselves as a person, and we judge them accordingly: I'm not so good, I shouldn't feel this way, I should be more responsible, I shouldn't be so selfish, I should be this, I shouldn't be like that, I shouldn't feel this way.... These are thoughts, aren't they?

Thought is a creation. So in this very present moment, what is it that isn't a thought? Awareness isn't a thought. When you try to become aware, you're grasping at the idea of awareness—that you're somebody who isn't aware and has to try to be more aware. That's another creation. Yet I've seen people desperately trying to be mindful and they don't see what they're doing. They've got some idea about mindfulness in their heads, something they've imagined mindfulness is, and they're trying to become like that. And of course it doesn't work that way. The more you think you should be mindful, the more you tend to be heedless. I've made some hilarious mistakes in my effort at trying to make myself mindful. Because once you get caught, you're so intent on trying to be mindful, you trip over your own feet.

Mindfulness isn't something difficult or a refined state of being that depends on very specially controlled conditions. It's very ordinary—most ordinary! If you weren't mindful you'd be dead by now. I mean, it's mindfulness that keeps you going, whether you're aware of it or not. But it's just not noticed. Awareness is not a concept. Even though I thought I understood the word when I first started meditation, I didn't really know what it was. They talk about "being mindful," and then they talk about "concentration." The first method I used when I was a layperson in Bangkok, was one where everything was done in slow motion. So I thought to be mindful you had to do everything in this exaggerated slowness. And so I used to practice doing everything that way. That's not a very useful way to live one's life. You can only do that under certain conditions. If you're trying to catch the train and make it to Heathrow Airport on time and you're into slow motion, you're never going to make it. Can you run for the bus mindfully? These are mindfulness practices: it was a method for developing a kind of intense concentration on slow movement of the body, and so I assumed that that was what they meant by mindfulness, but then I realized that wasn't it.

Mindfulness is ordinary. It's just being aware of the movements of your body—sitting, standing, walking, lying down, breathing—or being aware of your mood or mental state. Sometimes we have ideas about trying to practice but we're scattered, all over the place—and then we try to do *ānāpānasati* (awareness of breathing). It's an endless, hopeless task because when the mind is scattered like that, it's impossible to concentrate on something as refined as the sensation of breathing. That's why I encourage you to really notice the mood you're in, just to bring attention to the quality of mood—so you recognize, "Well, it's like this." Then, from there, as you recognize it, you become more peaceful—and if you're peaceful and calm it's easy to do ānāpānasati, the awareness of breathing. You can develop samatha (calm), jhānas (meditative absorptions), all these kinds of concentrated states—but if your mind is scattered and you're in a state of confusion or excitement, or you're restless or in physical discomfort, or you're feeling angry or upset by something, don't do ānāpānasati. So what do you do then?

Maybe go out and run around the field. Or you could be patient and just accept this state of mind you're in. Because if you just leave it alone, it'll settle. It's impermanent, it'll change. And so your relationship to any mood you're in is one of witnessing, not judging. When you judge it, then you're back into the phenomenal world of "I don't like this mood I'm in—I want to get rid of it. How can I get rid of it? I don't want it!" And then you're struggling with it. You not only have it, but you're creating negative feelings onto it: "I don't like it! I don't want it!" So you're in a bad mood, and you don't like yourself for being in a bad mood—it's increasingly complex. We get more and more confused, and that's why we're so neurotic in modern life. In countries like this we're not with the natural forces and the conditions just as they are; we're caught in a complicated network or a web of illusions that we impose on ourselves: judgments, criticisms, ideals. Reflecting on these natural conditions—getting in touch with "the way it is," which is, of course, not trying to control everything—takes patience.

Being patient and enduring means that even if we create something painful and unwanted and we don't like it, we're willing to let it be that way. When I say, "Accept it for what it is," I'm not asking you to like it. Acceptance doesn't mean you like something. It means, at this moment, if you're feeling scattered and confused, then accept that—it means you're allowing that to be what it is. You can also try to hold on. If you try to hold on to it in a deliberate way, you find that you can't keep it. If you don't know what you're doing then it seems like you're never going to be composed ever again. It's like stirring water with mud in it—if you keep agitating the water, it stays muddy. If you just leave it alone for a while, the mud will settle. So this is why knowing yourself is important, like in formal meditation practices, just noticing, paying attention—the mood or the state of mind is like this.

The body is like this. The breath is like this. Being aware of the body means we're aware of it as such, because it is sensitive. The whole thing is sensitive, every bit of it. Fingertips, toes—everything. It's a totally sensitive form. A lot of what we feel—like the pressure of clothing on the skin—is very neutral. We hardly ever notice a neutral sensation, because it doesn't draw our attention to it. What draws our attention is usually extreme, like pain. If your clothes or your belt is too tight, it feels very uncomfortable; you notice it. If the belt on your trousers is perfect—it's not too tight, not too loose—you'd probably never notice it, until you pay attention. It's not waiting for something to reach some extreme state so we have to pay attention. We're bringing attention to the ordinariness of the body in the here and now—to pleasurable sensations as well as painful ones. We're developing the witnessing, the Buddho.

Awareness is sati-sampajañña, *sati-paññā* (mindfulness and wisdom), and this wisdom faculty is not judgmental. It does not evaluate the quality of things—saying this is better than that. It discerns the way it is. This is what we call intuitive awareness. I use the words "intuition" and "apperception" or (another good word) "intuitive moment," to embrace everything in the present. When I start thinking, then I exclude. I go to something and judge its quality. I form an opinion: "I like this" or "I don't like this." But apperception, intuitive awareness, is not criticizing or judging. It's certainly aware and it's discerning, and so this is where the development of wisdom takes place, in this discernment. To really discern the conditioned phenomena is like this. So we have *anicca, dukkha, anattā* (impermanent, unsatisfactory, non-self)—the three characteristics of existence, or of all phenomena. These aren't qualities, are they? They're not qualities of phenomena; they're characteristics. And these characteristics are not judgments or criticisms of phenomena but ways of looking at phenomena when we're no longer involved with their qualities.

We're discerning the way it is: "all conditions are impermanent"—*sabbe saṅkhārā aniccā* is the Pāli phrase. *Sabbe saṅkhārā* is a Pāli word that means "all conditions, all phenomena," and they are impermanent—anicca. So this is a reflective discernment, a noticing and this helps us to lose that identity—that personal commitment, the momentum of habit—that binds us to the conditions of the body and mind, because that's where we suffer, isn't it? On a personal level we suffer. So then the second phrase—*sabbe dhammā anattā,* "all dhammas are not-self"—what does that mean? The Pāli word *dhamma* doesn't have a very good equivalent in English. That's why we have to take it and use it in the English context—dhamma—but it means *everything!* Conditioned, unconditioned and so what does *that* mean?

There's a condition and then we say "*un*condition"—the negation of a condition. Or the Deathless—*Amarāvatī,* the name of this monastery. *Amarāvatī* means "the Deathless Realm." Deathless—what does *that* mean? All conditioned phenomena are going to die or cease. So I chanted at the beginning in Pāli: "Apārutā tesaṃ amatassa dvārā ye sotavantā pamuñcantu saddhaṃ" (*Mahāpadāna*

Sutta, Dīgha Nikāya 14), which means, "The gates to the Death-less are open." Now what is the gate to the Deathless? This aware-ness, that is the gate. Awareness is the only possibility we have to get out of saṃsāra—out of the birth-and-death cycle. Any other way is an illusion—it's always here and now. That's why "I'll do it tomorrow" is another illusion you're creating here and now.

Awareness: you don't create it, you recognize it. And so this is what I'm pointing to all the time, recognizing this Buddho, this knowing. It's like this—the mood is like this, the body is like this, the breath is like this. And the more you reflect in this way, then the sense of "myself as a person" is also like this. When I start feeling self-conscious and start creating myself, then the self is like this. "Me" as a person. You have a personality that's conditioned. It has certain good qualities, certain not-so-good qualities. As a person I can be quite rational and reasonable, and at other times I'm totally stubborn and irrational and emotionally a kind of basket case!β In meditation I watch myself go crazy. In fact, several times I went kind of mad on the personal level.

I can be aware when stupid thoughts enter consciousness, or intelligent ones. There's a discerning that is not judging. As soon as I have some stupid thought and start to judge it—"That's a stupid thought!"—I'm taking a personal stand against it. Stupid thoughts, intelligent thoughts, emotional maturity, emotional immaturity—whatever you want to call it—our relationship now is through awareness and wisdom; it is what it is, what arises and ceases. So it's not self, it's anattā. Even though it says it's "me," it's not. It just has this habit of saying, "You're really like this!" But that's because the personality is conditioned to say that.

Am I going to take refuge in my personality, which gets me into trouble every time I do something, or take refuge in the awareness? Obviously there's no choice. Every time I take refuge in my personal feelings, views, and opinions, I get myself into all kinds of trouble. I create endless suffering, unnecessary anxiety around me. Why do it? Especially if you know you don't have to. So this is the way—the power of meditation. As you develop confidence in this awareness, you're freeing yourself from being enslaved, from the habits you've acquired. You're no longer a victim of your habits. You're not getting rid of them; you're not trying to be someone with no personality whatsoever. You're *recognizing* things as they are. So whatever you're thinking or feeling in the present, you receive and recognize it and accept it for what it is. We're patient with it—we receive it—and then we let it just be what it is. Then it can change accordingly. But we're not trying to kill it off.

This is where the Buddha's teaching is so direct. It always pointing to the here and now. Awareness here and now, liberation here and now, nibbāna here and now. It's not about "If you practice hard during this retreat you might attain nibbāna by the end of it." That's another perception, isn't it? It's learning to recognize, realize, reality: "all conditions are impermanent—not-self." The unconditioned, then, isn't something you can find as an object—you *are* that. Unconditioned awareness, the Deathless, is our refuge. That's an intuition, and through intuition, through awareness, we recognize, realize, the Deathless, or the Dhamma: the *amata dhamma,* or "the Deathless truth."

Now, all that I've said is for reflection, contemplation. I don't expect you to believe it. I'm just sharing what I've learned and hoping that it'll be of use to you. But the encouragement is always toward this awareness. We need encouragement because we're so critical of ourselves. We bind ourselves to such negative perceptions, and we never really trust ourselves at all. We might assume a certain confidence while doing a certain thing, but on a personal level we tend to mistrust or doubt endlessly, or just criticize or disparage ourselves. That's a habit of the mind—that's a habit that you create through thinking and conceiving yourself as this or that. So the transcendence of all that is through awareness. That's what your true nature is; that's peaceful, that's stillness. I experience that as stillness—as a stillness that one begins to recognize. A very natural stillness—it's not a precious stillness that is destroyed as soon as there's a loud noise. It's a natural stillness that we don't notice because we're so caught in the saṃsāra of birth and death, love and hate.

Just as space is not
established anywhere,
so too,
develop meditation
that is like space;
for when you
develop meditation
that is like space,
arisen agreeable
and
disagreeable contacts
will not invade
your mind.
(*Mahārāhulovāda Sutta* 62.17, Majjhima Nikāya)

IN CONTEMPLATING right understanding *(sammā-diṭṭhi)* I like
to emphasize seeing it as an intuitive understanding and not
a conceptual one. I have found it very helpful just contemplating the difference between analytical thinking and intuitive
awareness, because there is a huge difference between the use
of the mind to think, to analyze, reason, criticize, to have ideas,

perceptions, views and opinions, and intuitive awareness, which is non-critical. Intuitive awareness is an inclusive awareness. It's not that it doesn't allow criticism; rather, it sees the critical mind as an object. The critical mind is the tendency to criticize or compare, to hold one view that this is better than that, or this is right and that is wrong, to criticize yourself or others or whatever—all of which can be justified and valid on that level. We're not interested in just developing our critical faculty, because usually in countries like this it's highly developed already, but to trust in intuitive awareness (sati-sampajañña).

Sampajañña is often translated as "clear comprehension," which is so vague and, even though it says "clear," it doesn't give me a sense of the broadness of that clarity. When you have clear definitions of everything, then you think you have clear comprehension. That's why we don't like confusion, isn't it? We don't like to feel foggy, confused, or uncertain. These kind of states we really dislike, but we spend a lot of time trying to have clear comprehension and certainty. But sati-sampajañña includes fogginess, includes confusion, includes uncertainty and insecurity. It's a clear comprehension or the apperception of confusion— recognizing it's like *this*. Uncertainty and insecurity are like *this*. So it's a clear comprehension or apprehension of even the most vague, amorphous, or nebulous mental conditions.

Some people find this approach frustrating because it's easier to be told exactly what to do, to have a more methodical approach. But many of us have done that, and even though it can be very skillful, it can also become addictive. We never get to the root of the cause, which is "I am this person that needs something in order to become enlightened." This intuitive approach does not exclude methodical meditations. It's not that I'm against the methods of meditation in our tradition of Theravāda Buddhism—not at all.

I am trying to put them into perspective. If you go to different meditation retreats, courses, or whatever, intuitive awareness will help you to do the method in a much more skillful way than if you just start from faith in a method and never question or see beyond the ignorant perceptions of yourself. This encourages you really to question, to look into these perceptions you have of yourself, whatever they might be: If you think you're the best, the greatest, God's gift to the world, or you think you're the absolute bottom of the stack; or if you don't know who you are and what you want; or if sometimes you think you're superior but sometimes you feel that you're inferior—all these things change.

The *personality view (sakkāya-diṭṭhi)* with *sīlabbata-parāmāsa* (attachment to rituals and techniques), and *vicikicchā* (doubt) are the first three fetters that hide the path and keep us from seeing the way of non-suffering. Trying to figure out how to be aware is an impossible task—"What is he talking about, anyway?" "Wake up, be aware"—and then trying to figure it out and think about it, you just go around in circles. It's frustrating. Intuitive awareness is frustrating to an analytical person whose faith is in thought, reason, and logic. Awareness is right now. It's not a matter of thinking about it, but being aware of thinking about it. How do you do that?

My insight came when I was a *sāmaṇera* (novice monk). "How do you stop thinking? Just stop thinking. Well, how do you stop? Just stop. *How* do you just stop?" The mind would always come back with "how can you do it?" wanting to figure it out rather than trusting in the immanence of it. Trusting is relaxing into it; it's just attentiveness, which is an act of faith *(saddhā),* a "trustingness." It gives you perspective on anything you want to do, including other styles of meditation. Even training the physical body with these various mindful practices—yoga, Tai Chi, Qigong, and things like that—can fit well into the intuitive approach. Ultimately, when we develop these techniques, we learn to trust in the mindfulness rather than in just "me and my willful efforts" trying to do all these things.

I remember when I started hatha yoga, years ago, I'd see these pictures of yogis doing all these fantastic postures, and I wanted to do them, the really impressive ones. I had a big ego and didn't want to do the boring kind of things that you start out with, but really aimed at the fantastic. Of course, you're going to damage yourself trying to make your body do what you want before it's ready. Intuition is also knowing the limits of your body, what it can take. It's not just willfully making it do this and do that according to your ideas or ideals of what you want it to do, because, as many of you know, you can damage the body quite badly through tyrannically forcing it to do something. Yet mindfulness, sati-sampajañña, includes the body with its limitations, its disabilities, its sicknesses as well as its health and its pleasures.

In Theravāda Buddhism, as celibate alms mendicants especially, we can easily see sensual pleasure in terms of something we shouldn't enjoy. The Western mind will see Theravāda Buddhism in terms of denying pleasure, happiness, and joy. We do the *asubha* practices; we say the body is foul, loathsome, and filled with excrement, pus, and slime and things like that. If you're a monk you should never look at a woman; you keep your eyes down, and you shouldn't indulge in the pleasures of beauty—of anything. I remember in Thailand hearing that I shouldn't even look at a flower, because its beauty would capture me and make me think worldly thoughts. Because I'm from a Christian background, which for me has a strong puritanical ethic, it was easy to assume that sense pleasure is bad and that it's dangerous—you've got to try to deny it and avoid it at all costs. But then that's another opinion and view that comes out of an analytical mind, isn't it?

From my cultural background, the logic in seeing the foulness and loathsomeness of the body, the *asubha* practices, is easy to misinterpret in terms of being repelled and seeing the body in terms of something absolutely disgusting. Sometimes you can look at yourself and feel disgusted, even when you're fairly healthy—at least I can. It's a natural way to feel about yourself if you identify with the body and you dwell on its less appealing aspects. But for the word *asubha*, "loathsome" is not a very good translation, because to me "loathsome" is feeling really repelled and averse. If something is loathsome, it's dirty and foul, bad and nasty; you develop aversion and want to get rid of it. But *asubha* means "non-beautiful." *Subha* is beautiful; *asubha* is non-beautiful. That puts it in a better context—of looking at what is not beautiful and noticing it. Usually we don't notice this. We tend to give our attention to the beautiful in the worldly life, and the non-beautiful we either ignore, reject, or don't pay any attention to. We dismiss it because it's just not very attractive. So the vowel *a* in *asubha* is a negation, like *Amarāvatī*, "the Deathless." *Māra* is death; *amara* is Deathless. I found that a better way of looking at asubha practice.

Some of you have seen autopsies. I do not find that these lead to depression or aversion. Contemplating a dead human body at an autopsy when they're cutting it up, if you've never seen it before, it can be pretty shocking. The smells and the appearance—you can feel averse to it at first. But if you can stay beyond the initial reaction of shock and aversion, and with sati-sampajañña be open to all of this, then what I find is a sense of dispassion, which is a "cool" feeling. It's very clear, very cool, and very pleasant to be dispassionate. It's not dispassion through dullness or just through intellectual cynicism: it's just a feeling of non-aversion. Dispassion arises when we no longer see the human body in such a standard way as either very attractive and beautiful or ugly and foul, but of being able to relate to it, whether our own, somebody else's, or a corpse, in terms of sati-sampajañña. Sati-sampajañña opens the way to the experience of dispassion *(virāga)*.

Lust, on the other hand, is a lack of discrimination. The experience of sexual lust is a strong passion that takes you over and you lose your discriminative abilities. The more you absorb into it, the less discriminatory you get. It's interesting that critical people, the *dosacarita* (anger-aversion) types, usually like the asubha practices. They like very methodical meditations, especially when well presented intellectually: "You do this and then you do that." Stage one, then stage two, in a nice little outline. If you're critical, it's easy to see the body as foul and disgusting. A *kāmarāga-carita* (lustful-greedy) type of person likes *mettā* (loving-kindness) meditation the best. You teach mettā and they go "ooh!" with delight because mettā is not critical, is it? With mettā you are not being critical about anything.

So these are *upāyas* (skillful means) to get perspective. If one is a lustful type, then the asubha practices can be very balancing. They can be used skillfully to develop a more discriminative awareness of the unpleasantness, of the non-beautiful. For the dosacarita, then, mettā: being able to accept what you don't like without indulging in being critical, rejecting and averse to it. Mettā meditation is a real willingness. It can be done in a kind of stylized way, but basically it's sati-sampajañña. Sati-sampajañña accepts, it includes. Mettā is one of those inclusive things, much more intuitive than conceptual.

When you try to conceive mettā as "love," loving something in terms of liking it, you can't sustain mettā when you get to things you can't stand: people you hate and things like that. Mettā is very hard to come to terms with on a conceptual level. To love your enemies, to love people you hate or can't stand, is on the conceptual level an impossible dilemma. But in terms of sati-sampajañña, it's accepting, because it includes everything you like and dislike. Mettā is not analytical; it's not dwelling on why you hate somebody. It's not trying to figure out why I hate this person, but it includes the whole thing—the feeling, the person, myself—all in the same moment. So it's embracing, inclusive, and noncritical. You're not trying to figure out anything but just to open and accept, being patient with it.

With food, for instance, we eat here in the *dhutaṅga* tradition— that is, eating from alms bowls. I, at least, can no longer convince myself that I'm eating only one meal a day anymore because of this breakfast thing. But however many meals a day you eat, there's a limitation. Not because there's anything wrong with enjoying a meal; it's not that food is dangerous and that any kind of pleasure you receive from eating will bind you to rebirth again in the *saṃsāra-vaṭṭa* (the circle of birth and death)—that's another view and opinion—but it is a matter of recognizing the simplicity of the life that we have. It simplifies everything. This is why I like this way.

Just notice your attitude toward food. The greed, the aversion, or the guilt about eating or enjoying good food—include it all. There's no attitude that you have to have toward it, other than an attitude of sati-sampajañña. So it's not turning eating into a hassle. When I used to go on fasts, Luang Por Chah would point out that I was making a hassle out of my food. I couldn't just eat; I was making it more difficult than it needed to be. Then there is the guilt that comes up if you eat too much or you find yourself trying to get the good bits. I remember trying to get the good pieces for myself and then feeling guilty about that. There's a greed that really wants the tasty bits and then feels guilty about it.

Then it gets complicated. I couldn't just be greedy and shameless; I also had to have a strong sense of guilt around it and hope that nobody would notice. I had to keep it a secret, because I didn't want to look greedy, I wanted to look as if I wasn't.

I remember that while staying with Luang Por Jun, I was trying to be a really strict vegetarian, really strict. At the monastery, Wat Bung Khao Luang, they had certain kinds of dishes that didn't have any kind of fish sauce in them, or any kind of meat or fish. But as most of you know, in Thailand most of the food has fish sauce or some kind of animal mixtures in it. So it was difficult because I had very little choice and people would always have to make special things for me. I always had to be special. It had to be Phra Sumedho's food and then the rest. That was hard to deal with—to be a foreigner monk, a *phra farang,* and then to have a special diet and special privileges. That was hard for me to impose on the group. As I was helping to pass out the food, I'd get very possessive. The vegetable dishes they did have, I felt I had a right to have a lot of, because the other monks were eating all the fish, chicken, and things like that. I found myself aiming for the vegetarian dishes first so that I could pass them out according to my own needs. It brought up a really childish tendency in me. Then one day another monk saw me doing this, so he grabbed the vegetarian dish first and gave me only a little spoonful. I was so angry when I saw that. I took this fermented fish sauce, this *really* strong stuff, and when I went past his bowl, I splattered it all over his food! Fortunately, we were forbidden to hit each other. This is an absolute necessity for men—to have rules against physical violence!

I was trying to live up to an ideal of vegetarian purity, and yet in the process having these really violent feelings toward other monks. What was *that* about? It was a vindictive act to splatter all that strong chili sauce with rotten fish in it over some monk's food. It was a violent act done so I could keep a sense that I'm a pure vegetarian. So I began to question whether I wanted to make food into such a big deal in my life. Was I wanting to live my life as a vegetarian or what? Was that the main focus that I was aiming at? Just contemplating this, I began to see the suffering I created around my idealism. I noticed Luang Por Chah certainly enjoyed his food, and he had a joyful presence. It wasn't like an ascetic trip where you're eating nettle soup and rejecting the good bits; that's the other extreme.

Sati-sampajañña, then, is inclusive, and that's the attitude of a *samana* (monastic), rather than the ascetic, which is: "Sensual temptations, the sensual world, sensual pleasures are bad and dangerous. You've got to fight against them and resist them at all costs in order to become pure. Once you get rid of sexual desire, greed for food, all these other kinds of greedy sense things, these coarse, gross things, you don't have any more bad thoughts, you don't have any more greed, hatred, and delusion in your mind. You're absolutely sterilized from all those things. They're eradicated, totally wiped out, as if you used those toilet cleansers that kill every germ in sight—then you're pure." But then you've managed to kill everything including yourself! Is that the aim? That's taking asceticism to the *attakilamathānuyoga* position of annihilation.

Or is the opposite extreme the aim, the *kāmasukhallikānuyoga* one of eat, drink, and be merry, for tomorrow you may die? "Enjoy life. Life is a banquet, and most of the suckers are starving to death." This is a quote from a fifties movie called *Auntie Mame*. Auntie Mame managed to really enjoy life. She's a kind of icon, not a real woman but an icon of intelligence and beauty, one who just lives life to the hilt and enjoys everything. That's a very attractive idol: to see this life as something that is meant to be full of pleasure, happiness, and love. So grasping that is the kāmasukhallikānuyoga.

For the samaṇa, it's a matter of awakening to the two extremes; it includes both. It's not like taking sides: that we're rejecting or condemning Auntie Mame and "life is a banquet" or the extreme ascetic, the life-denying annihilator. But we can see that these are conditions that we create in our minds. Always wanting life to be at its best, a party, a banquet, one pleasure after another, or thinking that pleasures and enjoyment are wrong or bad, that they're unworthy and dangerous—these are conditions that we create. But the samaṇa life is right now; it's like *this*. It's opening to what we tend not to notice when we're seeking these two extremes as our goal.

Life is like *this*. You can't say it's always a banquet. Breath going in and out.... I wouldn't describe it as a banquet, or that the sound of silence is life at its best, where it's just one laugh after another. It's just like *this*. Most of our experience is neither one extreme nor the other; it's like *this*. Most of one's life is not peak moments, either in the heights nor in the depths. It's neither-nor; it's that which we don't notice if we're primed for extremes.

I find it helpful in terms of beauty, for example, to come from sati-sampajañña rather than from personal attachment. So with beautiful objects, beautiful things, beautiful people, whatever—coming from personal habits is dangerous because of the desire to possess them, to have them for yourself. When you experience beauty from a place of ignorance, you can be overwhelmed by desire. Then with experiencing beauty from sati-sampajañña, one can just be aware of the beauty as beauty. It also includes one's own tendencies to want to own it, take it, touch it, or fear it; it includes that. But when you're letting go of that, then beauty itself is joy.

We live on a planet that is quite beautiful. Nature is quite beautiful to the eye. So seeing it from sati-sampajañña I experience joy from that. When we speak from personal habits—then it can get complicated. It's complicated, no doubt, by wanting and not wanting, by guilt, or by just not noticing. If you get too involved with what's in your head, after a while you don't notice anything outside. You can be in the most beautiful place in the world and not see it, not notice it. So then beauty as experience, or sense pleasure, is seeing something for what it is. It is pleasurable. Good food does taste good; tasting a good, delicious flavor is like *this,* purely enjoyable. That's the way it is. So you may contemplate, "Oh, I shouldn't...." Then you're adding more to it. But from sati-sampajañña, it is what it is. It's experiencing the flow of life from this centerpoint, from the stillpoint that includes rather than from the point that excludes, the extreme positon of where we want only the beautiful and the good, just to have one banquet after another. When we can't sustain that delusion we get depressed. We go to the opposite, wanting to kill or annihilate ourselves in some way.

Just like this weather we've been having, the kind that people think England has all the time: cold, wet, damp, drizzly, and gray. This is the worldwide perception of England. I decided to open to these conditions with sati-sampajañña. It is what it is, but I'm not creating aversion to it. It's all right, and isn't like this very often. I've lived in this country for twenty-four years. Some of the most beautiful weather I have ever experienced has been here in England. Perfect days, so beautiful, the greenness, the beautiful flowers and hills and things like this. So sati-sampajañña includes the cold, wet, drizzly, and gray weather. There's no aversion created in it. In fact, I find I like it in a way, because I don't feel compelled to go out in it. I can sit in my *kuṭi* (hut) and keep

warm. I quite enjoy feeling that I don't have to go out anywhere just because the weather is so good. I can stay in my room, which I quite like; it has a nice feeling to it. When the weather gets really good I always feel I should be outdoors. These are ways of just noticing that even with physically unpleasant things like cold and dampness, the suffering is really in the aversion. "I don't like this. I don't want life to be like this. I want to be where there are blue skies and sunshine all the time."

With the body-sweeping practice, I found paying attention to neutral sensation very helpful because it is so easily ignored. When I first started doing it years ago, it was difficult to find, because I'd never paid attention to neutral sensation, even though it's quite obvious. My experience of sensation was always through the extremes of either pleasure or pain. But noticing just how the robe touches the skin, just one hand touching the other, the tongue in the mouth touching the palate or the teeth, or the upper lip resting on the lower, investigating little details of sensation that arethere when you open to them. They are there, but you don't notice them unless you're determined to. If your lips are painful you notice; if you're getting a lot of pleasure from your lips, you notice. But when it's neither pleasure nor pain, there's still sensation but it's neutral. So you're allowing neutrality to be conscious.

Consciousness is like a mirror; it reflects. A mirror reflects—not just the beautiful or the ugly but whatever is there: the space, the neutrality, everything that's in front of it. Usually you notice only the outstanding things, the extremes of beauty or ugliness. But to awaken to the way it is, you're not looking at the obvious but recognizing the subtlety behind the extremes. The sound of silence is like a subtlety behind everything that you awaken to; you don't notice it if you're seeking the extremes.

When you're seeking happiness and trying to get away from

pain and misery, then you're caught in always trying to get something or hold on to happiness—like tranquillity. We want tranquillity; we want samatha and jhānas because we like tranquillity. We don't want confusion, chaos, or cacophony, abrasive sensory experiences, or human contacts; we don't want that. So we come into the temple and sit down, close our eyes, and give off signs saying "don't bother me," "leave me alone," and "I'm going to get my samādhi." That can be the very basis for our practice—getting my samādhi so I can feel good, because I want that." That leads to an extreme again—wanting, always grasping after the ideal of some refined conscious experience. Then there's the others who say, "You don't need to do that. Daily life is good enough. Just in-the-marketplace practice—that's where it's at. Where you're not doing anything extreme like sitting, closing your eyes, but you're just living life as an ordinary person and being mindful of everything." That also can be another ideal that we attach to.

These are ideals; positions that we might take. They are the "true but not right, right but not true" predicament that we create with our dualistic mind; it's not that they're wrong. In George Orwell's novel *Animal Farm* there is the slogan "Everyone is equal but some are more equal than others." In the conditioned realm, this is how we think. We think all human beings are equal, ideally. All human beings are equal, but with the practicalities of life, some are more equal than others. You won't find the affluent Western world willing to give up much for the sake of equality in the Third World.

Reflect on the monastic form. It's a convention, and its aim is connected to the world through its alms mendicancy. We need society; we need the world around us; we need the lay community for our survival. They are a part of us.

Monasticism is not an attack on or a rejection of lay life. If we're living in the right way, then the lay community brings forth its good qualities: generosity, gratitude, and the like. We can also move toward silence—this is encouraged—toward meditation and reflection. We can combine both samatha and *vipassanā* (calm and insight meditation), both solitude and worldly life. It's not a question of rejecting one and holding on to the other as the ideal, but of recognizing this is the way it is; it's like *this*. The world we live in, the society we live in—we're not rejecting it, turning against or away from it, but including it. So we can include it in the silence and the solitude.

THE WAY IT IS

DEDICATION OF OFFERINGS

(Yo so) bhagavā arahaṃ sammāsambuddho

To the Blessed One, the Lord, who fully attained perfect enlightenment,

Svākkhāto yena bhagavatā dhammo

To the Teaching, which he expounded so well,

Supaṭipanno yassa bhagavato sāvakasaṅgho

And to the Blessed One's disciples who have practiced well,

Tammayaṃ bhagavantaṃ sadhammaṃ sasaṅghaṃ

To these—the Buddha, the Dhamma, and the Sangha—

Imehi sakkārehi yathārahaṃ āropitehi abhipūjayāma

We render with offerings our rightful homage.

Sādhu no bhante bhagavā sucira-parinibbutopi

It is well for us that the Blessed One, having attained liberation,

Pacchimā-janatānukampa-mānasā

Still had compassion for later generations.

Ime sakkāre duggata-paṇṇākāra-bhūte paṭiggaṇhātu

May these simple offerings be accepted

Amhākaṃ dīgharattaṃ hitāya sukhāya

For our long-lasting benefit and for the happiness it gives us.

Arahaṃ sammāsambuddho bhagavā

The Lord, the Perfectly Enlightened and Blessed One—
Buddhaṃ bhagavantaṃ abhivādemi
I render homage to the Buddha, the Blessed One.

(Svākkhāto) bhagavatā dhammo
The Teaching, so completely explained by him—
Dhammaṃ namassāmi
I bow to the Dhamma.

(Supaṭipanno) bhagavato sāvakasaṅgho
The Blessed One's disciples, who have practiced well—
Saṅghaṃ namāmi
I bow to the Sangha.

PRELIMINARY HOMAGE

(Handa mayaṃ buddhassa bhagavato pubbabhāga-namakāraṃ
karomase)
[Now let us pay preliminary homage to the Buddha.]
(Namo tassa) bhagavato arahato sammāsambuddhassa.
Homage to the Blessed, Noble, and Perfectly Enlightened One.

THE MORNING CHANT reproduced above—this continuous recollection of Buddha, Dhamma, and Sangha—is a way of internalizing, of seeing, this reality within yourself, rather than being just some kind of traditional chanting. Over the years this chanting does have a rather good effect on consciousness. It develops our vocabulary. One of the great advantages of a tradition such as Theravāda is that it has an agreed vocabulary. Pāli is a scholastic language now, it's not a living language that changes. So it kind of holds concepts and then allows us to use words, to have an agreed vocabulary, ways of expressing and thinking that aren't just bound into cultural conditioning or personal descriptions of experience.

When we develop awareness, we're coming from intuitive awareness rather than from personal experience. So when we express everything in a personal way, it tends to give the impression of something; it reinforces the sense of "me and mine" as a personality, as "my" reality. Whereas Pāli terms are not meant to be taken in a personal way. "Buddha, Dhamma, Sangha" is not some personal mode of expression but points to the reality we experience here and now. So when I use this word "Buddho" or "Buddha," this is not meant to be some kind of personal achievement or identity; it points to the pure knowing, pure subjectivity, before the personality arises. This is like intuitive intelligence—it's universal intelligence, not a personally acquired knowledge. So I just keep pointing to this "Buddho" that we recognize through being fully present, fully attentive to the present moment. Then it is like composing, bringing your scattered mind to this one point, here and now.

So in the present moment we're experiencing reality from this point. Each of us is a point of conscious experience, and we're experiencing, recognizing Dhamma, the way it is. And that's different than me sitting here experiencing my life through my memories and my emotions and my views and opinions. Because I'm no longer looking at it in a personal way: "my" life and what's happened to "me" and the way I think and what I hold is right and wrong. Getting beyond that to an awareness before the personality can arise or cease—that's awareness or sati-sampajañña. So the relationship of *Buddha* to *Dhamma* is rather different from the relationship of *me* to *my feelings*. It's a difference of attitude, the act of taking refuge in Buddha-Dhamma, rather than in my particular personal scenario. So my personal scenario, then, is seen in terms of Dhamma—what arises, ceases, personal feelings, memories...all these arise and cease.

I'm not dismissing anything whatsoever but changing from the highly emotive, painful, personal position to the awareness of the "Buddha knowing the Dhamma." I'm explaining this and how to use the Buddhist convention as a skillful means, not as an end in itself. And it's difficult to separate: to recognize the difference between pure subjectivity and the personal feeling—the sense of me as a person, a personality. That's why by a patient attentiveness in the present you begin to recognize the natural state of being and are able to recognize the personality as a mental object. Personality is a creation, it's not the subject of anything, and yet we tend to interpret experience always through personal feelings, personal opinions.

So now composing yourself, bringing your attention to the here and now, to the breath, the posture of the body, the mood: just reflect on them, on the mental state you're experiencing. There's a sense of awareness, and this includes the mental state, the posture, and the breath, so it's not just going to one without paying attention to the other. Trust in the awareness as that which holds you, which you're resting in, in which you can observe. Witness the observer, the emotional quality or mood, the breathing of the body, the posture.

So with awareness, for example, and visual consciousness, sitting here I can see the bell, the clock, my glasses, the chanting book—awareness means they're all here, present in one moment. Then I can notice, pay attention to, the chanting book or the glasses or the bell accordingly; this intuitive awareness embraces

everything here. Recognizing this—liberation is not going just to
one thing and shutting out everything else. Once I recognize this
awareness as the gate to the Deathless, to liberation, then I can
pay attention to the things, the particular objects that are present. Awareness includes visual consciousness and sound, smell,
taste, touch. It includes the mood you're in, the state of mind; it
includes the breath and the posture, the body and its sensations.

Now just to reiterate: I'm more interested in an attitude than in
a technique of meditation. Different teachers and different schools
have different techniques, different modes of meditation practice.
If the attitude is right then the techniques can be very useful, but
if we don't have the right attitude, then no matter what technique
we're using, we can only condition ourselves, bind ourselves to
a particular meditation technique. We become habituated to a
technique. The attitude, then, is of relaxed attentiveness, a sense
of opening, receptivity—a poised attention. Now, because I've
been meditating forty years, this opening to the present moment
has become, I find, my lifestyle as a Buddhist monk. So having
devoted forty years to mindfulness I'm very much aware at this
moment—just the bare attention, the mindful state of being, this
receptive state.

I notice the kind of background sound which I refer to as the
sound of silence, a resonating, vibratory sound. Is it a sound?
Whatever it is—"sound" isn't quite accurate—I begin to notice
a high-pitched kind of vibration that's always present. Once you
recognize this point—at which one is fully open, receptive; when
you recognize this sound of silence your thinking process stops—
you can rest in this stream. It's like a stream. It isn't like ordinary
sound that rises and ceases or begins and ends. The sound of the
bell has a beginning and ending, and so does the sound of the
birds, the sound of my voice. But behind that, behind all other

sounds, is this sound of silence. It's not that we create it or that it comes and goes—in my explorations of this it's always present, it's just there whether I notice it or not. So once I notice it—and it sustains itself, I don't have to create it—then it's just present, pure presence.

Earlier I referred to the body as four elements. So investigating this, in a non-personal way, the reality of a physical body—the four elements: solid element, fire element, liquid element, wind element; earth, fire, water, wind. Using these particular terms is a way of contemplating the nature of your physical body in the present. Bones, the solid bits of the body, the liquid water element, the fire or warmth, the air, the breath: it is looking at the body in a different way than if you evaluated it, whether you're male or female, young or old—the way we tend to regard ourselves, our bodies, in these very personal terms.

Then there's the space and consciousness elements. So there are six elements—earth, fire, water, wind, space, and consciousness—and notice that the body is in space, there's space all around it. Space is ever present, but if we're just concerned with the things in the space then we tend not to pay any attention to the element of space. Now we're going to the immeasurable, because space has no boundary. Earth, fire, water, and wind are contained and have limits and boundaries; they arise and cease. But visual space—where is the boundary to it? We might think that the walls of the room contain space—but space contains this room. There's space outside—where does it end? We're not looking for scientific explanations of space, but just in terms of experience here and now. When we begin to observe space we're not trying to get rid of the things in the space, but by withdrawing our absorption and fascination and habit of just looking at this and then that, going from one thing to another, we begin to notice that the reality of space is real. It's not created. I don't create this space—the word "space" is a creation, but it's pointing, getting me to look at, the here and now.

Being aware of space: space has no other quality than being spacious, it is boundless *(appamāṇa)*. So you're beginning to recognize, realize boundlessness, the unlimited, infinity. One can see, recognize the sound of silence, the reality of consciousness—it has no boundary because it takes consciousness to be aware of this subtle, ringing, resonating vibration—and as we explore that, it has no boundary. We don't create it, it's like space, it's infinite.

When you're identified on the level of "I am the body and I am my feelings, thoughts, and memories," you're always limiting, binding yourself to unsatisfactory conditions. These conditions can never satisfy you, because they're changing. When you try to find security and permanent happiness in things that are forever changing, you're going to be terribly disappointed. You're going to feel this dukkha or this sense of lack, and we tend to take that as a very personal flaw: "There's something wrong with me. What's wrong with me that I should feel lonely, inadequate, incomplete, or unfulfilled?"

So you see, the Buddha is pointing to the human problem, and this is an ancient teaching, not a modern New Age approach. Two thousand five hundred years of this teaching have existed. Because it's about the human condition—how we, as human individuals, can awaken to ultimate truth. If our identities are always with the conditioned, we're always going to feel some sense of lack and fear. Anxiety haunts our lives. So the Buddha says, "Wake up! Pay attention to life itself! Open to it. Observe. Witness." And so right here in this room we observe the way it is on a conditioned level: the body's like this, the breath is like this, the personal mood... the state of mind...space...consciousness is like this.

You're getting the full spectrum from this point, here and now right where you are. I'm sitting here, you're sitting over there. I experience it from this position here. You don't have to sit up on this seat here to experience it. It's not the place but the attitude. So then the inevitable question: Who's experiencing what? What is it? And then you're back into the world of thinking again: Who's the one that experiences all this? There's nobody—it's not a person, is it? Because the personality arises according to conditions. So somebody comes in and says, "Ajahn Sumedho?" and I say, "Yes." Then the conventional role of being Ajahn Sumedho can operate. Those roles depend on conditions for their existence. But this awareness doesn't depend on conditions for its existence. So you're seeing it in terms of Dhamma: All conditions are impermanent, all dhammas are not-self. Now, putting ourselves in the Buddha position—the Buddho, the knowing—I'm in that position where the awareness includes, opens me to the unconditioned. It's the unconditioned itself, in which the conditioned is seen in perspective. It's seen as *ārammana* (mental objects)—it is objectified, it's recognized.

From the position of awareness then, here—in Pāli, the Theravāda language—are the five *khandhas* (groups): *rūpa* is translated as the body; *vedanā* is feeling; *saññā,* perception; *saṅkhārā,* mental formations; and *viññāṇa,* consciousness. We experience consciousness through the senses—through seeing the bell, the clock, the glasses; or through consciousness of what we hear, smell, taste, touch. Form and consciousness, rūpa and viññāṇa, we don't create that—that's the package we arrive in when we're born. The rest of the sense realm, the vedanā—the pleasure, pain, or neutral sensation through the senses—we don't create that; it's like this. The cultural conditioning—the personality and language—is conditioned after we're born; we don't come with that. That means we're programmed by our parents and the society that we're born into. Our identities and so forth are conditioned. Our conventional reality is programmed like a computer, isn't it? We get that program.

So now we're going back to before the program begins, to the pure awareness—consciousness that isn't bound. We're not projecting or experiencing the consciousness through perceiving any particular thing but through awareness. That's why I keep pointing to this sense of attentiveness and listening, like the sound of silence. I use this listening or hearing; it means that I'm open, on that level of poised attention, to this resonating vibration that is easily not noticed. If we're always going into things, into thoughts, then we don't notice it. Some people have never noticed it. Some people, when they recognize it, develop aversion to it—they think it's tinnitus or something.

I was giving a retreat in the United States four years ago and talking about this. The participants were practicing the method where they label everything—and so they all noticed this sound of silence, but then they kept labeling it "sound...sound...sound," trying to get rid of it. Its how you relate to it—you can take an aversion to it or you can use it because it's expansive. When you relax into this sound of silence it's like resting and floating in a stream. It's just learning to pay attention and recognize what awareness really is. Now from this position you can reflect, because it isn't an absorption; you're not sinking into it and going into a trance of any sort. It keeps you fully present. Right now I'm fully aware of it, and I can speak at the same time. It's not like I have to stop speaking. I can include everything here. I don't have to close my eyes or shut out everything to be with this sound of silence.

In this stillness, then, the thinking process can arise and cease, but you're not caught in habitual, obsessive thoughts. Thinking is a habit. When you start thinking, one thought-moment connects to another, and so it's going from one thought to the next. We become absorbed in our thinking. Our thinking takes over consciousness—what we're experiencing through consciousness. But in this you recognize non-thinking. And as I said before, you have to *think* to create yourself as a person. With non-thinking, there's no longer a person.

Reflecting on this, anattā (not-self) is like this—it's not a destruction of personality or annihilation of anything. Anattā can sound like you are annihilating yourself. It's not an attack on the personality. It's putting the personality into perspective so you are not limited to your personality habits that you've acquired after birth. I'm reflecting at this moment myself, recognizing this natural state of being—the Buddho, the Buddha—knowing the truth of the way it is, knowing the Dhamma.

This is the point: present-moment awareness of the infinite that embraces the finite. To me the great gift of being human is that we can do this. This is within the human capability—not to perfect myself as a personality, become president of the United States or something like that. The Buddha's teaching is for human beings—it's not an ethereal teaching for only super-beings. Just take for granted that we are here and have taken the three refuges and the eight precepts. Human beings do things like this. In the animal world they can't take the eight precepts—trying to get the cat to stop killing the bird, "Give him the first precept!"

We might have the cat's inclination to kill a bird, but we humans can reflect on that feeling. We see a spider—we want to kill it. In England we are not into bird killing, but spiders, garden pests, we are quite willing to murder. But we can reflect on that, the impulse to kill some spider. So we can agree and make moral agreements. We have a reflective mind; we can observe our impulses. We are not trying to make ourselves into nonviolent persons but are also observing the violent impulses we have at times, not as personal flaws but just as impulses—things that arise and cease—agreeing not to act on that impulse.

So this morning is an opportunity to explore this, to center yourself in the present moment, the position of awareness, receptivity, acceptance. From that position we can focus on the breath or the body, reflect on Dhamma, as we begin to notice the arising and ceasing, noticing how moods change, how thoughts come and go, how sensation arises through the senses. We contemplate the reality of change—anicca—and then remember this natural state of awareness, which allows us to observe, to recognize, to witness the change that is happening through the body and our senses.

I N THIS THIRD DAY of our retreat you can be aware of the result of two days of noble silence, keeping the eight precepts, and being mindful. The reflections I give are for encouragement. The only way I can really help you is to encourage this sense of being awake, because although it's easy to say and understand conceptually, the reality is to realize what awakenness really is: sati-sampajañña, sati-paññā. So it's bringing attention always to the here and now. These words convey the sense of really observing, noticing and reflecting on the way it is.

Reflecting, then, is using consciousness as a kind of mirror so that you begin to recognize consciousness—realize the consciousness—because we're all conscious at this moment of what arises and ceases: the thoughts, the emotions, pleasure, pain, sensory experiences through the eyes, ears, nose, tongue, body. Then you can also see how, in terms of meditation, when you confine yourself to the eight precepts in a meditation retreat, where you have to sit for long periods of time and be quiet, it seems to increase the dukkha of your life, the suffering. Because if you were at home you wouldn't probably do this. There would be nothing to make you sit for a solid hour—in pain! When we get a little restless or experience a little discomfort then we can distract ourselves. In our homes usually we have a kind of routine where we know where things are, where the refrigerator is, the television, and then there's always duties and things that need to be done, the telephone rings...

Any kind of restriction seems to increase the suffering. We're creatures of habit, so we become very used to our own way, the place we're living in. When that changes in some way, we have to restrain ourselves or live in a way that we're not used to emotionally—and the body's not used to it. During the first three days I encourage you to let your body get used to this way of living. And mentally to surrender to it. The daily life situation has changed—it's *like this*. This atmosphere, the environment here at the retreat center at Amarāvatī—we can become used to that. In fact we can get so used to it after a ten-day retreat that you'll find going home rather traumatic. It'll seem too coarse. You get used to the restrained life and the orderliness here, the stillness.

People I've known have gone on a six-month silent retreat and then had to return to London. They usually suffer enormously—just from going back to London, back to the family and the chaos of family life. We get accustomed to things. I lived in Thailand for quite a few years before going back to the United States for a visit. I became so accustomed to Thailand, to the monastic life in Thailand. My senses, everything adjusted to the forest monastery and the Thai appearance, Thai features, and so when I found myself back in a country of big noses and big chins, I could understand what Thais feel like!

We have an amazing ability to adapt to things, to get used to and adjust to situations. The atmosphere of a meditation retreat here is like this. I'm not telling you anything about the way it is— just trust your own reflection, "It's like this." You begin to open to the way it is. Not criticizing and comparing it with something else but just being more conscious and observant of the kind of conditions that you experience during this ten-day retreat—and the effect it has on your mind. It's not habituating you, using some kind of sensory deprivation to calm you down—so that when you go back home you'll be even more upset. But here the atmosphere is restrained, contained. The absence of our customary distractions gives us a chance to reflect in a way that we might not elsewhere. Recognize this as a special situation.

These are special conditions. It's not like daily life, is it? It's not ordinary life that one lives. We live this way just to make it very conscious that this is a special situation, designed to give you as much time and opportunity as possible to reflect on what's going on, what's happening to you. We see it in terms of Dhamma rather than in terms of "me" and "mine." So that's why we use this Buddhist language. As I said, we don't really have a proper English translation for "Dhamma." It's a profound word. It's not a concept that we have in the English language. The best we can do is to translate it as the truth of the way it is. "Refuge in the truth of the way it is" does sound a bit strange, doesn't it? To me at least, "I'm taking refuge in the truth of the way it is" sounds strange. And then I want to know, "What way is it? Tell me the way it is!"

I'm not going to tell you the way it is! You can observe yourself. I'm putting it back onto you. *Wake up and observe* the way it is!—rather than ask me to tell you how it is. And then you might get into how things *should* be. Maybe you've gone on meditation retreats somewhere else—with other teachers—and you've got a standard of what you think meditation retreats should be. So then you come up to me: "Ajahn Sumedho...I think you should..." Maybe your standard for meditation retreats differs from what you're experiencing here. But that's also observable, we're not saying this is the ultimate, the highest standard for meditation retreats, or that there's no other possibility that is worth your bother. We're not trying a hard sell or conversion. So in a retreat the annoying, irritating, or frustrating things that happen are a part of this experience—we're awakening to the way it is, rather than idealizing how it should be.

Going back to the concept of anattā or non-self, this I personally found one of the more difficult concepts to understand. The concept of aniccā I found quite obvious. If you pay attention for long, you see that everything's changing—that's not a difficult one to recognize. But with anattā, it seems like if there's any reality here, it's *me!* I'm the one sitting here, feeling the things, this body here. I have to *live* with it, so it *must* be mine—it must be really happening to me. That seems like an obvious fact.

So then we can say "not-self" is a kind of a doctrinal position; we think we've got to get rid of our self. We've got to make our self into a kind of no person, no personality. On a conceptual level what does that mean? Can you imagine not having any personality? Just nothing really—it sounds like you're almost dead! Every personal opinion, every personal feeling, we would need to reject. But that's not it. It's not an annihilation of self. It's seeing that the self that we tend to cling to is our own creation. We create ourselves. And so with awareness we're beginning to see that. We're beginning to notice how I create myself as a person. Just out of habit, out of not awakening, out of being caught up in thinking habits, emotional habits, and identities that I never notice let alone question.

With sati-sampajañña we begin to notice what the sense of "me" and "mine" is. Because we have subjectivity, we have the sense of being aware. You're all objects in terms of this moment, in terms of visual consciousness here—you're objects in my consciousness.

Yet on a conventional level we wouldn't recognize that. We think we're all just people sitting here, on a meditation retreat, and we tend to see it from a very conventional position. But if I take that too into awareness, actually you're in my consciousness. I can't see my own face but I can see yours! That seems like an obvious fact, but it's worth contemplating. My right eye can't see my left eye—even when I cross my eyes! But I can see your eyes—so this is a reflection, observing the way it is. How many of you observe the fact that you can't see your own face right now? And then you go to a mirror: "I can see my face!" But that's a reflection, isn't it? That's not one's face—that's a reflection in a mirror. But we assume, just on a conventional level, when we want to shave we look into a mirror—so we can see, the reflection will help us to not shave off our nose or cut ourselves. This sounds so obvious and matter-of-fact, yet how many of you have ever really contemplated in this way?

Usually we're operating from a conditioned sense of self, what is called *sakkāya-diṭṭhi*—personality view. The Pāli word that we translated as "ego" or "self-view"—personality view—is sakkāya-diṭṭhi, is a sense of oneself as a separate person identified with the body and with memories and thoughts, it's a habit. So then the question arises: is this really me? We're not trying to deny these things to take the opposite stance of denial, but rather awakening and observing the way it is. Anattā is a characteristic of existence. It's not a quality or a doctrinal position, and it's not an annihilationist belief.

The Pāli word *nibbāna* is also often translated as "extinction." Now when I first came across this definition in Theravāda literature, that the aim is to "extinguish oneself," it sounded very nihilistic—extinction is annihilation, isn't it? For me at that time "extinction" meant total extinction—oblivion. Because that's the cultural conditioning of the mind and the English word "extinction," when I read that word, it means you "extinguish" something—you're getting rid of it, annihilating it. So when trying to explain to people what this word *nibbāna* means, we say, "Well, it means 'extinction.' Our main practice is to 'extinguish' things—become extinct!" That doesn't sound very inspiring.

So what does *nibbāna* really mean? In Buddhist countries nibbāna is often raised to a high level of attainment and achievement. You hear in Thailand about nibbāna as if it was some kind of high experience. It becomes a superlative in our language, almost equated with heaven: "I went into nibbāna, just went up on high and blissed out." The Buddha wasn't pointing to a high state but an awakened state. This awakened state is a natural state of being that we all can recognize if we pay attention, if we observe the way it is—if we observe things in terms of Dhamma. And this is what happens with religious conventions; they stay on the intellectual plane, they get fixed in this dualistic structure. So God and Satan are opposed to each other. I remember that when I was growing up as a Christian I said, "Um, well, Satan must be kind of a God too?" And my mother said no. So I asked, "If God created everything, why did God create Satan?" And she said, "Well, Satan disobeyed God, and he got sent to Hell!" That somehow didn't satisfy me. That's what you do with your mind, when you think and you're stuck on that linear level.

So I keep pointing out what thought is, what thinking is. It's a function that we have—one thought goes on to another. I have the thought "I am Ajahn Sumedho, a Buddhist monk," and then I get carried away, telling you all about my past and my plans for the future—the wandering mind. So long as we remain on the level of concept and convention—this has its function—we cannot liberate ourselves because the conventions themselves are conditioned; they're created and depend on language. So, rather than trying to get a perfect English definition for sati-sampajañña, rather than spending your life trying to define it, use it. It's something to use here and now. It's not something that you have to find somewhere else. If you define it too much then you become caught in trying to grasp the concepts or your definitions, trying to become like you think that should be.

So with mindfulness, sati, it's not like a thought or something that you need to develop or get hold of by controlling conditions—it's a matter of just using it. Awakened, observing, listening; attentiveness, openness. Now if I just stay in observing my thinking process I can choose to deliberately think, I can think very positively. I've experimented with developing positive thinking in the past. All is love and good, loving-kindness and compassion, and I put everything in a positive mode. Or just practicing mettā on a conceptual level, where I don't allow negative thoughts into consciousness. I keep concentrating on positive concepts, and that makes me feel very good—the power of positive thinking. That was a bestseller back in the forties in the United States, by Norman Vincent Peale. Everybody was buying *The Power of Positive Thinking*.

Thinking positively is certainly good advice. I'm not condemning it or making fun of it. If I think in very positive ways all the time, I do experience a happier life and I tend to be more positive. You can feel good and get very high, very blissed out on positive thinking. But the trouble is that you have to be continually, compulsively positive about everything to keep feeling good. To sustain the illusion of happiness that you get from positive thinking, you can't allow doubt, skepticism, or negative concepts to enter your mind. As soon as you become aware of this act of compulsive positivity, you stop winding yourself up.

Now, apply that same principle to negative thinking: "Life is no good. It's all a joke, everybody's corrupt, and there's not an honest person on the planet. All religions are phony; all politicians are corrupt.... My mother had me only because she was selfish and greedy, because she was filled with lust and..." And then what happens? I get depressed: "Life, what's the point of it? It's just a waste of time!" You can get stuck in depression. Doing this intentionally is a way of mindfully reflecting on the way it is; one can feed positivity or negativity. The result of positive thinking is happiness, of negative thinking is unhappiness. Positive thinking is heaven; negative thinking is hell.

That which is aware of the positive and negative—awareness— does not take sides, does not make judgments. It just notices the way things are, the way experience really is at this present time. So if Buddhist meditation were merely a kind of positive experience, certainly that can be quite skillful, but then when the conditions don't support your positive views, you crash. You can lose it; you can go into hell when the conditions and the people around you don't support positivity. So now observing this, you begin to recognize that there's just this dualistic ability to think—positive or negative. This is a construction, a convention.

So how to use thinking, rather than just be caught in the thinking process with no perspective on thought? Thinking becomes habitual and you can easily wander away in thought. Then intentionally think, listen to yourself thinking. Now that takes sati-sampajañña. It's skillful means to be aware of thinking rather than being caught up in it. We usually become our thoughts if we're not aware. And that's why I suggest intentional thinking, so that you're not trying to think about thinking. What we tend to do is get ideas about non-thinking and then think it or think about thinking, and think our way around anattā, and think our way around nibbāna—and so we never get out of that trap of our own thoughts—until we *observe* thinking. How do you observe thinking in your own mind?

In the present moment I find that, to intentionally think, I make a determination: "I'm going to think right now." Then I listen—you can hear yourself thinking, or at least I can—I listen to myself speaking. So then I can say, "I am a human being." Now this is not a thought that inspires me—it doesn't carry me up into bliss, nor is it depressing. So it's a kind of neutral statement, it's a matter of fact. You're now observing thought from this position of sati-paññā—the observing, awakened consciousness. You're beginning to recognize that you're not a thought—you're not what you think at all. Most of our thinking is acquired thinking habits, and our sense of self, of self-worth, comes from experience in life and from culture and society: family, education, ethnic conditioning, religious conditioning.

When I started studying Buddhism all my thinking processes were conditioned through Christianity. I'm from a devout Christian family—it was part of the cultural package I got from my mother and father and the society I grew up in. I didn't ask for it. Christian concepts, values, morality, love—Christian everything. So when I first started reading Buddhist scriptures, it was natural to be influenced by my conditioning because the thinking process was very much connected to Christian values, Christian ideas. By the time I discovered Buddhism I was off Christianity and I no longer considered myself a Christian. I didn't make Buddhism into another form of Christianity; I just tried to recognize the way my mind was conditioned and the way we tend to interpret words.

I found the Pāli teachings very helpful, because it's a different language. Using Pāli terms helps us to reflect—you have to translate them, so you understand the words. The terms are helpful, not for conditioning you to a Buddhist mind-set where you adopt Buddhist ideas and concepts and become a Buddhist, but for reflecting on the way it is. At first, religion for me meant inspiring things like unconditioned love, God's love and sacrifice, and exalted, inspiring terms—in contrast to the Buddha who talked about the noble truth of suffering, dukkha, and said nothing about eternal love. And so this was very interesting to me—a totally new approach. The Four Noble Truths aren't a doctrine; they aren't a dogma or metaphysics. They point to a very common experience, suffering, that every one of us can recognize with no trouble at all. It takes suffering out of being just a nasty experience that one wants to get rid of, and putting it in the context of a Noble Truth *(ariya-sacca).*

Why does he put "noble" in front of "suffering? Or call the First Noble Truth "the truth of suffering?" Then you reflect, "Why? Is there something noble about suffering, that I must believe in suffering?" If I start believing in suffering I get depressed: "It's all suffering. Everything is impermanent. There's no self, no God, and no soul. It all ends up in extinction." I find that depressing. It's so negative. If you hang on to this word, you become a wet blanket, a sour, grumpy person, not very pleasant company.

The word *dukkha* is interesting because even though the common translation is "suffering" it means much more. Usually *du* is a negative prefix in Pāli: *dukkha* means "what is hard to bear," "unsatisfying," or "unsatisfactoriness." It conveys a sense of incompleteness, a wanting or longing for something, or something that is missing or lacking, as in the thought "I'm not good enough." Once we turn our critical mind toward ourselves we can see all kinds of flaws and defects, inadequacies, and faults. I know what I would like to be if I could be just perfect, making myself into an ideal: the perfect man. I can imagine, being honest, brave, noble, kind, sensitive, intelligent, and strong. Then I look at myself and think, "I'll never make it."

"Why didn't God create me with the best? Why did he give me this burden to bear?" I used to feel quite annoyed: "It's not fair! God created everybody, so why are some people better off than others? Why do some people have such unfortunate conditions: bad health, bad parenting, and horrible places to live in? Not fair, is it?" So dukkha, being a noble truth, is for reflecting on—on one's sense of something being missing, inadequate, unsatisfying, or incomplete. When I contemplate myself as a person, I've never been able to convince myself that I'm all that good. I'm more aware of what I lack, the mistakes I make, the failures of my life. I'm more aware on that level than of my own goodness or my great gifts—or my good *kamma* (actions).

So on the level of conditioned personality it seems to be a critical personality that is very much aware of what's wrong—it obsesses itself with what's wrong—with me or with you or with the world in general. This can be observed, can't it? If I'm being self-disparaging and self-critical, this is a form of suffering because there's always a sense of "I shouldn't." "There's something wrong with me—who can I blame it on?" "Why can't I be this noble man, that's the way I should be." And yet this is what I find myself with, which I can only criticize and feel inferior or guilty about. So this is a reflection on the First Noble Truth. Being aware of this—of the negative way one regards oneself. "I am a human being": reflection on this does not create any strong emotion, I notice—it's rather neutral. I explore that before I think in terms of "I." When you're intentionally thinking a sentence or a word, there's a space there; there's no thought. Now that's an awareness, isn't it? Awareness of non-thought.

Then I think, "I..." and there's another space there. So this noticing, paying attention, no longer taking an interest in the things but the space around the object. This, I found, was one way of investigating the sense of myself, by taking a rather neutral attitude. "I'm a human being"—this is neutral. But "I...am... an...inadequate person.... I'm somebody with a lot of faults"— that's a little more emotive. That hurts a little bit—to see myself as somebody with a lot of faults. But I'm interested in the space around the words rather than in the words themselves. When I start thinking, "I'm somebody with a lot of faults," the feeling there is definitely different than when I think, "I am a human being." This is reflecting on how words affect our emotions. We're sensitive creatures; thought does affect us.

So "I'm a human being"—that's neutral. "I am a flawed man"—that's not neutral, that's a criticism. That's a negative observation. Then I can say, "I'm a very good person." I find that is not an easy one to think. I'm not used to thinking about "I'm a good person"—it seems a bit bland and dishonest. Somehow I was brought up to think that knowing all that's wrong with you is being honest. But that which is aware of this, the awareness of the "I" that arises, that "I" is a creation, isn't it? I mean, in different languages you have different words. In English, fortunately, it's just this one letter "I"—and so it's quite symbolic actually. This "I" in consciousness, the awareness of "I," that awareness isn't "I," is it? It doesn't have a word for it, because it's real. "I" or "me" is an artifice, a habit—it is due to language.

I find "I" doesn't have the strong ego quality of "me" or "mine" in statements like "This is mine! These things are mine! What about me?" But "I" can also be... "What *I* think"... "If you want my opinion" and "*I* really..." then the "I" becomes very big. So just in the tone of voice, you're aware of an emphasis on this sense that "I am this person and my view is like this." What I'm pointing to is an awareness of this through investigation. Just by observing and reflecting: "Is this I, me, or mine?" I create these words; they're conventions. But I don't create that which is aware of them. I'm not creating mindfulness. I'm just being mindful. So mindfulness isn't "I" or "me" or "mine"—it's anattā, not a self. It's not a man, not a human, not a woman, not a Buddhist monk. So by reflecting in this way you begin to value this ability to be aware. It's very important to recognize awareness and then really value that.

Awareness is the way out of suffering, the gate to the Deathless. And it's not a creation, not a personal quality. So as you practice, as you investigate, you begin to objectify language and thought as a mental object—and the emotions that arise such as "What about me?" I assert myself as a person: "I've got my rights! Got to stand up for myself! I'm not going to be bullied by anybody!" If my refuge is in the awareness then that sense of a person is an object in consciousness. It becomes conscious; it arises and ceases. So the "self" or the sakkāya-diṭṭhi is an artifice—it's artificial and created. We create it; we create ourselves as persons, as personalities.

So it's not a question of getting rid of the personality but of recognizing its limits, of freeing ourselves from it—because when you really look at it, our personality is very limiting. We have all kinds of views about ourselves, our abilities, our worth and all that. And so we tend to get stuck in neurotic fears, anxieties, and worries, about who we are. In middle-class society especially, we get so neurotic, because we've so much time to think about ourselves. Society tells us that we have certain rights, that we should do certain things, that we should believe certain ideals—and then we acquire all of those concepts. We then tend to make judgments—value judgments about ourselves and others and the world. So see this retreat as an opportunity to step back from creating yourself as somebody. Just exploring this sense of self—not getting rid of it, not annihilating it—but recognizing you're not what you think. I find that a relief, not believing my thoughts at all.

Thoughts still come and go. Sometimes they're useful and sometimes they're just habits. Certain conditions arise and make you happy, and you feel everything is going well. Then everything seems to fall apart, somebody disrobes, and on and on like this. People praise you and you feel good, and then people blame you and you feel bad—on a personal level. Awareness, then, doesn't get caught in the ups and downs of praise and blame, happiness and suffering. Awareness is a refuge that can recognize these qualities in terms of Dhamma—all conditions are impermanent and not-self. This is for reflection. This sense of sakkāya-diṭṭhi that I translate as "personality view." During this time you can experiment with "I am." You can be anything you want to create yourself into; but listen to it, don't believe it…. "I am God!"…"I am nobody, I'm not worth anything, I'm just another one of the ants in the anthill. I'm nothing, a cipher in the system, a cog on the wheel"—that's another creation, isn't it?

I can build myself up into being the almighty, powerful, one God or just a hopeless case. But these are creations, and this awareness doesn't believe in any of those conditions. It sees them, it recognizes them, but it doesn't attach to them. This is one way that I found of getting very clear insight. What is pure awareness, and what is personality? It is important for you to know the difference, to have that confidence, not in some kind of belief, but the insight. Recognize this awareness is here and now. "I am…Ajahn Sumedho" comes and goes. "I am a good person, I am a bad person." Memories come and go, but the awareness is self-sustaining—it's not created and it's always dependable. It's always here and now. To have this insight, then, frees you from the attachment to the sakkāya-diṭṭhi—to the ego—and it's not a denial of it. I still come across as a personality, don't I? And you see me as Ajahn Sumedho—"he's a personality." So it isn't as though I somehow become a zombie or some kind of neutered, bland nothing. It's being able to recognize a personality rather than become it and get lost in its habits.

IDENTITY

IS THERE ANYONE, any person or any condition that is absolutely right or absolutely wrong? Can right and wrong, or good and bad, be absolute? When you dissect it, when you really look at it in terms of the way it is now, there is nothing to it; it's foam on the sea, it's soap bubbles. Yet this is how we can get ourselves completely caught up in illusions.

We'll sacrifice our life for an illusion in order to protect our identities, our positions, our territories. We're very territorial. We think that this England here belongs to the English. When we take that apart, does this plot of land here say it's England? When I do *jongrom* (walking meditation) outside, does the earth come up and say, "You're walking on me—England." It's never said that. Yet I say I'm walking here in England. I'm the one who's calling it England, and that is an identity, a conventional identity. We all agree to call this plot of land here "England," but it's not really that; it is what it is. Yet we'll fight, torture people, and commit the most atrocious acts over territory, quibbling about just one inch of property on a border. The land doesn't belong to anybody; even if I own land legally—"this belongs to Ajahn Sumedho." It doesn't really; that's just a convention.

When we bind ourselves to these conventions and these

illusions, then of course we're troubled because illusions are unstable and not in line with Dhamma. We end up wasting our lives trying to increase this sense of identification, this sense of "it's mine, it belongs to me, and I want to protect it and hand it down to future generations." We create a whole realm of illusion, personality, and identity through the perceptions that we create in our minds, which arise and cease and have no real core, no essence.

We can be very threatened when these illusions are challenged. I remember first questioning the reality of my personality. It scared me to death. When I started questioning, even though I wasn't particularly overconfident and didn't have great self-esteem (I have never been prone to megalomania; usually the opposite, very self-critical), I felt very threatened when that security, that confidence in being this screwed-up personality, was being threatened. There is a sense of stability, even among people who identify themselves with illnesses or other negative things like alcoholism. Being identified with some sort of mental disease like paranoia, schizophrenia, or whatever gives us a sense that we know who we are and we can justify the way that we are. We can say, "I can't help the way I am. I'm a schizophrenic." That gives us a sense of allowing us to be a certain way. It may be a sense of confidence or stability in the fact that our identities are labeled and we all agree to look at one another in this way, with this label, with this perception.

So you realize the courage it takes to question, to allow the illusory world that we have created to fall apart, as with a nervous breakdown when the world falls apart. When the security that is offered, and the safety and confidence that we gain from that illusion starts cracking and falling apart, it's very frightening. Yet within us there's something that guides us through it. What brings us into this monastic life? It's some intuitive sense, a sense behind the sense, an intelligence behind all the knowledge and the cleverness of our minds. Yet we can't claim it on a personal level. We always have to let go of the personal perceptions, because as soon as we claim them, we're creating another illusion. Instead of claiming, identifying, or attaching, we begin to realize or recognize the way it is. This is the practice of awareness and paying attention, sati-sampajañña. In other words, it's going to the centerpoint, to the Buddho (the one who knows) position. This *Buddha-rūpa* (statue of the Buddha) here in the temple: it's the stillpoint. It's a symbol, an image representing the human form at the stillpoint.

Then there is this encouragement to what we call meditation. This word "meditation" can mean all kinds of things. It's a word that includes any kind of mental practices, good or bad. But when I use this word, what I'm mainly using it for is that sense of centering, establishing, resting in the center. The only way that one can really do that is not to try and think about it and analyze it; you have to trust in just a simple act of attention, of awareness. It's so simple and so direct that our complicated minds get very confused. "What's he talking about? I've never seen any stillpoint. I've never found a stillpoint in me. When I sit and meditate, there's nothing still about it." But there's an awareness of that. Even if you think you've never had a stillpoint or you're a confused, messed-up character that really can't meditate, trust in the awareness of that very perception. That's why I encourage, whatever you think you are, to think it deliberately; really explore the kind of perceptions you have of yourself, so that they're not just habitually going through your mind and you're either believing in them or trying to get rid of them. The more we try to get rid of personalities, the more confused we get. If you assume that you have to get rid of your personality in some way because it's an illusion, then you're caught in another illusion: "I'm someone that has a personality that I've got to get rid of; I'm the personality that's got to get rid of my personality." This doesn't go anywhere, and it's ridiculous. Personality is not something to get rid of but to know.

Be a personality, then; really intentionally be one; take it to absurdity. That's a lot of fun. Take your personality to where it's totally absurd and listen to it. Your relationship is not one of identity but of recognizing that you are creating this personality, this changing condition. I can't create any kind of personal perception that lingers, that stays. There's nothing that I can create through my mental powers that has any staying power on a personal level. It's all very illusory, very changing, very ephemeral.

However, there is that which can be aware of the personality as a construction. I deliberately think, "I am a screwed-up person that needs to meditate in order to become enlightened in the future." I think that, but I'm listening to it; I'm deliberately thinking it and I'm investigating it. I have created that perception. I have chosen to think that and I can hear myself thinking it. That which is aware and listens to that perception, I don't create. It's not a creation, is it? I create this perception, but not that which is aware of the perception. You can investigate, begin to know the difference between awareness and thinking. What is the stillpoint, the center, the point that includes? This kind of thinking is reflective, isn't it? I'm just asking myself this question to bring attention to it. I'm not looking for somebody to give me an answer, but it's a reflective question that clarifies my attention; it helps me to focus, to be aware.

The more I pay attention and am aware, the more I recognize that in this stillpoint there's this resounding sound of silence. I didn't create that. I can't claim that the sound of silence is some personal creation of mine, that it belongs to Ajahn Sumedho. It's like trying to claim the air, to claim space: "all the space in the world belongs to me," that kind of ridiculous thing. You can't create a person around it, you can only *be*—this sense of *being* the stillpoint; of resting, opening to, and allowing the personality, the body, and the emotional habits and thoughts that arise. Our relationship to them now is understanding or embracing rather than identifying.

As soon as we identify, we have a negative thought and it hooks us. I feel some negative feeling: "Oh, here I go again, being critical and negative about somebody. I shouldn't do that. I've been a monk all these years and how can I stop doing that? I've lost it." I've identified with a negative thought and it triggers all kinds of feelings of despair. "I shouldn't be like this, I shouldn't think like this. A good monk should love everybody." Then, with awareness, I suddenly stop and I'm back in the center again.

So just to recognize, no matter how many times you go out on the wheel, it's just a very simple act of attention to come back to center. It's not that difficult or remote; we're just not used to it. We're used to being on the turning wheel; we're used to going around and around and becoming all kinds of things. We're used to that; we're used to delusions, fantasies, dreams. We're used to extremes. And what we're used to, we incline to, if we're not attentive, not vigilant. When we aren't aware, vigilant, and attentive, we fall back into the realm of suffering. But when we cultivate awareness, we deprogram those habits. We don't feed these illusions anymore. We're not believing, not following, not resisting. We're not making a problem about the body as it is, or about the memories, thoughts, habits, or personality that we have. We're not judging or condemning, praising, adulating, or exaggerating anything. It is what it is. As we do that, our identity with it begins to slip away. We no longer seek identity with our illusions; we've broken through that. When we've seen through that illusion of self, of what we think we are, then our inclination is toward this centerpoint, this Buddho position.

This is something you can really trust. That's why I keep saying this, just as a way of encouraging you. If you *think* about it, you don't trust it. You can get very confused because other people will say other things and you'll hear all kinds of views and opinions about meditation, Buddhism, and all that. Within this Sangha there are so many monks and nuns, so many views and opinions. So it's a matter of learning to trust yourself, the ability to be aware rather than think "I'm not good enough to trust myself. I've got to develop the jhānas first. I've got to purify my *sīla* (morality) first. I've got to get rid of my neurotic problems and my traumas before I can *really* meditate." If you believe that, then that is what you'll have to do. But if you begin to see what you're doing, if you see that very illusion, then you can trust in that simple recognition. It's not condemning the illusion. It's not saying you shouldn't do those things. I'm not saying you shouldn't purify your sīla or resolve your emotional problems, shouldn't go to therapy, or shouldn't develop the jhānas. I'm not making any statement about "should" or "shouldn't," but rather I'm pointing to something that you can trust—this awareness (sati-sampajañña) here and now.

Suppose you come to me and say, "Ajahn Sumedho, I'm really screwed up. I was very badly treated when I was a child. I've got so many neurotic problems and fears. I really need to go to therapy and get these things straightened up somehow because I can't really meditate the way I am." If I replied, "Well, yeah, you should. You're really screwed up! I think you should go to a therapist and straighten yourself out first, and then meditate after that," would that be very helpful? Would I be pointing to the stillpoint or perpetuating your own self-view? That view might even be right on a worldly level, and I'm not saying you shouldn't get therapy. This is best: not to tell you that you are this way or that way, not to give you some kind of identity to attach to, but to empower or encourage you to trust in your own ability to wake up, to pay attention. What will result from that I don't know. I hope it will be good. But what's true is that your true identity isn't dependent upon any condition.

Pointing to the present, the *paccuppanna-dhamma,* we can grasp that idea, so then we think we don't need to do all those things. "We don't need to be monks or nuns; we don't need therapy. We can just meditate. Pure meditation will solve all our problems." Then we grasp that and become antireligious: "All religion is a waste of time. Psychotherapy is a waste of time. You don't need that. All you need to do is be mindful and meditate." That's another viewpoint, isn't it? Those kinds of opinions are not pointing to the center; they're judging the conditions or the conventions. "You don't need religion; it's all a bunch of rubbish." And even though you can say it is true that ultimately all that you need to do is to wake up—as simple as that—that is in itself a convention of language. This empowerment or encouragement points to an immanent act of awakening—not to tell you that you are some kind of person, that you're asleep and should wake up, or that you should grasp that idea—but to the sense of actually being that.

In the Western world we get very complicated because usually we don't have a lot of saddhā, or faith. The Asian Buddhists tend to be more culturally attuned to this. They have a lot of faith in Buddha, Dhamma, Sangha, a teacher, or something. Most of us come to Buddhism or become samaṇas (monastics) when we're adults—and we're skeptical. Usually we've gone through a lot of skeptical doubts and strong self-images, a hard, strong sense of individuality. My personality was a doubting, skeptical one. Doubt (vicikicchā) was one of my greatest obstructions. That's why I couldn't be a Christian, because I couldn't believe what I was supposed to believe in. It was just totally impossible for me to believe in the kind of doctrines that you have to believe in to be a Christian. Not only was I a skeptical, doubting character, I was also, at the age of thirty-two, quite cynical. I'd been through a lot and had quite a lot of bitterness about life. I was not pleased with my life at thirty-two. I was disappointed with myself and a lot of others. There was despair, bitterness, and doubt, and just a faint light at the end of the tunnel was in Buddhism. That was one thing I still had some hope for.

That was a sign that drew me into this life. The good thing about being highly individualistic, skeptical, and doubtful is that you do tend to question everything. That which is sacred, and never questioned in most religions, is open to question. One thing I appreciated with Luang Por Chah was that everything was up for questioning. He was never one for a peremptory approach of "you have to believe in this and you have to believe in that." There was never that hard, heavy-handed, dictatorial style; it was much more this reflective questioning and inquiry. One of the problems with Westerners is that we're complicated because of our lack of faith. Our identities get so complicated in so many ways, and we take everything personally. Sexual desire and the sexual forces in the body are regarded as very personal. The same is true with hunger and thirst; we identify with them in a very personal way.

We take on other basic, natural forces and judge ourselves: "We shouldn't be cowardly and weak, pusillanimous." We get complicated because we judge ourselves endlessly, criticize ourselves according to high, noble standards that we can never live up to. We get very self-disparaging, neurotic, and depressed because we're not in touch with nature. We've come from the world of ideas rather than from realizing the natural law.

So in meditation it is a matter of recognizing the way it is, the Dhamma or the natural law, the way things are—that sexual desire is like *this,* it's not mine. The body is like *this;* it's a sexual body so it's going to have these energies. It has sexual organs, it's made like this, this is the way it is, so it's not personal. I didn't create it. We begin to look at the most obvious things, the basics, the human body, in terms of the way it is rather than identifying with it personally. Hunger and thirst are like *this*—we investigate the instinctual energies, the urge for survival. We have strong survival and procreative instincts: hunger and thirst, the urge to protect ourselves, the need for safety. We all need to feel some kind of physical safety, which is a survival instinct; these are basic to the animal kingdom, not just the human.

So now it is time that it needn't be seen in this way. No matter how complicated it is, the practice is very simple. This is where we need a lot of patience, because when we're very complicated, we may lack patience with ourselves. We've got clever minds, we think very quickly, and we have strong passions, so it's easy to get lost. It's very confusing for us because we don't know how to transcend or to see it all in perspective. So in pointing to this centerpoint, to this stillpoint, to the here and now, I'm pointing to the way of transcendence or escape. Not escape by running away out of fear, but the escape hatch that allows us to get perspective on the mess, on the confusion, on the complicated self that we have created and identify with.

It's very simple and uncomplicated, but if you start thinking about it, you can make it very complicated: "Oh, I don't know if I can do that." But that's where this trust comes in. If you're aware that "oh, I don't know" is a perception in the present, that "I don't think I'll ever realize nibbāna" is a perception in the present—trust in that awareness. That's all you need to know. It is what it is. We're not even judging that perception. We're not saying, "What a stupid perception!" We're not adding anything. And that awareness of it, that's what I'm pointing to, the awareness. Learn to trust in that awareness rather than in what the perception is saying. The perception might even be common sense in a way, but the attachment to it is where you get lost. "We should practice meditation. We should not be selfish and we should learn to be more disciplined and more responsible for our lives." That's very good advice, but if I attach to that, what happens? I go back to thinking, "I'm not responsible enough, I've got to become more responsible and I shouldn't be selfish. I'm too selfish and I shouldn't be"—and I'm back on the turning wheel again. One gets intimidated even by the best advice. What to do? Trust in the awareness of it. "I should be responsible"—it is seen and one's relationship to it is no longer that of grasping. Maybe if that resonates as something to do, then I'll be more responsible. It's not a matter of denying, blotting out, condemning, or believing but of trusting in the attitude of attention and awareness rather than endlessly trying to sort it out on the turning wheel with all its complicated thoughts and habits, where you just get dizzy and totally confused.

The stillpoint gives you perspective on the conditions, on the turning wheel, on the confusion, on the mess. It puts you into a relationship to it that is knowing it for what it is, rather than some kind of personal identity with it. Then you can see that your true nature is this knowing, this pure state, pure consciousness, pure

awareness. You are learning to remember that, to *be* that: your real home, what you really are rather than what you think you are according to the conditioning of your mind.

BODY CONTEMPLATION II

AS SOON AS I think of the posture of sitting, I'm aware of the pressure the body feels while sitting. Awareness includes that, the whole body in this one moment: the pressure felt in the body while sitting, or just noticing the hands, the feet...any kind of stress. If you feel stress or discomfort, just receive it rather than think you have to get rid of it. It's like learning just to receive, noticing the way it is without reacting in a habitual way.

I encourage a lot of body contemplation because the body is a heavy, coarse condition, since it is made up of earth, fire, water, and wind, the four elements. It seems more solid, more real, than, say, thinking a thought or emotion, which tend to be very fleeting and very changeable. So we're bringing attention to just the experience of sitting—"the *body* is sitting" rather than "*me*," "*my* posture" and "*my* sitting practice." I'm treating the body as an object, not putting it in personal terms of "*my* body, *my* posture," just "the body is like this," which helps us to look at it in this more objective way, to see it for what it is. So this is an intuitive knowing of the way it is: "the body is like this."

Notice the abdomen and any kind of holding there. We create a lot of tension through holding here in habitual ways, stressing that part of the body, the abdominal area. Just let it relax, so that you feel the sense of letting go of the body, not trying to hold it or control it. Now notice the heart area, the chest, where the heart is, just bringing attention to that. And then the throat, bring attention to it.

Noticing the body, reflecting on it—the way it is, the way the body responds. We try to make it follow our will or our desires. When you're young, you can get away with a lot, making it do all kinds of things that it's really not meant to do. It's not very good for it. This noticing is not trying to fit your body to some kind of ideal, or deny it or ignore it; you're bringing it into consciousness as an experience. Because wherever you are, your body's going to be here and now, isn't it? It's a kind of mettā practice, receiving the body. It's noncritical, nonjudgmental. It's accepting this form, this natural condition, for what it is right now, without creating any conditions about how you'd like it to be. Even if it's not the way you want it to be, accepting it the way it is—that's a receptive attention.

This can be a way of dealing with illness, pain, and other conditions of the body, because desire tries to get rid of things; it tries to ignore the body. We can live in a totally artificial mental world that we create, and then we forget about the body until it gets so miserable and sick and painful that it forces you to pay attention to it. Then you may want to just get rid of the pain, get rid of the disease as quickly as possible—you don't want to be bothered with this formation if it's going to be troublesome. Old age is very good for this because you're reaping the result of what you've done with your body.

Now using the body as an object of contemplation, you become aware that the body is not-self. It's quite capable of adjusting to circumstances, if you don't impose your will on it or ignore it. The body possesses a kind of instinctual intelligence that knows what it needs. I remember going on some of these retreats where you do the body sweeping, which I found quite useful. You contemplate the sensations, starting with ānāpānasati at the nostrils and then sweeping from the top of the head, the face, and back of the neck on down to the shoulders, arms, hands, trunk, legs, and feet and then back up again. What you're doing is really allowing the body to be received in consciousness, which it seems to appreciate.

Then there is the breath, here and now, the inhalation and exhalation. If you are seeking tranquillity then the nostrils are the place to focus on, the tip of the nose, the inhalation and then the exhalation, just sustaining attention on the breath as the body breathes in and out. When the mind wanders away in thought, just gently bring it back to the breath or the body, to that which is here and now, which isn't a thought or an idea or anything. This is a way of grounding yourself in the present, and being with what is, the body, the posture, sitting like this, with the breath. But then the mind will wander off again.

When you realize you're thinking about something, gently go back to the breath or the body. If you say, "I don't want my mind to wander, I've got to develop this practice," you've set an agenda for yourself that you're going to fail at, and then you'll feel despair. So it's not a matter of being successful at any of these practices—just moment by moment, the here and now, just staying with this sense of being with the present, and then when the mind wanders, to acknowledge that and return to the body as present experience.

Often we try to get in a samādhi or a jhāna because we have the idea that this is something to attain. Just notice this, any goal you've set for yourself, or any idea of getting concentrated or getting samādhi or jhāna. If we don't see this, then we tend to operate from desire and compulsiveness, and meditation becomes quite compulsive and controlled. What I'm pointing to now is not controlling but freeing: kind of relaxing, opening, resting in the moment. There's no need to get or achieve or attain anything in your meditation practice! These are worldly goals and aims.

Now, *mettā* translates as "loving-kindness" or "unconditioned love." So it's noncritical. I mean, it's not about projecting loving thoughts, but it's an attitude of receiving, allowing things to be what they are, not picking, choosing, judging, or criticizing. So it's an attitude of receiving, welcoming, allowing it to be what it is. Even if you don't like it, receive your dislike in this attitude of the knower, the Buddha knowing the Dhamma; rather than having to struggle with negative thoughts or unpleasant states of mind or physical problems. So this attitude of mettā is not just a sentiment that we create; it's an attitude of noncritical non-aversion.

Now, focusing on the body and the breath is like this, on the four elements: they are objects. So this relationship of subject–object is the experience of life, isn't it? This is what we live from—the subjective and the objective. The subjective knowing, from this point here, knowing the posture, the body's like this, the breath is like this, mental state, the mood you're in, is like this. And then just resting in this awareness, the sound of silence, this kind of vibratory sound or whatever it is—this cosmic sound of the universe. It isn't an object, it's not to be seen as something to focus on but to recognize.

So we're developing this in order to contemplate the way it is. We have the Four Noble Truths, which the Buddha names in his first sermon, given after his enlightenment to the five disciples in Sarnath in India. His first sermon is very interesting, pointing to suffering, its causes, its cessation, and the Eightfold Path. So when we reflect on these, we are beginning to recognize this. There is a natural sense of suffering, like the sensory impingement that we experience. But the suffering of the First Noble Truth is not the pain itself but what we create around it—wanting something we don't have, not wanting what we have, not wanting it to be like this.

The cause of suffering, the Second Noble Truth, is desire *(taṇhā)*—attachment to desire out of ignorance. Here we're not trying to rid ourselves of desire, or become somebody who doesn't have any desires. We're recognizing desire: desire is like this, it's an object. So you begin to notice the desire to get something, desire to get rid of something, desire for sense pleasures. Desire is a kind of energy, it takes us over. If we're not aware of it, if we don't recognize or understand it, we become slaves to it. If you're cynical or want to put down humanity, you could think of all human beings as just desire-formations. In this position of the Buddha, that of the Buddho or awareness, desire becomes an object; you can actually notice it. It's that compulsive feeling of having, wanting. It's ambition, isn't it? It's that driving sense of "I've got to get something I don't have" or "I've got to get rid of desire or anger or greed." These desires for becoming, desire for annihilation, sensual desires, illustrate the way we create desires. When we see something beautiful then we create a desire: "I want it." Or we see something ugly and we want to get rid of it.

This is knowing the way it is; desire arises and ceases, changes. So it's not self. Desire is a natural condition, it arises, ceases. We create it when we're heedless, and then we get caught in the power of the sensual—in the sense world and habit formations. When we get caught in desire, we have no perspective, no understanding. So from this position of knowing, of awareness, then desire—the Second Noble Truth—is recognized; you understand it, you know it for what it is. This is not judging. We can desire good things: world peace and altruistic goals. It's not that desire always means something negative or bad, but it's important to recognize it, to be the knower of desire rather than become the desire.

The insight into the Second Noble Truth is a letting go. Once you see that attachment to desire is the cause of suffering you don't get rid of desire, but you let it be. You see the suffering you create by following it or trying to get rid of it. So you know desire—not making a problem about it, letting it be what it is. Then you're aware of its nature; desire is impermanent, not-self, it ceases. Desires can't sustain themselves—they cease. So the Third Noble Truth is realizing, recognizing desirelessness, a natural state of being.

As you begin to cultivate this awareness, desire ceases to be a problem. We're no longer blinded, victimized, enslaved, exploited, or persecuted by desires. Then the Eightfold Path, the Fourth Noble Truth, is the way of awareness. What I'm doing is taking these Four Noble Truths and reflecting on them, when there's a level of calm and I'm not half caught in a mad mind, a monkey mind. We can start then reflecting on, observing, and using dukkha, the First Noble Truth, as a reference point—this sense of suffering or unsatisfactoriness—and investigate it with sati-paññā, or mindful discernment, rather than with our views and opinions.

So there is an opportunity to investigate, experiment, and develop—begin to recognize awareness. This is what you can really trust. This is perfection itself. It's something to value, to respect—not as some kind of personal quality, but within the experience that I'm having right now, of consciousness in a human form. It's just this simple attention to life that is the liberation from suffering. In worldly terms it doesn't seem like much of anything. Your worldly mind says, "So what? I want to get high, I want to feel blissed out, spaced out into a realm where I can forget all the coarseness and misery of life and live in a world of eternal bliss." But that's not the way it is. The way it is, is like *this,* so awareness isn't about making conditions, bargaining, or complaining, but recognizing. It seems to me the whole purpose of being a human is to understand the lessons we need to learn, to free ourselves from ignorance, and that's possible only through awareness, not through some kind of personal achievement.

TRUST YOUR INTUITION

REFLECT ON the mental state you are in. Just observe that it's like *this*. So the sense of the paccuppanna-dhamma, here and now, the truth of the way it is, is recognizing how the state of mind is. When you grasp things you become confused: "Should I practice ānāpānasati? Concentrate on the body? Listen to the sound of silence? What should I do next?" Just observe this kind of doubting, uncertainty, or mental confusion as a mental state, not trying to resolve it, but just recognize it's like *this*—not knowing what to do. So while feeling uncertain, not knowing, you observe this sense of not knowing or confusion.

With the intellect, with the reasoning mind, we want clarity, we want answers to questions, solutions to problems. There is desire to know "what should I do first?" I might say, "Well, do ānāpānasati first, and then after you get to a certain level of calm do the reflection on the body." So you are quite willing to follow instructions, because it gives you a sense of security if you know exactly what I expect you to do, because you don't trust yourself, your intuitive sense of how it is.

By no longer just wanting recipes or formulas or certainties for meditation, the more you meditate, you can understand right view as uncertainty, not knowing. Uncertainty is no longer something resisted or rejected or a source of suffering; it is just the way it is. It's what you can know directly at this moment and it may not give you a sense of exactly how it is right now, but it's like *this*. So that is putting the onus back on to you to trust your intuitive sense rather than always be doubting, wanting the teacher to tell you, or wanting to follow instructions—which we are all quite conditioned to do. Instead you open to the sense of uncertainty, insecurity, or confusion.

Investigation: getting to the root, looking into—they call it *yoniso manasikāra* in Pāli. Vipassanā implies investigating, looking into, not coming from a position or a premise—that's an intellectual condition—but recognizing the ability of awareness to observe the way it is, the Buddha Dhamma. So if you feel mentally or emotionally confused, look at that confusion—it is like this.

I found this very helpful with my own confusion, a feeling I didn't like. I wanted certainty and precision. Confusion is a state of mind that we generally try to resist, get rid of, or run away from. In the context of the four *satipaṭṭhānas* (foundations of mindfulness), there is the *kāyānupassanā*, that is the body, the four elements, breath; *vedanānupassanā*, pleasant, painful, neutral vedanā or feeling; and *cittānupassanā*, mental states. So just knowing confusion as confusion is like this, the knowing is the refuge and the confusion is the mental object—or doubt, feeling insecure, uncertain, not knowing, is like this.

You have other emotions—maybe you are angry or greedy— that have sharper forms, they are clearer to observe. But many of our mental states, such as confusion, dullness, sleepiness, restlessness, worry, uncertainty, and doubt, we tend to resist, use willful ways to get rid of them, and then feel that there is something wrong with us for feeling confused or uncertain or insecure. We take it all in a highly personal way because the ideal is that you shouldn't be confused; you want to know and be certain and clear in your life. These are the ideals. But this realm that we are living in is basically uncertain, its nature is uncertainty, and so it's like trying to demand certitude from what, by its very nature, is uncertain, which is going to be terribly frustrating for you. So Ajahn Chah always used to increase our uncertainty. There is the Thai phrase *mai nei*—meaning "uncertain, not sure." Ajahn Chah liked to use it, so much so that it has become common even here in England. You even hear English people say *"mai nei."*

There are various views about effort. Krishnamurti, for example, always emphasizes "no effort." And then you read the Theravāda scriptures, where there are several kinds of effort. In the Eightfold Path the sixth factor is *sammā-vāyāma,* which is right effort. So what do we mean by effort? Whatever we do we have got to put effort into it—grasping this idea that we have got to apply ourselves and really concentrate and put our effort into it—is, say, one extreme. Yet others like Krishnamurti would emphasize the effortless. Now these are opinions, aren't they?

Krishnamurti tends to criticize the effort style and there are those who are attached to views about effort who think Krishnamurti doesn't know what he is talking about. But these are the paradoxes that we are becoming aware of through meditation. In terms of too much effort, when we try too hard, then we have got to recognize the situation, the thing that needs to be done in the present, the way it is right now. If we need to do some heavy labor—say, you have to lift a heavy log up onto a truck—you need to put a lot of effort in all at once and very quickly to get the log off the ground and into the truck. That is appropriate effort for that kind of endeavor. That's just common sense, isn't it? "Krishnamurti said effortlessness," but if you just touch the log, you'll never get it onto the truck. So you rally an enormous amount of effort and then use it but you can't sustain it, can you?

So sometimes we are conditioned to try to use a lot of will-power in meditation to get rid of the defilements, to attain certain states. This is where recognizing the way your character operates, what you expect, or how you habitually approach tasks is import-ant. Meditation, or just the fact of having to do something, puts us into the habit pattern of exerting an effort, which can be trying too hard, and so we might be able to sustain a certain amount of effort up to a point, but then we can't do it anymore. So in the Dhamma, then, we are finding a balance between effort and concentration. This is intuitive, it isn't prescriptive. I can't tell you how to do it, I can only point to it. This is where you need to trust your awareness.

We tend to be so programmed into using a lot of willpower and effort that we are not aware we are doing something. This is where it is helpful to be aware, to see assumptions that we have about having to do something, having to meditate, having to get something, get samādhi, get concentrated. Now that is not wrong, it's good advice, but how does that affect us? Does it put us into a tense state of willfulness, where we are trying too hard? We get the ideas of meditation, understand the words, then we try to do it, grasping the ideas, and then we get frus-trated because it seems so obvious. People say, "You make it sound so easy, Ajahn Sumedho," and it *is* simple. Understanding Dhamma on that level is not difficult, but then for practice, for meditation, we are not coming from the intellect anymore, but from awareness—*sati*. And then you have effort, mindfulness, concentration.

Now sati, mindfulness, is always like the center of it all. Without sati we get lost in going from one extreme to the next, up and down. Sati isn't an extreme; it's learning to observe, witness, notice. I can have an intuitive sense of my mood at the moment, whereas a critical sense is where, if I am in a bad mood, I think "it's a bad mood" and then maybe try to get rid of it, because I feel that a bad mood is not good to have, "should get rid of it." So there is a kind of logic there but, in terms of awareness even a bad mood is recognized, through intuition. It's not dismissed, denied, or thought about. It's recognized, "it's the way it is," feeling uncertain, insecure, or confused is like this.

Doubt can make you feel very dull and half-alive. These states are a bit formless, they are kind of nebulous, like clouds. We like clearly defined images but when you are getting into doubt and confusion they are rather nebulous, formless. But they certainly can be recognized from the sati level: receptive, relaxed attention, recognition of the mental state is like this. With this, then, you can use patient endurance. Patience is an essential ingredient. It means that we are willing to let something be what it is. If we are impatient, then if it is a mental state that we don't like, we want to get rid of it. That is lack of patience. Endurance is the ability to endure something—pain or mental anguish, or whatever. Let it be the way it is. If we lack endurance, then we just try to get rid of it or get away as quickly as possible.

A meditation retreat is largely about patient endurance, learning to develop patience with yourself, with the way your mind is, the way your body is. Many of you might think that you can't meditate because you feel frustrated, or you look around and you think everybody else is in deep concentration and only you have a wandering monkey mind, and then you start thinking, "They can do it, but I can't." This is a self-view. We have the idea that we should be able to do this, or the fear that we can't do it because we are not advanced enough, or whatever. We believe that we have too many problems or are too restless. So I have always found the reflection on just the way I am—physically, mentally—is the path for me. The habits, the kamma, the personality, the physical condition, whether you're a positive or negative person, or a bright or dull one, or happy or sad, or however you see yourself—all of this is not to be attached to. We learn from the way we are, from the way we happen to be.

We may not be the way we would like. There are many things about my personality that I can be very critical of. I don't like myself that much or approve of myself on a personal level. I now see that as part of the path, not as an obstruction. So no matter what way you are right now—no matter how critical you might be, or how inadequate you feel—change the attitude to one of learning from the way you are right now. Rather than trying to become something—rather than trying to get rid of negativity, restlessness, or confusion because you think that these are flaws or defects that block you from enlightenment—just don't believe any of that. Your conditioned mind will say anything, it is totally untrustworthy. That which we can really trust is the awareness.

So in awareness we can be aware of self-view as an object; we don't put it in the subjective position anymore. Even when you are feeling utter despair about yourself—"I can't do it," listen to that. Make it more so that you are listening to what your personality is saying but no longer believing *in what* it is saying, recognizing that this is a condition, this is a creation. "I can't do it, I can't meditate, I've got too many obstructions, too many emotional problems." You are creating those assumptions or attitudes; you are producing them in the present. But if you have awareness of that, if you listen to yourself thinking, then

you get some perspective: a thought is an object in consciousness, not the subject. The fetter of sakkāya-diṭṭhi is being aware
of the thought "I can't do it, I'm not a good meditator." Don't
believe it. Be aware of it. Anything you think is conditioned,
it's not what you really are. Even question the view "I'm an
unenlightened person that needs to practice in order to become
enlightened in the future."

When I started meditation years ago, I felt that I was a mess.
"I'm totally confused about life, don't know what to do with
myself; I need to practice meditation and hopefully in the future
sometime I might get my life together and even might become
enlightened. I wouldn't count on that because I'm such a mess."
So there was a lot of doubt and feelings of self-aversion, disappointment, despair, and then the hope that meditation would help
me to deal with these personal issues, these emotional problems.

I had some direction at the time because South-East Asia and
Thailand was a possible destination. I was living in Malaysia, but
Malaysia didn't offer much in terms of meditation at that time, so
Thailand was the obvious place to go. I started meditation with
this attitude. So at least I had direction, I had faith, I loved Buddhist teachings. This was the one thing in my life that enthused
me, namely Buddhism, and then Thailand was a Buddhist country, nice and warm and nearby, so it was the obvious place to go.
But then I started to practice meditation, always from the sense
of "I've got to do this in order to get something in the future." I
was always practicing in order to develop or achieve something.
And because I have a strong will I can make myself do all kinds
of things. I can discipline myself; this is not difficult. But still,
even after using my willpower and my drive, I didn't feel that
much better. There were moments of tranquillity, and that was
the best I could expect.

Then I began to really understand Dhamma better. I began to recognize that it's not a matter of willpower and attainment but of right view and mindfulness. This word "mindfulness" used to mystify me. What is mindfulness really? And then it became apparent, this awareness here and now. We say, "Saṇḍiṭṭhiko akāliko ehipassiko opanayiko paccattaṃ veditabbo viññūhi" when we chant the reflections on Dhamma. *Saṇḍiṭṭhiko* means apparent here and now; *akāliko,* means timeless; and *ehipassiko,* encouraging investigation. "Encouraging investigation" doesn't quite get the spirit of *ehipassiko.* It's "come and see right now," "wake up right now." *Ehi* is the Pāli word for "come and see." "Encouraging investigation" doesn't have the sense of urgency to investigate the Dhamma for yourself. "Come and see right now" is a bit more immediate.

So *ehipassiko-dhamma:* right now investigate Dhamma. What should I do first to encourage investigation? It's certainly good to give advice, but notice that these reflections on Dhamma are not a kind of theoretical teaching; they're more like apparent here and now. "Oh well, we must study the way it is, what is apparent here and now, we can talk about it," but "What *is* apparent here and now at this very moment?" *Akāliko-dhamma:* timeless. We are conditioned to time. Personality is all about "I have a whole history, I can remember way back in childhood, more than seventy years of memories." When people invite me to give talks they want my CV: the American monk—born in Seattle, Washington, was in the navy (they sometimes get it wrong and say that I was a pilot in the army or something). "I was born in Seattle, Washington"—that is a memory, isn't it? It's not a person. Apparent right now, what is that? If I say, "I was born in Seattle, Washington, seventy years ago," that is a memory. So, "apparent" is looking at what it is, rather than getting caught in the memory, the quality of the memory. I'm seventy years old. That is time. There is when I was born, when I was young, when middle-aged, and now I'm old. It's all about time, about birth and growing up and aging. Dhamma apparent here and now, timeless. "Timelessness" is a word, but the reality of timelessness, the only possible way to recognize timelessness, is through awareness, not through analysis or any thought process. So it's putting it back into this center position of sati.

"If I practice hard I might get enlightened in the future" is another self-illusion, isn't it? "I'm unenlightened now—if I practice hard I might get enlightened in the future." This is a creation: words, concepts about me as a person, what I think I am and what I should do in order to become. This is all about time and personality, not Dhamma. When I get caught in personality and the sense of time, there is no sati anymore, but there is judgment, hope, despair—all this arises. So then sati is the gate to the Deathless. That is why learning to recognize, to realize this natural state of being, isn't about becoming enlightened in the future. It is about being: being the light itself, being awareness itself now, recognizing, not trying to become someone who is aware anymore, but just this, this sense of openness, receptivity, attentiveness.

The first ordination for bhikkhus (monks) at the time of the Buddha, before it got all complicated, was simply *"ehi bhikkhu,"* which means "Come, bhikkhu" and that was it. Now we have to go through a whole procedure. Ven. Subhaddo will become a bhikkhu on Sunday and go through that procedure. But according to the scriptures the original was just "Come, bhikkhu." Just like that. You know the kind of immediacy. So ehipassiko: come and see. There is always this sense of "wake up, pay attention." Sometimes meditation can seem like a cop-out. A lot of people think we are just contemplating our navel or our breath, not facing the real world. "You should be out there, trying to make everything right in society, and here you are sitting at Amarāvatī all these days watching your breath. What good is that to anybody?"

On the worldly level there are all kinds of things that need to be done. There are so many problems at this time, it is overwhelming. You just have total collapse and burnout when you start thinking about it—the problems that face humanity on this planet. And so this is not to dismiss this, but trying to make the world right is an endless process. You are not getting to the source of what is wrong: the delusion, the ignorance, the cause of the suffering. And now we are looking here, not blaming the government anymore but looking at the cause; we are not blaming someone else, but recognizing the ignorance in our lives, the illusions we create and operate from. We are learning to recognize that which isn't deluded. That takes a willingness to be patient with yourself, and being receptive and open to whatever you are feeling, whatever results you are having from your practice, whether you feel calm or confused, peaceful or angry. I'm not asking you to become anything, but—this: ehipassiko—come and see, trust this awareness more and more, recognize it. This is the real Dhamma. This is the refuge that I can always be, because I trust it more and more, I tend to be this way more and more. So be aware.

NO EXIT

THE ESSENTIAL TEACHING of the Lord Buddha is the Four Noble Truths. So there are four truths and three aspects of each truth, which make twelve insights. Three times four is twelve. And if you have all twelve insights, you are an *Arahant* (a fully enlightened person). So the three aspects of each noble truth: dukkha is the first aspect, and this is the First Noble Truth—there is dukkha. It's a statement. And then the second aspect is, this dukkha should be understood. The third aspect is, this dukkha, this suffering, has been understood. So notice this is the pattern of reflection: the statement, the practice—what you do about suffering—and the result of having done that. So you have the *pariyatti* (study), *paṭipatti* (practice), and *paṭivedha* (realization).

Pariyatti is the statement. Each noble truth is a statement—there is dukkha, there are the causes, the origin of dukkha, there is cessation of dukkha, and there is the Eightfold Path, or the way of no suffering. We learn this from the pariyatti level, we read it in a book, we memorize it: *dukkha, samudaya* (origin), *nirodha* (cessation), and *magga* (path) in Pāli. Then the second aspect of each noble truth is paṭipatti, or the practice: what to do about it, or how to realize this. The First Noble Truth says you should understand dukkha, so this means not just *thinking* you understand what suffering is, but it's more like to stand under, to really notice, to feel the suffering, to develop this awareness where you are embracing the suffering. It's not just something you understand with your brain. It's not just "Oh, I know what suffering is" and then get on with it. It's really admitting it, that suffering is like this, this sense of anxiety or restlessness, or anger or jealousy. You are looking at the reality of it, not just thinking about it but practicing, understanding. To understand something you have to really accept it.

So through this understanding, the third aspect—the paṭivedha, the result of the practice—is suffering has been understood. Notice there is the statement, the remedy, and the result. So the third aspect of each noble truth is the result of the practice. I call this the reflective style of the Lord Buddha. It's not grasping ideas, doctrines, dogmas, positions, or anything. It's pointing to dukkha, which is an ordinary, banal experience. Everybody experiences it. In modern life what we usually do with suffering is try to get rid of it. In the modern Western life here in Britain we want to seek happiness, we don't want to suffer—"Let's live it up, let's take drugs, let's go to good restaurants and enjoy life, have a lot of fun and security"—because suffering isn't something we want and seek. But it is part of this realm, it's the common bond of all humanity.

So instead of dismissing it, running away from it, denying it, or whatever, we understand it. To understand something, you accept it, you stand under it, you feel it, you are willing. It's "I'm willing to suffer," whereas before it was "I don't want to suffer, I want to be happy, why do I have to suffer?" It's not that I want to suffer. I'm not a masochist, not seeking to persecute myself because I enjoy misery and pain. I don't like misery and I don't want to suffer, but I'm willing to suffer, so I turn to the suffering rather than just find the quickest way to get rid of it. So in the first year, when I was a sāmaṇera, a novice monk, I lived alone in a little hut for a year, and the first few months were just nothing but seemingly unmitigated suffering. I was alone, nobody to talk to, nothing to do, no television, no radio, couldn't go anywhere. You are supposed to stay in these little huts, and you can go out and walk in this slow method outside. At first I rather liked it, you know, getting out of the rat race of Bangkok. I was teaching English in Bangkok, and so I was quite happy to get rid of all that. The first few days were fine, but then, day after day, nothing to do, just me and my suffering.

I found out that because I had spent so much of my life in a family where anger was never allowed to be shown—over thirty years of suppressing anger—suddenly I felt this almost continuous rage for about two or three months. Where did that come from? Nobody was making me angry there. It wasn't the situation, so I couldn't blame it on the place or the people or anything. I had some kind of intuitive sense to stay with it, and at first I tried to do a lot of intentional practice, really concentrating the mind in order to suppress the anger. But to do that for three months was impossible because I didn't have that strong a will. So I gave up trying to control it and just watched it, and then, through that, I began to understand. Then one morning I woke up and it was all gone. There was no anger and I was in a state of bliss. Everything was beautiful and luminous, and there was no anger. Even trying to bring it back, I couldn't. Nothing seemed to *be,* nothing would catch hold, nothing would grab me. So that happened just through patience and a willingness to suffer. I could have left anytime. I wasn't chained to the wall or held there as a prisoner, as a hostage with a gun to my head.

There was a terrible flood that year in Nong Khai, and for several days I didn't get any food. There wasn't enough to eat for anybody, so I was suffering from malnutrition. I could have left. I could have gone back to Bangkok, flown back to the United States, but I decided to stay. So I experienced malnutrition and all the mosquitoes and everything. This happened to me naturally—I wasn't seeking these situations, just living there during a natural catastrophe. Most of the people living there couldn't leave, but I could have. Yet I decided to stay and just meditate with the conditions I was in. The Second Noble Truth is the origin of suffering, *samudaya* in Pāli. *Samudaya* means that suffering is not an absolute, not a permanent state; it has a beginning, an origin. So this is pointing to the fact that things, saṅkhārā (mental formations), all have beginnings—this is the Buddha's teaching about sabbe saṅkhārā aniccā: all conditions are impermanent. Suffering is a saṅkhārā, it is impermanent. So this is the pariyatti (scriptural) statement; there is an origin to suffering, and that origin is ignorance of the Dhamma and attachment to desire. In this statement attachment comes out of ignorance, not just out of habit. In this way ignorance means being caught in the habit, never questioning, never looking, never using awareness. We become creatures of habit, programmed like a computer, we become fixed in our ways of looking at things.

Instead of being set in our ways, we start looking, watching, witnessing. So the origin of suffering is this attachment to desire. There are three kinds of desire. There is *kāma-taṇhā,* which is sensual desire for what we see, hear, smell, taste, and touch through the senses, and the pleasant, attractive impingements that we have. Then *bhava-taṇhā* is desire for becoming, wanting to attain, wanting to achieve. Desire is wanting—wanting something we don't have, wanting pleasure through the senses, wanting to become something. And then *vibhava-taṇhā;* the third kind, is wanting to get rid of, to annihilate. Genocide is a kind of vibhava-taṇhā, to get rid of the vermin, get rid of the pests. So these three kinds of desires are from just reflecting on desire, because even though I understood the words, I didn't really look at desire as it happened to me, as it arose in my consciousness.

I found kāma-taṇhā quite obvious. Sensual desire isn't difficult to recognize; you see something you like, and you want it. But bhava-taṇhā—wanting to become something, to get something, to attain states, to achieve—was less obvious. So I began to notice that even my meditation was motivated by bhava-taṇhā. Being a monk is not exactly the best place to experience kāma-taṇhā, but it can certainly be a hotbed of both bhava-taṇhā and vibhava-taṇhā, desire to get rid of. So I noticed that I'm more of an annihilationist. I'd like to get rid of everything: get rid of myself, get rid of pain and suffering and irritation and dukkha, get rid of faults and bad habits. And all this seemed right, too: shouldn't you get rid of all the evil, nasty habits? Shouldn't you get rid of selfishness, jealousy, and fear?

On the logical level it always seems that trying to become good and get rid of, annihilate the bad is a natural way of thinking. Especially when you've been brought up as a Christian, you fight, you resist, you beat the devil. You fight against the forces of evil; more like the heroic warrior, you kill the dragon. You're Saint George. I'm only a miserable sinner and I want to become a saint, or become at least something better than the kind of vulgar sinner I see myself being. So bhava-taṇhā, vibhava-taṇhā. This taṇhā really interested me. What is it? To see it in myself, not just think about it. The kāma-taṇhā wasn't so much of a problem but the bhava-taṇhā and the vibhava-taṇhā was quite subtle. They had a righteousness to them; it was good to try to become, try to get rid of, these were noble efforts. But then I began to notice that it's an energy.

Taṇhā is a pushy energy; it operates looking for something. In monastic life I began to notice this. Sometimes I would go back to my little hut and there would be a desire to do something. I would do anything. I'd rearrange the pillow; I was given presents when I was ordained, so I'd look at these presents. There was an embroidered pillow and a few other things. I was getting so bored living in that place all by myself that I would go around and put the pillow in another place just to do something, I was so desperate. But then always the desire to practice hard to become, to attain arahantship, full enlightenment—I began to notice this very compulsiveness, this conditioning when you have been in the American educational system. I was in graduate school and there was this incredible drive and enormous effort to will myself to achieve. And so this was still part of my conditioned character. Even in the meditation there was a lot of bhava-taṇhā; and also vibhava-taṇhā, trying to suppress or get rid of things.

I began to watch and observe the attachment to these desires, and this is where the Buddha's teaching is so precise, because desire is not really the problem. This is a desire realm that we are experiencing, so desire is part of the package that you get when you are born as a human being in the sense world. It's the ignorance of Dhamma, of the way it is, and the attachment to desire, attachment—the Pāli word, *upādāna*—identifying "I want, I need, I have to have, I must, I should, I shouldn't," all of this, these are ways of expressing kāma-taṇhā, bhava-taṇhā, vibhava-taṇhā. So I would think, "What if I don't have any desires? I'll be nothing." I thought, I *am* my desires. I couldn't imagine just letting go of all desires; I wouldn't do anything, I'd just lie there in a heap. Then recognizing this awareness; desire is an object, a condition. It arises and ceases; it's not a permanent state. So when the conditions for desire arise, it manifests, along with ignorance of it and attachment to it, which means that one is caught in it.

So we become the victim of our desires; we become those very desires. Of course they are always looking for something, the best thing. Desire is always looking for something to go toward, a womb for rebirth, and it will take anything that is available, like switching the pillow from here to over there. But that which is aware of desire is not desire. I recognize it, what is it that is aware? I began to trust in this awareness, and this puts desires in perspective. I began to see it in not such a highly personal way of being so bound into desire that I could get no perspective.

Before that, I'd use one desire to get rid of another. "I want to get rid of sensual desire, so I'm going to wear a blindfold, going to put plugs in my ears. I'm going to give up eating because food always creates a lot of desire. Got to fight against desire." That is the desire to get rid of sensual desire. You can't win that way. The more you try to destroy sensual desire it brings up more desire. It's a Catch-22.

So "let go" is the insight of the way of practice, the paṭipatti for the Second Noble Truth. To let go of desire you have got to understand and know what desire is. Otherwise you tend to just suppress desire again and use vibhava-taṇhā, use desire to resist desire, and it doesn't work, the result isn't very good at all. So it's a letting go, a releasing yourself: stop identifying with desire. You see it arise, you recognize it, you let it go.

Fear can also take over your consciousness, and then everything looks evil and if you are not aware, then it's attachment—isn't it?—attachment to this perception of evil and the desire to get rid of it, to run away from it. Fear has the power to make us run. Something frightens us and we want to get away. I realized that when I stopped creating desire. When I let go of desire, the fear was gone. So the result of that is "desire has been let go of," and that is the third aspect of the Second Noble Truth. It's reflecting on the result of the practice, or paṭivedha in Pāli—the result of having practiced is like this. Then the Third Noble Truth, *nirodha sacca,* which is the truth of cessation—suffering ceases, there is an end to suffering. This is where, after the letting go of desire, then actually the fear—the desire—ceases and there is the reality of cessation, what arises ceases. Cessation is like this, it is empty. When something ceases it's gone, but there is an awareness. If I am attached to conditioned phenomena, then I always fear death, because if I am my body then when it dies I am annihilated, that is the end of me, oblivion.

Because I haven't died yet, I can imagine anything at all about what happens then, such as rebirth or reincarnation. Will I go to heaven or hell? It's all speculation, isn't it? Right now, death for us, our physical death, is all speculation, probability. We might have preferences for certain scenarios of what happens when we die, but the reality is that we don't know at this point. Death is the unknown, physical death, but cessation is knowable now through the mind; cessation of suffering is like this. So then the statement "there is the cessation of suffering" and "it should be realized"—this realization or this reality is recognized. Connected awareness, when sati connects, when it's not just fragmentary but you have this continuity of awareness, then you are aware of when the fear is no longer present. When the fear ceases, there is still awareness, an awareness of non-fear. Noticing non-fear is like this.

The sense of fear made me feel I am somebody, there is a strong sense of self when you are frightened. "What am I going to do? Will I be killed, taken over? Will I go crazy?" and "Unknown dark forces will take me over. I'll go insane. They'll lock me up in a mental institution, chain me to the wall, shoot electric shocks into my brain, give me terrible drugs, who knows what, and I'll lose my mind." That's all self, isn't it? Fear creates this "anything could happen to me." But when fear ceases, there is still awareness which is not-self, and that has no sense of "Oh, now I'm free from fear and I'm a fearless man." There is awareness of non-fear which isn't a claim on a personal level. So then realizing this, recognizing this, non-fear, cessation is like this, non-hatred, non-greed, no greed, no hatred, no delusion, no fear is like this.

So you have *lobha, dosa, moha*—greed, hatred, and delusion—and their opposites, *alobha, adosa, amoha*. We tend to only notice when there is lobha, dosa, moha, but as you develop your awareness then you are aware that "no greed is like this." So right now, no greed. I'm watching my citta (mind): there is no greed; it's like this, sound of silence, awareness; I can't find any greed, don't want anything right now. There is a poised attention and a reflectiveness, observing: no hatred, don't want to get rid of anything or anybody, nonattachment, can't find any upādāna (clinging). So in this state of connected awareness we get perspective. We are not just arising and ceasing with the conditions, and identifying and feeling lost in the conditioned realm—we have perspective on it. With that perspective, then, we cannot be attached.

Developing, realizing cessation means that we realize the way of nonattachment. It doesn't mean we never experience greed, hatred, delusion, or fear or any of those. It doesn't mean that those mind states never arise, but with refuge in awareness, when they do arise you don't grasp anything; you recognize non-grasping, non-self, nibbāna; the reality of non-grasping is like this. So then cessation has been realized, the paṭivedha of the Third Noble Truth, the result of this practice. Then the Fourth

Noble Truth is the *majjhimā paṭipadā,* the middle way, the way
of non-suffering, or the Eightfold Path, and it always starts with
sammā-diṭṭhi, right understanding or right view.

Right understanding comes from these previous insights, and
so it's not a verbal or a contextual understanding. It's intuitive,
empty, not something you can write down: it's something that you
recognize and realize. To me sammā-diṭṭhi is like ground zero, the
starting point of awareness, here and now. Then *sammā-saṅkappa,*
right intention—from this point wisdom is operative, the way of
wisdom. Then comes *sammā-vācā, sammā-kammanta,* and *sammā-
ājīva:* right speech, right action, and right livelihood. We have to
live our life, get food and survive as a human being in the world.
We have to speak; we don't cut our tongues off or have frontal
lobotomies. We are still normal human beings, but we are taking
responsibility for right speech, right action, and right livelihood.
Nonviolence: not using the body for harming or doing things that
are cheating or illegal. So this is the moral aspect, or sīla.

Then *sammā-vāyāma, sammā-sati,* and *sammā-samādhi*—this
aspect then is equanimity, you have this balance between vāyāma
(effort), samādhi (concentration), and sati (mindfulness) as the
point of balance. This is an emotional equanimity, a coolness, a
calmness. You are no longer a helpless victim of circumstances
yo-yoing up and down with praise and blame, success and failure. Before I meditated I was like that. I was a helpless victim
of circumstance. Somebody would praise me and I would be
happy; somebody would criticize me and I would be depressed.
I'd pass an exam, I'd be happy. I'd fail an exam, I'd be depressed.
When everything was going well, I'd be happy; when everything
seemed to be falling apart, I'd be upset. These things can make you
become frightened of life, and then you get into very controlling
and manipulative situations. "I have to control everything so I'll

have security." The sense of "everything is going to be all right," so you desperately avoid anything that might upset or humiliate you or that you might fail at.

So long as I was controlling life, I had a lot of fear, self-consciousness, and misery, because I was emotionally unstable, helplessly going up and down depending on how the world impinged on me. Then with this insight about developing the Eightfold Path, I found greater emotional balance, equanimity. Not that I don't have emotions, but I'm no longer attached, identified, or frightened; I no longer need to suppress, deny, or follow them or identify with them. So then this Fourth Noble Truth is what meditation is all about, it's *bhāvanā*. This Pāli word *bhāvanā* is the Pāli word for "meditation." In Thailand they use *bhāvanā* meaning "meditation." Bhāvanā is the way of awareness, mindfulness: connected awareness, realizing, recognizing, appreciating, developing, and cultivating it.

The lifestyle of a Buddhist monk is very conducive toward bhāvanā. That is what it was designed for. The whole structure of monasticism is for developing awareness, not to become a "Buddhist monk" but to assist awareness. So bhavana should be developed and the result of that insight is the Eightfold Path has been developed: the realization of the Arahant. In Thailand they believe that Arahants can fly through the air, that they are super-men or magicians. *Arahant* is another word like *nibbāna* that gets put into a very extraordinary position, for instance we hear about "arahants" that fly in the air and perform miracles, have psychic powers, can read your mind, and can do all kinds of fantastic psychic feats. That's not an Arahant. An Arahant is one who has the knowledge from investigating the Four Noble Truths. That's the scriptural meaning, not just Ajahn Sumedho giving his view about what Arahants are.

I have reflected on the Four Noble Truths for so many years that I know them backward and forward, it's been like a paradigm, a form that is easy to keep in mind. The Four Noble Truths are pretty easy to remember. It gets a little more complicated with three aspects, twelve insights, but that's not all that difficult either. So once you understand how it works, it's a reflective form for observing, developing awareness, understanding. You start out with something quite common, some coarse object of suffering. You are not looking high up for God or for angels, or anything like that. You are looking at something very basic, which I am sure some of you have experienced during this retreat. Even though by looking at you no one would ever know.

Investigating, getting to the source, or yoniso manasikāra, getting to the source—not just the peripheral, the surface of things, but getting to the cause. Insight is like gut knowledge, not mere intellectual symbolic knowledge; you know the reality of it through insight. So there are these twelve insights. That is why these Four Noble Truths are not just a beginner's practice, or not just a preliminary to something else, but a lifetime's practice, because of the law of kamma. When your kamma ripens this is what happens. Through all these years of being a monk, various things happened to me quite unexpectedly. So you think, "If I could just solve all these, have all these twelve insights, then the rest of my life is just going to be an easy ride. I won't suffer anymore, just be mindful and float..."

What happens then is the *kamma-vipāka* (result of action): unexpected things happen, challenges of various sorts, because this is life in this realm. It's not a *deva-loka,* a heavenly realm, just living on your good kamma until it expires. It's like this, it's about praise and blame, success and failure, happiness and suffering; it's about old age, sickness, death, and loss. We all lose; in the end we lose everything. You see your parents get old and die, your teachers die, and your friends die, and this sense of loss is just a natural part of this realm. As these things happen to us, it's not that you don't feel anything—that you're indifferent, that when your mother dies you don't even notice. You feel it, but your relationship to it is through wisdom rather than through personal attachment and being caught in grief.

You experience grief, but you're not attached to it. In the life of awareness, you experience ups and downs, good fortune and bad fortune, praise and blame, and you still feel it. You feel it even more, but your relationship to the feeling realm is one of nonattachment: no longer identifying, no longer being blinded and victimized and caught in the vortex of emotions the way it was on a personal level before.

WHEN YOU'RE AN EMOTIONAL WRECK

RIGHT NOW we're in a situation where everything is under control and perfect for a proper formal retreat. In contrast, next week there will be a lot of comings and goings and things happening that we can't control. Just be aware of expectation, a view about what a proper, formal retreat should be. Whatever views or opinions you may have, just know the way they are. Whatever kind of irritation, frustration, or aversion you might feel, you can use that for meditation. The important thing is the awareness that *it is the way it is*—rather than trying to suppress or ignore your feelings or getting upset and angry about things not going the way you want, and then not looking at that, not taking the opportunity to observe the way it is. If you are upset about the way it is, you can use that as a part of your meditation.

Unwanted things happen in any retreat. Take, for example, the window in the temple: the electric motor that opens and closes it doesn't work. High-tech, isn't it? We could use a long pole, or we could get knotted ropes and hang them from the beams and learn to climb them to open and close the windows. It would be good physical exercise. Then the spotlight went out. I notice that when things go wrong, things break, or things make me feel frustrated or irritated, then I like to use those situations. If the window doesn't close and the spotlight doesn't go on, I notice I feel a certain way. I'm aware of that feeling of not wanting the spotlight to be broken or the window or whatever. Or a feeling of wanting to get it fixed right away: "We can just get somebody in to do it right now between breaks so it doesn't interfere with my practice." But notice in all of this that mindfulness is the important factor. Concentration can get disrupted, but mindfulness, if you trust it, opens to the flow of life as an experience with its pleasure and pain.

So sati-sampajañña, awareness, apperception, or intuitive awareness: I keep reiterating all this so you can really appreciate the difference between intuitive awareness and the thinking or analysis coming from trying to get something or get rid of something with a controlling mind. With the thinking process—if you're caught into that, you'll end up with "well, it should be like this and it shouldn't be like that" and "this is right and that is wrong" and even say, "the Buddha's teachings are right." We then get attached to the idea that Buddhist teachings are right, and the result of that—if we don't have enough sati-sampajañña along with it—is that we become Buddhists who feel *we are right* because *we're* following the *right* teaching. Thus as a consequence of attachment and the way we perceive the Buddha's teaching, we can become self-righteous Buddhists. We can feel that any other form of Buddhism that doesn't fit into what we consider right is then *wrong,* or that other religions are wrong. That's the thinking behind self-righteous views. Notice how limiting it is. You're often stuck with these thoughts and perceptions and often very inferior perceptions of yourself. We can be attached to very negative perceptions of ourselves and think they're right. "Apperception" means being aware of perception. Perception of myself, or that Buddhism is right, is like *this*. "Buddha's teachings are right"—that all arises and ceases, and what's left is *this*. There's still consciousness, awareness, intelligence. It's pure, but it's not *my* purity as a personal achievement. It's naturally pure.

Notice that this includes the body, the emotions, and the intellect. This is the Noble Eightfold Path—sīla, samādhi, paññā; morality, concentration, and wisdom. Sati-sampajañña includes everything, so the body is included now. It's not dismissing the physical condition that we're experiencing; it includes the emotional state and whatever state your body is in, whether it's healthy or sick, strong or weak, male or female, young or old. The quality is not the issue; it's not saying how your body should be but including the body in this moment. Apperception is the ability to embrace that which *is,* so the body *is* right now. This is my experience, the body is right here—I can certainly feel it. Awareness includes emotional states, no matter what they are. Whether you're happy or sad, elated or depressed, confused or clear, confident or doubtful, jealous or frightened, greedy or lustful, it includes all those, just by noticing in a way that is not critical. We're not saying you shouldn't have lustful emotions or anything like that. We're not making moral judgments, because we're using sati-sampajañña. If you get caught up in your brain, your intellect, then it says, "Oh, you're having lustful thoughts in the shrine room! You shouldn't do that. You're not a very good monk if you do things like that. You're impure!" We're very attached to these judgments, this judgmental, critical function that we have, but sati-sampajañña includes that; it includes the judgment. It doesn't judge judgment; it just notices the kind of tyrannical, self-righteous superego that says, "You shouldn't be the way you are. You shouldn't be selfish. You should be compassionate and loving," and all that kind of thing. "Buddhism is right," "I'm getting nowhere in my practice"—sati-sampajañña embraces that. It's just noticing the way it is. I can listen to my intellect, my superego, emotional states, the body—"I know that, I know you." It's a matter of being patient with all this. It's not trying to control or make any problem out of it. But when we relax and open to these things, we allow them to change on their own. They have their own kammic force, and we're giving them that opportunity. Our refuge is not in thinking or emotions or the physical body. We just see our refuge as this simple ability to listen, to be attentive to this moment.

I always use the practice of listening to the sound of silence— that subtle, continuous, inner ringing tone in the background of experience—because every time I open to the mind, that's what I hear. Its presence contains and embraces the body, the emotional quality, and the thinking mind all at once. It's not like A-B-C or anything in tandem or sequence, but in just the way it is, as a whole, it includes; it doesn't pick and choose, as in "I want this but I don't want that." Just noticing, trusting, and valuing this ability that each one of us has. It's something to really treasure and cultivate.

You can reflect on intuition as the point that includes or embraces. We have both this intuitive ability and the thinking ability that excludes, the single-pointedness you get through concentrating on an object. With a single point for concentration you focus on it in order to exclude distractions, but intuitive awareness includes all that is there. The single point you get through concentration is just a perception, isn't it? When you take it literally, it means one naturally excludes anything that's not in that point. That's the rational, logical way of looking at it. One-pointedness can be seen in terms of the one point that excludes everything, because that's the logic of thought. Intuition, on the other hand, is nonverbal and non-thinking;

so the point is everywhere, and it includes everything. This is sati-sampajañña, sati-paññā; these are the words that the Buddha used to describe the path to the Deathless. That's why you can't do it through thinking or analysis, through defining or acquiring all the knowledge in the Abhidhamma Piṭaka (the analytical teachings of the Buddhist canon) or in the *suttas* (discourses), or through becoming an expert on Buddhism, because although you might know a lot *about* it, you won't know it. It's like knowing all about honey without tasting it—chemical formulas, different qualities, which honey variety is rated the best and the sweetest, which is considered common and vulgar, lower-realm honey. You might know all that but not know the flavor. You can have pictures and portraits, the whole lot. The taste of honey in terms of intuition is like *this*. But if you just taste the honey, then you are intuitively aware that it tastes like *this*.

Paññā (wisdom) comes from intuition, not from analysis. You can know all about Buddhism and still not use any wisdom in your life. I really like the word combinations *sati-paññā* and *sati-sampajañña,* as you might have noticed. Sati-sampajañña is not something that you acquire through studying or pursuing with willpower. It's awakening, learning to trust this awakening, and paying attention to life. It's an immanent act of trust in the unknown, because you can't get hold of it. People ask, "Define it for me, describe it to me, tell me if I have it." But nobody can tell you, "Well, I think you have it, you look like you're mindful right now." A lot of people who look mindful are not necessarily mindful at all. It's not a matter of someone telling you or learning all the right definitions for the words, but in recognizing the reality of it and trusting it.

I used to experiment with this because of my background. I spent many years studying in university and was conditioned to define and understand everything through the intellect. I was always in a state of doubt. The more I tried to figure everything out (I'm quite good at figuring things out), the less certain I was that I got it right, because the thinking process has no certainty to it. It's clean and neat and tidy, but it is not liberating in itself. Emotional things are a bit messy. With emotions you can cry; you can feel sad or sorry, angry or jealous; you can feel all kinds of messy feelings. But a nice intellectual frame of reference is pleasurable because it's tidy and neat. It isn't messy, doesn't get sticky, wet, and soggy—but it doesn't feel anything either. When you're caught in the intellect, it sucks you away from your feelings. Your emotional life doesn't work anymore. You suppress it because you're attached to thought, reason, and logic. The intellect has its pleasures and gifts, but it also makes you very insensitive. Thoughts do not have any sensitive capability, do they? They are not sensitive conditions.

One of the ideals we sometimes talk about is "all is love," or the concept of universal compassion, but the words themselves have no ability to feel that emotion, compassion or anything like that. We might attach to the most beautiful, perfect ideals, but attachment blinds us. We can talk about how we must all love each other, or have compassion for all sentient beings, and yet we may be unable to do that in any practical way, unable even to feel it or notice it. Then going into the heart—where often it's amorphous, where it's not clean, neat, and tidy like the intellect—emotions can be all over the place. Then the intellect says, "Oh, emotional things are so messy. You can't trust them," and feels embarrassed. "It's embarrassing! I don't want to be considered emotional. Ajahn Sumedho is very emotional." Whoa, I don't want anyone to think that. "I'm reasonable." Now I like that. "Intelligent, reasonable, kind." But say, "Ajahn Sumedho is emotional" makes me sound weak and wimpy, doesn't it? "Ajahn Sumedho is emotional. He cries, he weeps, and he's wimpy. He's all over the place. Ugh!" So maybe you think of Ajahn Sumedho as mindful. *That's* nice.

Emotions are often ignored or rejected and not appreciated; we don't learn from them, because we're always rejecting or denying them. At least I found this easy to do. So sati-sampajañña is like opening up and being willing to be a mess. Let a mess be a mess; a mess is like *this*. Wet, weak, all over the place, foolish and silly, stupid, it's all like this. Sati-sampajañña embraces it all. It doesn't pass judgment or try to control, to pick or choose, but just the act of noticing that it's like this. Whatever emotion is present, this is the way it is, it's like this.

So the point that includes—notice that it's the here and now (paccuppanna-dhamma), just switching on this immanent kind of attention. It's a slight shift, just relaxing and opening to this present, listening, being attentive. It's not going into some kind of real super-duper samādhi at all, it's just like *this*. So it doesn't seem like much at all. As you relax, trust and rest in it, you'll find it sustains itself. It's natural, and you are not creating it. In this openness, in this one point that includes, you can be aware of emotions that you don't usually bother with, like feeling lonely or sad, or subtleties such as resentment or disappointment. Extreme ones are quite easy because they force themselves into attention, but as you open, you can be aware of subtle emotions. Not judging this, just embracing it, so that it's not making a problem about the way it is, it's just knowing the way it is. It's like *this,* at this moment the feeling, the vedanā-saññā-saṅkhārā (feeling, perception, mental formations) are like *this,* the body (rūpa) is like *this*.

Notice what it's like when you open to emotional feelings, to moods, without judging them, without making any problem out of them, without trying to get rid of them, change them, or think about them. Just totally accept the mood you're in, the emotional state, or the physical sensations like pain, itching, or tension, with this sense of well-being, of embracing. When I do this, I notice the "changingness." When you are willing to let something be the way it is, it changes. Then you begin to recognize or realize nonattachment. We say "embracing": in this way sati-sampajañña is not attaching (upādāna) to them, it's embracing. This sense of widening is inclusive, not picky-choosy. It doesn't say, "I'll pick only the good things, not the bad ones." It takes the bad along with the good, the whole thing, the worm and the apple, the snake and the garden. It allows things to be what they are, it's not approving. It's not saying that you have to love worms and want them in your apples and like them as much as you like apples. It's not asking you to be silly, ridiculous, or impossible, but it encourages you to allow things to exist, even the things we don't allow, because if they exist, that's what they do: they exist. The whole thing, the good and the bad, *belongs*. Sati-sampajañña is our ability to realize that, to know that in a direct way, and then the processes take care of themselves. It's not a case of Ajahn Sumedho trying to get his act together, trying to cleanse his mind, free himself from defilements, deal with his immature emotions, straighten out his wrong, crooked views, trying to make himself into a better monk and become enlightened in the future. That doesn't work, I guarantee—I've tried it!

From this perspective you can use upāya (skillful means) for particular conditions that come up. One could say, "Just be mindful of everything." That's true, but some things are quite obsessive or threatening to us, so we can develop skillful means with that. I got a lot of encouragement from Ajahn Chah to develop skillful means, and that takes paññā, doesn't it? It's using paññā to see how to deal with emotional states, especially difficult emotional

habits. Don't be afraid to experiment. See what comes up using catharsis, or talking it out with somebody who will listen to you, or thinking it out deliberately.

One of my skillful means was listening to my thoughts as if they were neighbors talking on the other side of the fence. I'm just an innocent bystander listening while they carry on these conversations. All this gossip, opinions, and views I'm actually producing in my own mind, but I'm listening to it. I'm not involved, not getting interested in the subject matter, but just listening as it goes on and on about what it likes or doesn't like, what's wrong with this person or that one, why I like this better than that, and if you want my opinion about this... I just kept listening to these inner voices, these opinionated, arrogant, conceited, foolish voices that go on. Be aware of that which is aware and notice, make a note of that which is aware. The awareness is my refuge, not this gossiping, not these arrogant voices or opinions and views. That's a skillful means, I've found.

We can learn to help each other by just listening. Learning to listen to somebody is about developing relationship rather than preaching and trying to tell somebody how to practice and what to do. Sometimes all we need to do is learn how to listen with sati-sampajañña to somebody else, so that that person has the opportunity to verbalize his or her fears or desires without being condemned or given all kinds of advice about them. These can be very skillful means. Some kinds of therapy can be skillful means that help us to deal with what is usually an emotional problem. Where we tend to be most blind and most undeveloped is in the emotional realm.

Upāya, skillful means, is learning that you do have the wisdom to do it. If you consider that "I'm not wise enough to do *that*," don't believe it! But also don't be afraid to ask for help.

It's not that one is better than the other, but just trust your own experience of suffering. If you find you obsess, things suddenly obsess your consciousness, memories come up, certain emotions or really silly things just pursue you, foolish thoughts or whatever, we say, "I don't want to bother with that stupidity, I'm trying to get my samādhi and be filled with loving-kindness and do all the right things"—and not see what we are doing; we're trying to become, we're trying to make ourselves fit into an unreal image, something imagined, an idealized image. The Buddha certainly did not expect that. Whatever way it is for you is the way it is, and that's what you learn from, that's where enlightenment is—right there—when you're an emotional wreck.

SUFFERING SHOULD BE WELCOMED

O NE OF THE EPITHETS for the Buddha in our chanting is *lokavidū* (knower of the world). Of course we can see that this is a quality of the Buddha, but something more practical than simply chanting the positive qualities of somebody called "Buddha" is to reflect on what is the world, the situation that we are experiencing now. This entails contemplating or reflecting on life as we experience it rather than describing how life should be. If we're rationalists, we have theories about how things *should* be. But in reflective awareness we're noticing how things are.

Breathing is like *this* when we become aware of the breath. We're not saying you should breathe a certain way, that there's some standard of breathing that is ideal, that we must all strive for. We contemplate the experience of "sensitivity is like *this*." When we begin to notice that the human body—this body that we're in with its eyes, ears, nose, and tongue—is sensitive and that sensitivity is like *this,* then we look inward. What is it to be sensitive? We're looking at and noticing what it is to feel, to see, to hear, to smell, to taste or touch, to think, to remember. We can have ideas about being sensitive, about "our" sensitivity, or we can try to make ourselves insensitive because we might see it as a weakness. To be sensitive, for some people, is a sign of weakness. We're not placing any judgment on sensitivity, but just noticing that it's like this.

As we notice the world that we live in, the environment—the way it is—we find that it leads toward just recognizing the impermanent nature of our conscious experience, how things arise and cease, begin and end. This is "knowing the world," not judging the world according to some standard, but seeing that the world is like *this:* it is sensitive. The world is about birth and death, about meeting and parting, coming and going, good and bad, right and wrong, beauty and ugliness, and all the various gradations of experience and qualities that we are subject to in this form.

Even though this seems to be an obvious reality when you recognize it, how many people really are aware of the world in terms of experience? We interpret it usually in a personal way. The habitual pattern is to interpret it all in terms of personal limitations, personal feelings or personal ideas. In noticing the world as it is, we're seeing that it is not a personal thing. A person is a creation of the mind, to which we remain bound if we don't awaken. If we just operate within the emotional conditioning that we have, then we see it in terms of "This is happening to me," or "I am good...bad..."

It is very important to recognize and to know that the world is the world. It's a very strong experience, because having a human body is a continuous experience of being irritated. Contemplate what consciousness is in such a form as a human body, which is made up from the four elements of earth, water, fire, and wind. From birth to death, from the time you are born, the moment you cry when you're out of your mother's womb, you start screaming. Then the sensitivity, impingement, and the irritations come through this sensitive form until it dies. I encourage you to contemplate what birth into this world is, rather than to judge it according to any ideals or ideas that you might have. This is called the state of awakened awareness. To "wake up" means to know the world as it is; it's not judging the world. If we have ideas about how the world should be, then our critical mind often sees it as "this shouldn't be." When you see how countries should be, how governments should be, how parents, partners, or whatever should be, then you are coming from ideals, usually quite high standards of "if everything were perfect." But this realm's perfection doesn't lie in taking conditioned experience to some kind of peak moment. Peak moments are just that; they're wonderful in their way, but they're not sustainable. The flow and movement of our life is around the "changingness" of the conditioned realm that impinges on us, that we're involved in, that we're immersed in, in this conscious form.

Notice how irritating it is just to be able to see, hear, taste, smell, and touch. There's always something that isn't quite right. It's too cold or too hot; we have a headache or backache; unwanted noises, odors, and suchlike impinge or come into contact with this form—and as a result of this we experience its beauty and ugliness, pleasure and pain. But even pleasure is irritating when you think about it. We like pleasure, but having a lot of pleasure is also very exhausting and irritating. This is not a criticism. It's just noticing that having a human body is like this; breathing is like this; consciousness is like this.

Just consider how sensitive we are in relation to words and thoughts. One can say things and upset everybody just through a certain tone of voice. Using certain words can be very distressing. We remember things of the past that are pleasant or unpleasant. Our minds can obsess about things we shouldn't have done in the past. We get a lot of guilt and remorse or self-aversion because of mistakes, failures, or unskillful acts that we remember. We can get really neurotic, because in the present moment we can be totally obsessed with something we shouldn't have done twenty years ago. We can drop ourselves into real states of depression and despair.

Being born as a human being is a real challenge in terms of how to use this experience of birth, this human experience, this sensitive state that we're living in. Some people think about committing suicide: "Just get it over with"—it's just too hard to bear, too much to stand, a lifetime of this continuous irritation and guilt, remorse and fear of the unknown. It can be so utterly depressing that we think it's better to kill ourselves. The Buddha encouraged us to wake up to it, learn from it, see it as an opportunity, as a challenge. We can develop wisdom through the conditions and the experiences that we have in this life—which are not guaranteed always to be the best. Many of us have had to experience all kinds of frustrations, disappointments, disillusionments, and failures. Of course, if we take all that personally we want to end it very quickly. But if we put it in the context of knowing the world as the world, we can take anything. We have an incredible ability to learn from even the most unfair and miserable, painful, and nasty conditions. These are not obstructions to enlightenment; this issue is whether we use them to awaken or not.

Some people think that it's good kamma just to have an easy ride, to be born with wealthy parents and high status, beautiful appearance, intelligence, an easy life, all the benefits, all the blessings, all the good things. It is good merit, good *pāramī* (virtue), and all that. But when I look at my own life, incredible challenges have come to me that have shaken me, have really upset me, disappointed me to the point where I have contemplated suicide—"I just want to get this over with. I don't want to spend more and more years in this realm. I can't take it." But awakening to that, I realized that I'm quite willing to take what life presents and to learn from it. That's the challenge: seeing this as an opportunity that we have as human beings, as conscious beings.

Now the teachings of the Lord Buddha are teachings pointing to this. They're here to awaken you rather than to condition you. It's not a matter of trying to grasp them as doctrinal positions to take hold of but of treating them as expedient means for developing and encouraging awakened awareness, mindfulness, intuition. Rather than fear sensitivity, really open to it: be fully sensitive rather than trying to protect yourself endlessly from possible pain or misfortune.

Knowing the world as the world is not a resignation in a negative way—"Oh, you know how the world is"—as if it is bad, that there's something wrong with it. That's not knowing the world as the world. "Knowing" is a matter of studying, and taking an interest, investigating, examining experience, and really being willing to look at and feel its negative side. It's not about seeking sensory pleasures, pleasurable experiences, but about seeing even your most disappointing ones, your worst failures, as opportunities to learn, as a chance to awaken: one can say that they're *devadūtas* or "heavenly messengers" that tap us on the shoulder and say, "Wake up!" That's why in Buddhism, aging, sickness, disabilities, and loss are seen not as things to fear and despise but as devadūtas. This word *devadūta* is a Pāli word; *dūta* means a "messenger" of some sort, *deva* is "angelic" or "heavenly"; so they're heavenly messengers sent to warn us. A Christian asked me once if we had angels in Buddhism. "We have angels in Christianity," he said, "all kinds of white and beautiful beings that play harps. They're very radiant, light beings." I replied, "Well, Buddhist angels are not like that. They're old age, sickness, and death!" The fourth devadūta is a samaṇa: a contemplative, a human being who is having the spiritual realizations.

It has always interested me, and I've found it quite amusing, to see an old person as an angel, or to see the sick, the mentally ill, corpses, or monks and nuns as devadūtas. Let's look at one another as devadūtas. Otherwise we become personalities, don't we? In looking at the shaven heads and the saffron robes, this is seeing them in terms of devadūtas rather than in terms of monks and nuns, senior and junior, and all that, which gets into personality view (sakkāya-diṭṭhi). Do we see ourselves actually helping each other to awaken, or do we see each other as persons? "This monk is like this, and that nun is like that." We can either see others in a very worldly way or change our perspective and see them as devadūtas.

You can see old people as devadūtas. Like me: I'll be sixty-seven in a few days. Not only a devadūta on the level of a samaṇa, but an old man too. As I get sick and senile, I'll be even more of a devadūta; and when I'm dead, I'll be four all in one. Just reflecting in this way we can see how to use life—the malleability of our human mind is endless. We can be so set and conditioned by the dualistic thinking that we get from our cultural background. For example, I was brought up with a very dualistic way of looking at everything as a result of my Christian background. Things were *absolutely* right or wrong, good or evil. These were very fixed ways of looking at everything. You had a very limited use of your mind, because it tended to move only between two extremes.

Notice in some of the Buddhist meditation exercises, they offer ways of visualizing, of using your mind to create visions of things. One of these exercises is the contemplation of the thirty-two parts of the body. I remember when I was first faced with this in Thailand, I kept wanting to think of the thirty-two parts of the body as being physiologically accurate according to Western science. For me, it was easier to find a book on anatomy and look at a picture than to contemplate the reality of those organs and conditions, here and now in this form that I call myself and that I assume to be me; it is a different use of learning. It requires us to flex the mind a bit.

I was talking to a monk about how difficult it sometimes is to see yourself in terms of positive qualities, because we're so used to seeing ourselves in terms of the negative, what's wrong, what our faults are. I notice especially with Western people, Europeans and Americans, that we spend so much time criticizing ourselves and dwelling on what we feel is wrong, bad, or weak in us. We think it's wrong to admit our good qualities. I used to feel like that: I was being honest when I was admitting my weaknesses and faults, but if I admitted my virtues, that would be bragging. Here in Britain, it's very bad taste to brag and tell people how wonderful you are, how much money you make, how many important degrees or titles you have. In Thailand some monks have these name cards that have all their titles on them—B.A., M.A., Ph.D., Chao Khun, Head of Province, Vice-President of the World Fellowship of Buddhists and World Congress of Buddhists, Trustee to this and that—it's quite all right there to present yourself in terms of your accomplishments. But here we think that it is very bad taste; it's embarrassing. In an English home you never see framed university degrees hanging on the walls, do you? People would be too embarrassed because it's like boasting. There is a sense of modesty here which is quite lovely in many ways. But it can be taken to the extreme where you have no way of acknowledging any goodness in yourself or appreciating your own successes, virtues, and good qualities.

Are we going to become inflated egotistical monsters if we admit that we love good things? Why did I become a bhikkhu? Why would I choose to live a celibate life in this monastic order? I could give you reasons like "I've got to shape up and get my act together. I can't do it any other way. I have to do something in order to make myself do it." I can look at it in terms of weakness and inability, telling myself that I need external support because I can't do it by myself. But I can also look at it in terms of being attracted to what is good, virtuous, and beautiful. Both perspectives have their points. I can be fascinated by lower things and the darker side of life. It's not that I'm so good that I gravitate to everything that's light and beautiful, I've certainly had my fascinations for that which isn't. I would say that it's something of a character tendency that my preference leans toward the light and the good, the true and the beautiful. This is the movement that I'm interested in. It's something to respect. I see it as something very good in my character.

In terms of personal qualities, it's learning to be honest, to admit to and make a conscious appreciation of your own humanity and your individuality. It helps to give you a confidence that you don't have when you're obsessed with self-criticism and negative perceptions. We use our critical mind and discriminative abilities, not to analyze and compare one thing with another, but to examine and investigate our experience. We awaken to the breath—it's like *this*. We awaken to the sensitive state that we're in—it's like *this*. We awaken to the irritations that we experience as conditions that contact our senses, and to our obsessions and emotional habits, whatever they might be. We put them in perspective rather than seeing them as something to get rid of. It's something to awaken to, a change from resistance and denial to awakening, acceptance, and welcoming.

In the First Noble Truth, the Buddha proclaimed that there is dukkha, suffering. It is put in the context of a noble truth rather than a dismal reality. If we look at it as a dismal reality, what happens? "Life is just suffering, it's all just suffering. You get old, you get sick, and then you die. You lose all your friends. All that is mine, beloved and pleasing, will become otherwise, will become separated from me. That's what it's all about; it's just dukkha from beginning to end." There's nothing noble in that, is there? It's just pessimistic and depressing, seeing it in terms of "I don't like it. I don't want suffering. What a bad joke. What a lousy joke God played on us creating this mess, and me being born in it. What am I living for? Just to get old, get sick, and die." Of course, that's depressing. That's not a noble truth. You're creating a problem with the way things are. The noble truth is just "there is suffering." And the advice, the prescription to deal with this suffering, is to welcome it, understand it, open to it, accept it. This gives rise to the willingness to embrace and learn from that which we don't like and don't want: the pain, the frustration, and the irritation, whether it's physical, mental, or emotional.

To understand suffering is to open to it. We say, "We understand suffering because it's..." We rationalize it, but that's not understanding. It's welcoming and embracing the suffering that we are experiencing—our frustration, despair, pain, irritation, boredom, fear, and desire—just welcoming, opening, accepting. Then this is a noble truth. Our humanity then is being noble; it's an *ariyan* truth. This word *ariya* means "noble." The English word implies something grand, something that rises up. If you're noble, you rise up to things. You don't just say, "Oh, life is misery and I want to hide from it. I can't bear it." There's nothing noble in that. If you're brought up as Christian, you find yourself blaming suffering on God: "God, why did you create this mess? It's your fault." I used to feel furious with God. "If I were God, I would have created a much better situation than this." I remember as a child thinking that if I were God I wouldn't have created pain. You fall down and hurt yourself and you think, "Why does God allow this? Why did he create a realm where there is so much pain? If I were God and I created the world, I wouldn't have created pain." Or is pain a noble truth? Is old age a noble truth? Are loss, separation, and all these experiences that we always have in this form, in this human realm, a noble truth? Are we seeing it in terms of complaining and blaming or in terms of a noble truth? This is what I'm pointing to.

We can look at things in different ways. We can choose. We don't get stuck with a program and become its victim. The program we got from our parents and our culture may actually not be a good one. Sometimes it's all right. But still, why should we limit ourselves to that experience alone when we have an opportunity to explore, investigate, and know reality in a direct way. Enlightenment is not something remote and impossible. You might see it in terms of some very abstract state that you aim for but think you'll never achieve. But what's the basis for this way of thinking? You think of yourself as *this* kind of person.

If I depended on my personality, I couldn't do anything. I'd never hope to get enlightened because my personality can't possibly conceive of myself as a person that could be enlightened. My personality is conditioned to think of myself in terms of what's wrong with me, since I come from a competitive society where everyone is very much aware of who's better or worse, who's above or below. So I can't trust that. My personal habits are conditioned things, so they're not flexible in themselves. If you just attach to or interpret experience through those perceptions

and never learn to look at things in any other way, then you are stuck with a limited view, and that can be a very depressing way to live.

We can begin to wake up and see beyond our rigid, puritanical dualism, or whatever program we acquired through our family and social background. We can learn to trust in our own intuitive, awakened sense. Don't trust in your views and opinions about anything—about yourself, about Buddhism, about the world—for these views are often very biased. We get very biased views about each other: racial prejudices, class identities, ethnic biases, and feelings of social superiority. These are not to be trusted.

We don't always have to look at something from our acquired conditioning. So when the Buddha talks about the "Buddha-mind," it's very flexible and malleable; it's universal. We can see things in so many different ways. The mind has a radiant quality to it. Consciousness has a radiance; it has a light itself. So when we begin to let go of always limiting ourselves through the distortions of our conditioned mental states, then we begin to understand things as they really are, to know the Dhamma—enlightenment. This is not something remote and impossible, unless you want to hold to those views from a personal attitude about them. You can be holding your perceptions so high that they're way beyond your ability to achieve them. This is because you haven't awakened to what you're doing. You're merely operating from a conditioned view of everything.

There is dukkha (suffering), and dukkha should be welcomed. This is my new interpretation. The usual translation is "dukkha should be understood," and my new rendering of it is "dukkha should be welcomed." Try that one. You can experiment with these different words. You don't have to think, "Pāli scriptures say

'understand,' they don't say 'welcome.'" Pāli scriptures don't say
"understand," they use a Pāli word that we translate as "understand." Maybe we don't understand what "understand" means.
Did you ever think about that? Maybe we don't understand our
own language. We're so limited to a particular narrow view of
the word "understand" that we can't really expand it. If we have
a broader view then we can experiment with the words. Just
observe the effect.

I say "welcoming" not because I found the *real* translation for
this and therefore anyone who goes back to using "understand" is
wrong. That is getting into another rigid, arrogant approach. I'm
not interested in proving that I'm right, that my translations are
the best, but just seeing how they work, what the effect is here
and now. I am sharing this with you as a way of encouraging you
to have that right and that freedom to know for yourself. You
don't always have to fit yourself into the views and opinions of
our tradition with its orthodox forms or definitions, which are
our particular group's way of looking at things.

"There is dukkha, and dukkha should be welcomed. Dukkha
has been welcomed." What is that like? Try that one. I don't
know if it works for you, but it does for me, because my character
tendency is to push dukkha away. That's my conditioning, my
personality; "Suffering? Push it away; don't want it." Somebody
else's suffering—I see somebody suffering and I don't want to go
near them, I want to push away from them. If I encounter someone with a problem—"Ajahn Sumedho, I've got a problem"—I
push away. This is my character tendency, to resist. I don't want
to know about the suffering. Tell me about the good things. How
are you today? "I'm fine, Ajahn Sumedho. I just love it here at
Amarāvatī. I love being a monk. I just adore the Dhamma and
the Theravāda form and the Vinaya (monastic discipline). I love

the whole thing." Oh, that makes me feel so good. Tell me more. And I go to somebody else: How are *you* this morning? "Ugh! This life is such a dreary, miserable thing. I'm fed up. I want to disrobe." I don't want to hear that. Don't tell me that.

We can go around trying to get people to make us feel good. Tell me the good things, because that makes me feel good. Don't tell me the bad stuff, because that makes me feel bad. I don't want to feel bad. I don't want suffering; I don't welcome it, I want to get rid of it. I'm going to live my life so that I can get as much of the good stuff as I can and push away all the bad stuff. But in this new translation, "There's suffering, and suffering should be welcomed," it changes, doesn't it? You see the suffering—your own or others' problems, difficulties, and so forth—as things to welcome rather than avoid or push away.

We have been on retreat for the past week. I really like formal practice. I like to sit here and face the shrine. I like the temple; it's a very pleasant place to sit. I sit on this triangular cushion that supports the spine, so I can sit very comfortably for long periods of time. I look at the shrine and the mind goes very still and quiet. Then when I look around and face you… What happens when I'm looking at all of you? This is just a way of contemplating. When I look at the shrine, all the things on the shrine bring peace and calm. There are candles and incense and the Buddha image, things that aren't dukkha for me. They inspire, they're pleasing, they aren't irritating; and they do not cause me any kind of unpleasant feelings. If I don't particularly want to look at them, I can just close my eyes and not look at anything. But then turning around and you're all here—what happens? It brings up a sense of there being so many possibilities. All these different people, some of whom I don't know, others whom I think I know. I've got views about some of you—you're like this and you're like that. I've got memories and each person will bring up certain memories, some pleasant, some unpleasant. Some people have different ways of moving and acting and saying things that bring up different feelings in my mind, in my consciousness. If I think, "Oh, I can't bear this," then the world is like that. I have to immediately turn around again and look at the shrine. If, on the other hand, when I'm looking at the shrine, I begin to allow the awareness to take me to non-grasping, to the reality of non-attachment—if I really know this, rather than merely depend on the lack of stimulation for it, then rather than having to turn away from the community in order to get it, I can turn toward the community. It's not dependent on facing the shrine. In this way we're beginning to awaken to reality rather than to a conditioned experience that we become very dependent upon.

We talk of taking refuge in Sangha; we can define Sangha in terms of the four pairs, the eight kinds of noble beings. How many fit into that description? How many of your egos can think of yourself as *sotāpanna-magga* or *sotāpanna-phala*, *sakadāgāmi-magga* or *sakadāgāmi-phala*, *anāgāmi-magga* or *anāgāmi-phala*, *arahatta-magga* or *arahatta-phala*? [These are the eight kinds of noble beings, who have reached at least one of following realizations: the path of stream-entry, the fruition of stream-entry; the path of once-return, its fruition; the path of non-return, its fruition; the path of arahantship, its fruition.—Ed.] Which one are you? How can I take refuge in "four pairs and eight kinds of noble beings?" It's very abstract, these sages, ideal beings somewhere...or are they here? This monk, or that nun? What's the refuge in Sangha then? Do we want to make it abstract? Is it up to me to decide who's a sotāpanna or sakadāgāmi and so forth, to figure out who I can take refuge with? Then it's just a matter of my ego again. Here I am—this person, trying to decide what somebody else is.

It's taking these words like "Sangha" and making them work for you. Make it practical. We have the same refuge; we're the Sangha. Our refuge is in Buddha, Dhamma, and Sangha, not in personal attitudes or preferences, habits, or views and opinions. When we see each other in terms of Sangha or as devadūtas, it's a way of looking at each other that is beginning to appreciate, respect, and get beyond personal preferences, views, and personal reactivity. But we're not trying to annihilate these preferences, because the dukkha we welcome is all this personal reactivity. Why we feel angry, why we feel jealous, why we feel rejected or the like—we're not trying to dismiss all this. But as we trust in this awakened state, we welcome our foolish feelings and neurotic habits. We welcome them as a noble truth rather than as personal faults.

THE SOUND OF SILENCE

SOMEBODY referred to the sound of silence as a cosmic hum, a scintillating almost electric background sound. Even though it's going on all the time we don't generally notice it, but when your mind is open and relaxed you begin to hear it. I found this a very useful reference because in order to hear it, to notice it, you have to be in a relaxed state of awareness. When I describe this people try to find it. They go on a ten-day retreat trying to find the sound of silence, and then they say, "I can't hear it, what's wrong with me?" They are trying to find this thing. But it's not a thing you have to find—rather you just open to it: it's the ability to listen with your mind in a receptive state, which makes it possible to hear the sound of silence. You're not trying to solve any problems but just listening. You're putting your mind into a state of receptive awareness. Awareness that is willing to receive whatever is, and one of the things you begin to recognize in that is the sound of silence.

Some people become averse to the sound of silence. One woman started hearing it and she wanted it to stop, so she resisted it. She said, "I used to have peaceful meditations. Now all I hear is that blasted sound and I'm trying to stop it. Before I never heard it, now I sit down and immediately I hear *zzzz*." She

was creating aversion toward the way it is, "I don't want that." She was creating suffering around the sound of silence. But the sound of silence, rather than creating suffering, can help to focus the mind, because when the mind is aware of it, it's in a very expanded state. This state of mind is one that welcomes whatever arises in consciousness; it's not a state where you are excluding anything. The sound of silence is like infinite space because it includes all other sounds, everything. It gives a sense of expansion, unlimitedness, infinity. Other sounds come and go, change and move accordingly, but it is like a continuum, a stream.

I was once giving a retreat in Chiang Mai, northern Thailand, in a lovely mountain resort with a waterfall and stream. The meditation hall had been built right by the stream, and the sound of the waterfall was continuous and quite loud. Somebody on the retreat became very averse to the sound of the stream. "I can't meditate here, it's too noisy. The sound of the stream is just too much, I can't bear it." You can either listen to and open your mind to the sound, or resist it, in which case you are fighting and resisting, and that creates suffering.

I noticed the sound of the waterfall and the stream, and the sound of silence was in the background as well. In fact the sound of silence became the stronger and more obvious, but it did not obliterate the sound of the stream; the two sounds worked together. The sound of the stream did not obliterate or cover up the sound of silence.

So it's like radar. The mind is in a very wide, expansive state of awareness: inclusive, open, and receptive rather than closed and controlled. So notice and contemplate this experience, and then just concentrate your attention on the sound of silence. If you think about it, think of it like a blessing, grace, or a lovely feeling of being open, rather than as a buzz in the ear, in which case you think that it's tinnitus or some other disease. If you start contemplating it as the sound of angels, as a cosmic or primordial sound, blessing every moment as you open to it, you will feel then blessed. Reflecting in this way, in a positive way helps us to take an interest in it and get a good feeling from it.

Listening to the sound of silence, you can begin to contemplate non-thinking, because when you are just listening to the cosmic sound there is no thought. It's like this—emptiness, not-self. When you're just with the cosmic sound alone, there is pure attention, no sense of a person or personality, of me and mine. This points to anattā.

Relax into the sound, don't try to force attention onto it. Just have a sense of relaxing and resting, peacefulness. Try counting to say, ten, to sustain listening to the sound of silence: "one, two, three…nine, ten." The mind is not used to resting in that way, it's used to thinking and to restless mental activities. It takes a while to calm, to relax, and to rest in this silence.

In the silence you can also be aware of any emotions that arise. It's not an annihilating emptiness, it's not a sterile nothingness, it's full and embracing. You can be aware of the movements of emotions, doubts, memories, or feelings as they start to become conscious. Silence embraces them; it neither judges, resists, nor gets fascinated with them. It just recognizes and realizes the way it is.

We tend to use the word "sound" in terms of how the mind has been perceptually conditioned. We connect sound with the ears. That's why the sound of silence is heard as if it were a buzzing in the ears, because the impression of sound is always connected with the ears. But you can plug your ears up and you can still hear it. When you're swimming underwater you can still hear it. So what is it?

Then you start to realize that it's everywhere and not just in the ears. That perception of the sound of silence as something heard in the ears is the same misperception as thinking that the mind is in the brain. You're changing from that very conditioned way of experiencing life, which arises through this sense of self and the culturally conditioned attitudes we hold, to a much wider understanding of the way it is.

It's like the perception of the mind as being in the body. Through intuitive awareness we can see that the body is in the mind. Right now you are in my mind; all of you in this hall, you're in the mind. On the conventional level, for each one of us, our mind is in our head—you're sitting over there with a mind in your head—all these different heads with minds in them. But then in terms of mind, I'm sitting here on the high seat, I can see you with my eyes, and you're in the mind, you're not in my head. I can't say you're all in my brain. The mind has no limit to it.

So then one can see that the body is more like a radio, more like a conscious entity in the universe that picks up things. Being born as a separate entity in the universe, we are a point of light, a conscious being in a separate form. We tend to assume we are a fixed, solid, physical person, but are we something greater than that—not so limited, heavy, and fixed as our cultural conditioning makes it sound, or as we tend to perceive.

The sound of silence isn't mine, nor is it in my head, but this form is able to recognize it and know things as they are. This knowing is not a cultural knowing; it's not like interpreting everything from my cultural conditioning; it's seeing things as they are, in a direct way, which is not dependent on cultural attitudes. So we really begin to understand anattā, not-self, which enables us to see that we are all connected, all one. We are not, as we appear to be, a collection of totally separate entities. If you start contemplating like this, you begin to expand your awareness to include rather than to define.

So in terms of meditation, we are establishing awareness in the present, collecting, recollecting, contemplating one-pointedness in the present—the body, the breath, the sound of silence. Then we can bring to this an attitude of mettā (loving-kindness), which is a way of relating to and recognizing conditioned phenomena without judging them. Without this attitude we tend to make value judgments about what we experience on a personal level. One person is feeling peace, another person is feeling restless, another person is feeling inspired, another person is feeling bored, another person high, another low; or you're having good or bad thoughts, stupid or useful thoughts, judgments about the quality of the experience that each one of us is having. In terms of knowing, we are knowing that thought is a condition that arises and ceases. Bad thoughts or horrible thoughts arise and cease, just like good thoughts. It's not a matter of passing judgment about how bad you are because you are having bad thoughts; it's about the ability to recognize thought, and to see that the nature of thought is impermanent, changing, not-self. So now just use this cosmic hum, this gentle stream of flowing, scintillating sound. Just get familiar with it.

Sometimes with emotional experience we wind ourselves up about something and sometimes have strong emotional feelings such as being indignant or upset—"I'm not standing for that; I've had enough." When that happens, go into the sound of silence and count to five, to ten, and see what happens. Experiment with it, right at this moment. "I'm totally fed up, I've had enough, this is it." Then go into the silence. I used to like to play with this, when I used to suffer from indignation, exasperation, and being fed up. I like that word "fed up," you can say it with such conviction.

This cosmic sound, the sound of silence, is really a natural sound. That's why when you learn to rest with it, it's sustainable; you don't create it. It's not like you're creating a refined state that depends on conditions to support it. To sustain any kind of refined state you have to have very refined conditions supporting it. You can't have coarse, noisy, raucous, nasty things happening and still sustain a sense of refinement in your mind. To have a refined mental state you have to have silence, few demands, no noise, no distractions, no quarreling, wars, explosions, just a very lovely scene where everything is very precious and controlled. When we get into that state, we can get very precious. Everybody whispers to one another in gentle tones. Then when somebody says, "Agh" it really shatters us and we get very upset because we have become so sensitive.

With the sound of silence, you begin to hear it wherever you are—in the middle of London, in a traffic jam in Bangkok, in a heated argument with somebody, when the pneumatic drill, the lawn mower, and the chainsaw are all going at the same time, even when there is music. So learning to detect it and tuning into it is like a challenge. Sometimes people say: "I can't hear it; there's too much noise." If you are resisting the noise you can't hear the sound of silence, but if you open to it then you begin to hear the gentle scintillating hum, even with the pneumatic drill blasting away.

Listening to the sound of silence allows us to integrate mindfulness meditation into movement, work, business. If you are in the kitchen washing the dishes, or walking from here back to your room, or driving a car, you are able to listen to the sound of silence at the same time. It does not make you heedless. It allows you to be fully with what you are doing; it increases your mindfulness. It helps you to wash the dishes fully and really be with the washing of the dishes, rather than just washing the dishes and being with all kinds of other things. Walking back to your room, you could be thinking about anything. Using the sound of silence helps you to be with walking, being mindful and with the very action that's happening in the present.

Sometimes this sound of silence will become very loud and quite unpleasant, but it won't stay that way. I remember one time it was incredibly loud, ear-splitting. I thought, "something's going wrong." Then it changed and I tried to get it loud again and couldn't. It's not something that is dangerous. It depends how you look at it. If you resist it or are negative to it, you're creating that negativity towards it. If you relax and open, then you feel this gently scintillating background sound that is peaceful, calming, and restful. You begin to recognize emptiness—it's not some vague idea that if you practice meditation you might experience emptiness some day. It's not a vague kind of thing, its very direct.

Then in that emptiness contemplate what "self" is. When you become a personality, what happens? You start thinking, grasping your feelings, then you become a monk or nun, man or woman, a personality, Pisces or an Aries, an Asian or a European or an American, an old man or a young woman or whatever. It's through thinking, grasping at the khandhas, that we start getting wound up into that, and then we become something. But in this emptiness there is no nationality. It's a pure intelligence; it does not belong to anybody or any group. So then you start recognizing when you've become somebody and nobody, when there is attā (self) and anattā.

In the emptiness there is no self, no Ajahn Sumedho right now. "But I want to tell you about my personal history and all my qualifications and my achievements in the holy life over the past thirty-three years. I'm abbot of a monastery, considered a VIB, a Very Important Bhikkhu, and I want you to respect me and treat me properly because you get a lot of merit for being kind to old people!" That's Ajahn Sumedho! Or, "You don't have to respect me at all, it does not matter to me in the slightest, I can take it if you don't like me or if you criticize me and find fault with me. It's okay, and I'm quite willing to bear it because I've sacrificed a lot for all of you." But that's Ajahn Sumedho again. Born again and then gone! Empty.

Just by exploring this you really get to understand what attā is, how you become a personality, and you also get to see that when there is no person, there is still awareness. It's an intelligent awareness, not an unconscious dull stupidity. It's a bright, clear, intelligent emptiness. You become a personality through having thoughts like: feeling sorry for yourself, views and opinions, self-criticism and so forth, and then it stops—there is the silence. But the silence is bright and clear, intelligent. I prefer this silence rather than this endless, proliferating nattering that goes on in the mind.

I used to have what I call an "inner tyrant," a bad habit that I picked up of always criticizing myself. It's a real tyrant—there is nobody in this world that has been more tyrannical, critical, or nasty to me than I have. Even the most critical person, however much they have harmed and made me miserable, has never made me relentlessly miserable as much as I have myself, as a result of this inner tyrant. It's a real wet blanket of a tyrant. No matter what I do, it's never good enough. Even if everybody says, "Ajahn Sumedho, you gave such a wonderful *desanā* (Dhamma talk)," the inner tyrant says, "You shouldn't have said this, you didn't say that right." It goes on, in an endless perpetual tirade of criticism and faultfinding. Yet it's just habit; I freed my mind from this habit, it has no footing anymore. I know exactly what it is, and I no longer believe in it or even try to get rid of it. I know not to pursue it and just let it dissolve into the silence.

That's a way of breaking a lot of these emotional habits we have that plague us and obsess our minds. You can actually train your mind, not through rejection or denial but through understanding and cultivating this silence. So don't use this silence as a way of annihilating or getting rid of what is arising in experience, but as a way of resolving and liberating your mind from the obsessive thoughts and negative attitudes that can endlessly plague conscious experience.

THE END OF SUFFERING IS NOW

O N A CONVENTIONAL LEVEL we easily conceive the conditions that we attach to. With sati-paññā and sati-sampajañña we begin to awaken to the way it is rather than committing ourselves to conventional realities. This is just to emphasize the awareness, before you become something. I'm trying to get this point across, so I think it needs to be repeated many times, because even though it looks very simple, our mind-set is definitely geared to believe in the personality view as our reality. Most of you are very committed to yourselves as personalities, and the reality of yourself as a person is very much ingrained.

The term *sakkāya-diṭṭhi* can be translated as "personality view" or "the ego." It refers to the perceptions that we hold in regard to our identity with the five khandhas (groups)—body, feelings, perceptions, conceptions, and consciousness—as belonging to this person. In investigating this we are not grasping the perception of "no person" either. We can take the concept of anattā and grasp that, and say, "There's no self because the Buddha said there's anattā." But then we're also grasping a perception. Grasping a perception of yourself as a non-self gets to be a bit ridiculous. Grasping perceptions is not the way. If you grasp whatever conditions you create, you'll end up in the same place, suffering, as the result. Don't believe *me* either, this is for you to explore.

Instead of starting with a perception or a conception of anything, the Buddha established a way through awareness, through awakened attention. This is an immanent act in the present. You can grasp the idea of awakened attention and repeat that over and over, but the simple act of paying attention is all that is necessary. There is this attention, sati-sampajañña, an intuitive awareness where the consciousness is with the present moment: "it's *this* way." It's beginning to explore sakkāya-diṭṭhi in terms of the perceptions you are attached to as yourself. That is why I keep emphasizing deliberately to conceive yourself as a person. For example, "I'm this person who has got to practice in order to become enlightened." Just take something like that. "I'm an unenlightened person who has come here to Amarāvatī in order to practice meditation so that I will become an enlightened person in the future." You can have comments about this, form perceptions about these perceptions, but that's not the point. Deliberately think this: "I am an unenlightened person...." Deliberately say that to yourself with attention, listening. This deliberate thinking allows us to listen to ourselves as we think.

When you are caught in the wandering mind, you lose yourself; you just go from one thought to another. One thought connects to another and you get carried away. But deliberate thinking is not like wandering thinking, is it? It's intentional, for you are choosing whatever you are going to think. The important thing is not the thought, or even the quality of the thought, whether it's stupid or intelligent, right or wrong; it's the attention, the ability to listen to the thinking that you are deliberately doing. Being aware of thinking in this way—in my experience and I assume it will happen also to you—I don't know, maybe I'm an exceptional

case! Before you start thinking "I am an unenlightened person…"
there is a space, isn't there? There is an empty pause before you
deliberately think. So notice that. That is just the way it is; there
is no perception in that space, but there is attention to it, there is
awareness. You are certainly aware of this before "I am an unenlightened person" arises. Thinking about this is not wandering
thinking, it's not judging or analyzing, but just noticing: it's like
this. So when you deliberately think, you can also use thought to
keep pointing to this, noticing the way it is.

Consider the pronoun "I" in the sentence "I am an unenlightened person." If you listen to it and the words that follow,
you will realize that you are creating this consciousness of yourself through the words that you are deliberately thinking. That
which is aware of your thinking—what is that? Is that a person?
Is it a person that is aware? Or is it pure awareness? Is this awareness personal, or does the person arise *in* that? This is exploring,
investigating. By investigating you are actually getting to notice
the way it is, the Dhamma, that there is actually no person who
is being aware, but awareness will include what seems personal.

"I am an unenlightened person who needs to practice meditation in order to become an enlightened person in the future."
I assume that I am this body, with this past. I have this history. I
am so many years old, born in such and such a place. I've done all
these things and so I have a history to prove that this person exists.
I have a passport and a birth certificate, and people even want me
to have a website on the Internet. But really there doesn't seem
to be any person in the awareness.

I find that the more I am aware, the more my personal past
seems totally unimportant and of no interest whatsoever. It doesn't
mean anything, actually. It's just a few memories that I can turn
up. Yet taking it from the personal view, if I get caught in myself,

thinking about myself as a real personality, then suddenly I find my past important. An identity gives me the sense that I am a person. I *have* a past, I *am* somebody. I am somebody *important;* somebody that may not be *terribly* important, but at least I feel connected to something in the past. I have a home, I have a heritage. These days people talk about losing the sense of their identity because they're refugees and their parents are dead, because they're of mixed race, or they don't have any real clear identity of themselves as belonging to something in the past. The sense of a personality depends very much on proving that you are somebody, your education, your race, your accomplishments (or lack of them), whether you are an interesting or uninteresting person, important or unimportant, a Very Important Person or a Very Unimportant Person!

In meditation we are not trying to deny personality, we are not trying to convince ourselves that we are nonpeople by grasping ideas such as "I have no nationality (or no sex, no class, no race)" and "the pure Dhamma is my true identity." That's still another identity, isn't it? Now that's not it. It's not about grasping the concepts of no-self. It is realizing, noting through awakened attention the way things really are. Just in this simple exercise, "I am an unenlightened person...," it is quite deliberate. You can say, "I am an enlightened person." You can choose which you would like to be, enlightened or unenlightened. Most of us don't dare to go around saying that we are enlightened, do we? It's safer to go around saying, "I am an unenlightened person," because if you say, "I am an enlightened person," someone is going to challenge you: "You don't look very enlightened to me!" Anyway, the words are not really important. Whether you say, "I am an unenlightened person" or "I am an enlightened person," "I am an enlightened nonperson" or "I am an unenlightened nonperson," it's the attention that matters.

I have found this very revealing. When I did this exercise it became very clear what awareness is—sati-sampajañña, mindfulness, awareness, apperception. Then the thinking, the perceptions arise. Deliberately thinking "I am an unenlightened person..." arises in this awareness. This awareness is not a perception, is it? It's an apperception; it includes perception. Perceptions arise and cease. It's not personal; it doesn't have any "Ajahn Sumedho" quality to it; it's not male or female, Bhikkhu or *Sīladharā* (nun) or anything like that; it has no quality on the conventional, conditioned level. It is like no thing, like nothing. This awareness—"I am an unenlightened person"—and then nothing, no person. So you are exploring, you are investigating these gaps before "I" and after "I." You say "I"—there's sati-sampajañña, there's the sound of silence, isn't there? "I am" arises in this awareness, this consciousness. That, as you investigate it, you can question.

This awareness is not a creation, is it? I am creating the "I am..." What is more real than "I am an unenlightened person" is this awareness, sati-sampajañña. That is the continuous one, that's what sustains itself, and the sense of yourself as a person can go any which way. As you think about yourself and who you are, who you should be, who you would like to be, who you do not want to be, how good or bad, wonderful or horrible you are, all this whirls around, it goes all over the place. One moment you can feel "I am a really wonderful person," the next moment you can feel "I am an absolutely hopeless, horrible person." But if you take refuge in awareness, then whatever you are thinking does not make much difference, because your refuge is in this ability of awareness, rather than in the gyrations and fluctuations of the self-view, your sakkāya-diṭṭhi habits.

Just notice how being a person is really like a yo-yo; it goes up and down all the time. With praise you feel you're wonderful, you *are* wonderful—then you're a hopeless case, you're depressed, a hopeless victim of circumstances. You win the lottery and you're elated; then somebody steals all the money and you're suicidal. The personality is like that; it's very dependent. You can be hurt terribly on a personal level. Or you can be exhilarated: people find you just the most wonderful, thrilling, exciting personality, and you feel happy.

When I was a young monk, I used to pride myself on how well I kept the Vinaya discipline, that I was really, really good with the Vinaya. I really understood it and I was very strict. Then I stayed for a while on this island called Ko Sichang off the coast of Siraja with another monk. Later on this monk told somebody else that I didn't keep very good Vinaya. I wanted to murder him! So even Vinaya can be another form of the self-view: "How good a monk am I?" Somebody says, "Oh, Ajahn Sumedho is exemplary, a top-notch monk!" and that's wonderful. "He's a hopeless case; doesn't keep good Vinaya" and I want to murder. This is how untrustworthy the self is.

We can rise to great altruism and then sink to the most depraved depths in just a second. It's a totally untrustworthy state to put your refuge in, being a person of any kind. Even holding the view that "I am a good monk" is a pretty tricky refuge. If that is all you know, then when someone says that you are not a very good monk, you're angry, hurt and offended. Sati-sampajañña, despite all the fluctuations, is constant. This is why I see it as a refuge. As you recognize it, realize it, know it, and appreciate it, then that's what I call a refuge, because a refuge is not dependent on praise and blame, success and failure.

There are different methods to stop the thinking mind. For example, there's a Zen koan or self-inquiry practice like asking "Who am I?" These kinds of techniques or expedient means in

Zen and Advaita Vedanta are designed to stop the thinking mind, so that you begin to notice the pure state of attention where you are not caught in thinking and in the assumptions of a self, where there is just pure awareness. That's when you hear the sound of silence, because your mind is just in that state of attention; in pure awareness there's no self, it's like *this*. Then to learn to relax into that, to trust it, but not to try and hold on to it. We can't even grasp the idea of that—"I've got to get the sound of silence and I've got to relax into it." This is the tricky part of any kind of technique or instruction, because it is easy to grasp the idea. Bhāvanā (meditation) isn't grasping ideas or coming from any position, but in this *paṭipadā,* this practice, it's recognizing and realizing through awakened awareness, through a direct knowing.

When the self starts to break up, some people find that it becomes very frightening, because everything you have regarded as solid and real starts falling apart. I remember years ago, long before I was even a Buddhist, feeling threatened by certain radical ideas that tended to challenge the security of the world that I lived in. When it seems that somebody is threatening or challenging something that you depend upon for a sense that everything is all right, you can get very angry and even violent because they are threatening *your* world, *your* security, *your* refuge. You can see why conservative people get very threatened by foreigners, radical ideas, or anything that comes in and challenges the status quo or what you are used to, because if that's your world that you are really depending on to make you feel secure, then when you are threatened you go into panic.

Reading about the horrible earthquake in India recently, it's believed that a hundred thousand people were killed. It just happened out of nowhere. Some schoolgirls were practicing marching on the school ground for some festive parade they were engaging in, and the merchants were placing their wares out in their shops. Just an average, normal day. Then suddenly, within five minutes, these girls were all dead, killed from falling masonry. The whole town of twenty-five thousand people was completely demolished within five minutes, just out of nowhere. Think what that would do to your mind! It's really frightening to think what an undependable realm we live in. When you explore what's really going on in this planet, it seems pretty unsafe. Even though it looks solid, just looking around, we take it for granted, yet last week in Gujarat all of these people were killed. It seems like a solid and safe environment, then suddenly out of nowhere there's an earthquake and the whole lot collapses. We can recognize, even without earthquakes, how easily we can have a heart attack or a brain hemorrhage; we could be hit by a car or a plane could crash. In terms of this conditioned realm that we perceive, create, and hold to, it is a very unstable, uncertain, undependable and changing condition in itself. That's just the way it is.

The Buddha pointed to the instability of conditioned phenomena, to their impermanence. This is not just a philosophy that he was expecting us to go along with. We explore and see the nature of the conditioned realm in just the way we experience it, the physical, the emotional, and the mental. But that which is aware of it—your refuge—is in this awakened awareness, rather than in trying to find or create a condition that will give us some sense of security. We are not trying to fool ourselves, to create a false sense of security by positive thinking. The refuge is in awakening to reality, because the unconditioned *is* reality. This awareness, this awakeness is the gate to the unconditioned. When we awaken, that is the unconditioned, the actual awakeness is that. The conditions are whatever they are—strong or weak, pleasant or painful.

"I am an unenlightened person who has to practice meditation *hard*. I must really work at it, get rid of my defilements, and
become an enlightened person sometime in the future. I hope to
attain stream-entry before I die, but if I don't, I hope that I will
be reborn in a better realm." We go on like that, creating more
and more complications. People ask me, "Can we attain stream-
entry? Are there any Arahants?" We still think of stream-entry and
Arahantship as a personal quality, don't we? We look at somebody
and say, "That monk over there is an Arahant!" We think that
person is an Arahant or stream-enterer. That's just the way the
conditioned mind operates; it can't help it, it can't do anything
else than that. So you can't trust it, you can't take refuge in your
thoughts or your perceptions, but in awareness. That doesn't
seem like anything, it's like nothing—but it's everything. All the
problems are resolved right there.

Your conditioned mind thinks, "It's nothing, it doesn't amount
to anything. It's not worth anything, you couldn't sell it." This
is where we learn to trust in the ability to awaken, because if
you think about it you'll start doubting it all the time. "Am I
really awake? Am I awake enough? Maybe I need to be asleep
longer so that I can be awake later on. Maybe if I keep practicing
with ignorance I'll get so fed up that I'll give it up." If you start
with ignorance, how could you ever end up with wisdom? That
doesn't make any sense. Hitting your head on a wall, after a while
you might give it up, if you haven't damaged your brain. It does
feel good when you stop, doesn't it? But instead of looking at
it in that way, trust in this simple act of attention. Then explore
and have confidence in your ability to use wisdom.

Many of you may think, "Oh, I don't have any wisdom. I'm
nobody. I haven't had any real insight." So you thoroughly convince yourself that you can't do this. That's the way it seems on

the personal level. Maybe you don't feel that you have anything to offer on that level, but that's another creation. That's the same as "I am an unenlightened person." Whatever you think you are, whether it's the best or the worst, it's still a creation; you create that into the present. Whatever assumptions you have about yourself, no matter how reasonable, they're still creations in the present. By believing them, by thinking and holding to them, you're continually creating yourself as some kind of personality.

The awakeness is not a creation; it's the immanent act of attention in the present. That is why developing this deliberate thinking "I am an unenlightened person" is a skillful means to notice more carefully and continuously what it's like to be mindful, to have pure awareness at the same time that you are creating yourself in whatever way you want as a person. You get this sense that your self-view is definitely a mental object; it comes and goes. You can't sustain "I am an unenlightened person." How do you sustain that one? Think it all the time? If you went around saying "I am an unenlightened person" all the time they would send you to a mental hospital. It arises and ceases, but the awareness is sustainable. That awareness is not created; it is not personal, but it *is* real.

Also recognize the ending, when "I am an unenlightened person who must practice meditation in order to become an enlightened person sometime in the future" stops. Then there is the ringing silence; there's awareness. Conditions always arise and cease *now* in the present. The cessation is *now*. The ending of the condition is *now*. The end of the world is *now*. The end of self is *now*. The end of suffering is *now*. You can see the arising, "I am..." then the ending; and what remains when something has begun and ended is awareness. It's like *this*. It's bright, clear, pure, alive. It's not a trance, not dull, not stupid. So this is just an encouragement, an "empowerment" according to modern jargon. Do it! Go for it. Don't just hang around on the edges thinking, "I am an unenlightened person who has to practice really hard in order to become an enlightened person" and then after a while start grumbling, "Oh, I need more time." and go into the usual plans and plots, views and opinions. If you start with ignorance you will end up with suffering. *Avijjā-paccayā saṅkhārā* in the teachings on dependent origination *(paṭiccasamuppāda)*: *Avijjā* is ignorance; and that conditions *(paccayā)* the saṅkhāras (mental formations), that then affects everything and you end up with grief, sorrow, despair, and anguish *(soka-parideva-dukkha-domanass-upāyāsā)* as a result. This is a way of encouraging you to start not from avijjā, but from awareness *(vijjā),* from wisdom (paññā). *Be* that wisdom itself, rather than a person who isn't wise trying to become wise. As long as you hold to the view that "I'm not wise yet, but I hope to become wise," you'll end up with grief, sorrow, despair, and anguish. It's that direct. It's learning to trust in being the wisdom *now,* being awake.

Even if you feel totally inadequate emotionally, doubtful or uncertain, frightened or terrified—emotions are like that—*be* the awareness of the emotions: "Emotion is like *this.*" It's a reaction, because emotionally we are conditioned for ignorance. I am emotionally conditioned to be a person. I am emotionally conditioned to be Ajahn Sumedho. "Ajahn Sumedho, you are wonderful!" and the emotions go: "Oh?" "Ajahn Sumedho, you are a horrible monk with terrible Vinaya!" and the emotions go "grrrrr!" Emotions are like that. If my security depends on being praised and loved, respected and appreciated, successful and healthy, everything going nicely, everyone around me being in harmony, the world around me being utterly sensitive to my needs...then I feel all right when everything else seems all right. But when it goes the other way—the earthquakes, the persecution, the abuse, the disrobing, the blame, the criticism—then I think "Ugh! Life is horrible. I can't stand it anymore. I'm so hurt, so wounded. I've tried so hard and nobody appreciates me, nobody loves me." That's emotional dependency; that's personal conditioning.

Awareness includes those emotions as mental objects (āram-maṇa) rather than subjects. If you don't know this, you tend to identify with your emotions and your emotions become you. You become this emotional thing that has become terribly upset because the world is not respecting you enough. Our refuge is in the Deathless reality rather than in transient and unstable conditions. If you trust in awareness, then the self and all its emotions, whatever they might be, can be seen in terms of what they are: not judging them, not making any problem out of them, but just noticing: it's like *this*.

R EFLECTING ON "centering"—which means each one of us is the center of the universe at this moment. Now this is not personal interpretation but it is a reality at this moment. You are—in terms of this moment, as I'm experiencing it—the object; the center is here and now, from this point here. If I'm reflecting on this presence, this point where we experience life, consciousness is always from this point—awareness here and now. We are each separate conscious forms in the universe, but for our lifetime we experience the universe from this centerpoint, wherever we happen to be: here, in a kuṭi, on a mountain top, in an airport....

Reflecting on the center: it isn't a point in space, but it's the reality of our being. Taking it on a personal level, "I am the center of the universe" sounds like an inflated assumption that I'm the most important or I'm God or I'm claiming something special. This is quite ordinary, because each one of us, each creature, is in fact the center of the universe in terms of experience. Even a flea is a conscious being and experiences consciousness from this point, whether it is on the dog or on the cat. I don't imagine fleas have strong egos; they don't think that much. But not being a flea, I can't speak for them. So then we can see ourselves—I'm just an ordinary human being. There is nothing special about me, considering how many billion people live on this planet. This is a conventional way of thinking, "I'm just one other creature on the planet," which is certainly true. There isn't anything wrong or false about that, but is that really the way it is? What happens to this form is what I'm experiencing, and so that is important, even though on the level of the macrocosmic perspective I'm just like a flea of no great importance to the universe.

If I drop dead now it's not going to be any great loss to the universe. Only a few will ever notice. Like when a flea dies, who cares? In fact we might be glad. Seeing dead fleas might be better than seeing live ones. But in terms of experience, and this is what I'm pointing to, this point is the experience of here and now. So this awakened state, awareness, is our ability to reflect on this experience, not from personal preferences or opinions but from the position of the Buddha knowing the Dhamma. Consciousness in a separate form is the experience of knowing. Knowing, then, is what we have been doing on this retreat—knowing the way it is rather than knowing *about* the way it is or having views or opinions on a personal level of "I'm feeling, my feelings are like this," or "my body feels like this." Our thought habits and our language are very much based on the sense of me and mine. But transcending thought and language, when we have stopped thinking, there is still presence, isn't there?

When I think "I am Ajahn Sumedho"—and I can get caught in the associations of that thought and the attachment to that particular perception of me—there is still awareness, and that is the gate to the Deathless. That is the opening, the crack in saṃsāra, the escape hatch from being constantly propelled and enslaved to our habits. Thinking is a habit; the sense of myself as a person is a habit. Personal habits are sakkāya-diṭṭhi, sīlabbata-parāmāsa, and vicikicchā, the first three of the ten fetters, called *saṃyojana* in Pāli. So these first three fetters are to get beyond, to see through. Then one realizes the path: stream-entry, *sotāpatti*. So it is not getting rid of these three fetters by annihilating everything, going into a blank state—but in recognizing these fetters; being the observer of them rather than being taken over by them—becoming this personality and these conventions and thoughts, becoming the thinking process.

So things like self-inquiry, looking into self, observing self, rather than taking a position that we shouldn't have a self, that we shouldn't be selfish—which depends on thought...If I believe in anattā, in no-self, then I think of myself as something that I've got to get rid of rather than understand. So this is understanding in the First Noble Truth, understanding dukkha, understanding self, "standing under" or observing the self. The very thought "I am Ajahn Sumedho" is an object in my mind. I can think that, but there can also be an observation, a witnessing of that thought, if I'm aware. In the *Dhammapada,* the verse that I've reflected on for many years is *appamādo amatapadaṃ*—mindfulness is the path to the Deathless. *Appamādo* is not being heedless, paying attention, being mindful; the way to the *amatapadaṃ*. Now *amata* is the Deathless. I always found that very meaningful to me. When I read the *Dhammapada* or suttas these words seem to resonate very strongly with me; they stand out.

There is so much scripture in Buddhism; the Tipiṭaka (the Pāli canon) is enormous. You start reading it and you feel a bit over-whelmed—you will never quite finish it all. But then trust your own intuition, in your life, the things that are really meaningful to you, that stand out, that reach out to you when you are read-ing the suttas or the *Dhammapada*. In the *Sutta Nipāta* there is a quote: "There is an island, an island that you cannot go beyond"

(v. 1094). This particular metaphor always meant a lot to me. An island you cannot go beyond, this centerpoint—you can't get beyond it. When you reach the center, when you recognize the center, then if you go outside it you are off on the periphery again. So an island as a metaphor works in that way. Or the concept of axis mundi, the centerpoint of the universe, of the world.

If we don't recognize the centerpoint, then we are always out on the periphery, out in saṃsāra. We might be looking for the center, but we are looking for the center out on the periphery rather than being the center itself. So with awareness, this taking refuge in Buddha, Dhamma, and Sangha isn't taking refuge in something out on the periphery of thought or the universe, or some vague forces or unseen energies that we assume—or maybe doubt. They are concepts whose purpose is to recognize the center of this moment, the center of being present here and now. So then, from the center, if my personality is out in the saṃsāra, you know me as a person. The convention, even the Theravāda Buddhist conventions, are out there, that's the conventional world that is saṃsāra. So the aim isn't to bind yourself to the conventions of Buddhism but to use the conventions for awareness, for centering.

In sīlabbata-parāmāsa, the second fetter, this is attachment to conventions out of ignorance, we bind ourselves to the conventions. We in the Buddhist world all have different views. Here in Britain you have strong views, sectarian views, views for and against Hīnayāna, Mahāyāna, Tibetan Buddhism, Vajrayāna, Zen. Then there is Advaita, Bhakti, Sufism, Christian mysticism, Jehovah's Witnesses, Mormons. We are very much attached to a particular convention. We become the convention itself, and this is a fetter, an obstruction. And it is divisive. If my main identity is that I am a Theravādan Buddhist, then I feel Mahāyāna is different. So you hold opinions about being Theravādan, and then when you see somebody who says, "I am a Mahāyāna Buddhist," you see them as separate. Or somebody who is a Christian you see them as separate, or a Mormon. Even within Theravāda there are plenty of views and opinions.

"The Buddha's teaching is like this," "this is the true teaching," and these statements, kind of *ex cathedra* (from the chair) positions, let me make the pronouncement, "My way is the right way." In Theravāda a plethora of opinions and views creates division, separation, and attachment to conventions. It is divisive. So what is unitive at this moment, where I'm not dividing anything, not seeing through the self position, my own personal preferences? Personally I have preferences, I admit. I've chosen to follow the Theravāda tradition because it attracts me. It's a personal preference, but there is a knowing of this. It needn't be an attachment. The convention that attracts you, or that you feel an affinity with, usually is the one that you use. And then "You've got to do it exactly like I do, you can't do it except through Theravāda Buddhism, because that's the way I've done it and all the others are heretical or deluded," and that's separative, isn't it? That's a personal opinion again.

So then recognizing this, this centerpoint has no opinion. For an opinion to arise, I have to become "Ajahn Sumedho" and then come from that—so we're back in the three fetters of sakkāya-diṭṭhi, sīlabbata-parāmāsa, and vicikicchā. Even though things like the Theravāda convention are good, attachment to convention is a fetter. A fetter binds you, limits you, separates you. The fetter is not the convention itself but ignorance and attachment to it, because the conventions themselves are expedient means, skillful means; they are not ends. If I make the convention an end in itself, then I have to convince everybody to become a Theravāda

Buddhist; and if they don't, I cast them out as apostates, heretics, not *real* Buddhists. And that's division. I say I'm right, and if you don't agree with me you are wrong obviously.

Right and wrong come from thinking; true and false and good and bad, this is the thinking process, the discriminative intellect. The term *vicikicchā* is translated as doubt. Well, how does doubt arise? Through thinking. If you think too much you end up doubting all the time. Because language is like that, it is what we project; it's an artifice, a man-made creation, the convention, the ego, these things are created by us onto the present. I'm creating myself in the present. "I am Ajahn Sumedho, a Theravāda Buddhist." And then if I bind myself to those views, I am coming from this ignorance, avijjā, not knowing the Dhamma.

I might know all about Dhamma from a Theravāda conditioned mind. I might be a Pāli scholar or an expert on Theravāda Buddhism. I might know all about it, be able to write textbooks for universities and whatnot. So just reflecting on what the conventional world is like, *sīlabbata-parāmāsa* is an interesting word, usually translated as "attachment to rites and rituals." There is an arrogance among many Western Buddhists. We are not born into Buddhist cultures and Buddhist families; rather, we come to Buddhism. So all that hocus-pocus, bowing and chanting, lighting joss sticks—we are not attached to any of that. It's like we'd just as soon get rid of all that. I've never suffered from the delusion that rituals and chanting are going to enlighten me or purify me; it's not part of my cultural conditioning. So arrogant Westerners can have contempt for the devotional side of the Buddhist convention and assume that they are not suffering from attachment, that sīlabbata-parāmāsa is not a fetter for them. There is the story about spitting on the Buddha-rūpa or "Kill the Buddha if you see him" and these kinds of things. We are quite willing to do that because we can have the view that there were no Buddha-rūpas at the time of the Buddha. I've heard British Buddhists condemn Buddha-rūpas—"That's not real Buddhism, that's sīlabbata-parāmāsa," "We don't need Buddha-rūpas." That is another opinion, isn't it?

In terms of reflection, awareness, I can see if I have this thing against Buddha-rūpas, and I begin to be aware of it. What is it, why have I got this? I actually like Buddha-rūpas, so I surround myself with them—this has never been a problem with me, but for some people it is. There are purists, the Buddhist purists, who want to have everything according to their view of what the Buddha really was teaching according to the suttas, the scriptures. Like Luang Por Chah made a statement once, "True but not right, right but not true." I always found this very helpful, because it is so easy to be *right,* to be righteous, and in that very attachment to being right, you become heedless. If I insist that my view is right, then I become quite heedless to the present moment, I operate from a righteous position.

So this is the danger of all religious conventions, namely, righteousness. I'm right and therefore it has to be this way; otherwise it is wrong. This is dualism again, isn't it?—right and wrong, good and bad, true and false. Now the only way that one can get perspective on right and wrong, true and false, is through awareness. Because awareness does not criticize, does not discriminate. It doesn't say what is right or wrong, but it discerns the way it is. So if I come into a shrine room and I see a Buddha-rūpa and I feel this is sīlabbata-parāmāsa, just attachment to rites and rituals and ceremonies, I might be right: it could be just that everybody is attached to the forms of Buddhism. But one can attach to one's opinions, which is sīlabbata-parāmāsa also: attaching to my interpretation of the scriptures, attaching to the party line, to the tradition, to the viewpoint. So this attachment is what the Buddha is encouraging us to look at, the sakkāya-diṭṭhi—attachment to the illusion of a self as a kind of permanent separate soul or self; "me" as a kind of permanent person. And attachment to the convention—attachment to the rational process, the thinking process, to views and opinions about right and wrong, good and bad.

So on this retreat I emphasize the recognition of this: seeing the attachment, recognizing what they call upādāna—clinging or attachment out of ignorance—in order to have insight into the path or stream-entry. It isn't a matter of doing everything right, getting rid of the Buddha-rūpas and rites and rituals, or annihilating your personality and stop thinking so as not to be attached to thoughts. Try to do that, try to stop thinking by trying to think, "I shouldn't think," and then I'm still thinking. No matter how much I think I shouldn't think, I still think—that's not wrong, but I'm not awakened to what I'm actually doing, the way it is. The thinking process is an object in consciousness. Buddha-rūpas or no Buddha-rūpas, the ego, the sakkāya-diṭṭhi is then seen in terms of Dhamma.

Dhamma, then, is the way it is, the arising, the ceasing, of all conditions. Sabbe saṅkhārā aniccā is not holding to a *view* that all conditions are impermanent, it's observing, being the knower of impermanence. Impermanence is like this. The view that there shouldn't be any Buddha-rūpas is a view that arises and ceases, so your refuge is in the awareness of this view. The view can be, "You have to have Buddha-rūpas, you need to chant Pāli, and if we don't it's not real Theravāda."

The four stages on the path—the stream-enterer, the sakadā-gāmī, the anāgāmī, Arahant—this is all about reflecting on the ten fetters, not becoming, not "me" becoming any of these stages. What happens so much of the time—if you don't see through the sakkāya-diṭṭhi, sīlabbata-parāmāsa, and vicikicchā and get past them—is that you try to *become* a stream-enterer or *become* an Arahant. Or feeling you are not, "I can't do it, I've still got so many attachments I can't possibly do that. And are there any real stream-enterers in the world?" In Thailand when I lived there, Westerners used to come and ask about Ajahn Chah, "Is he an Arahant?" And the arrogance of Western Buddhists sometimes is appalling—they go around looking for Arahants in Thailand and then decide there aren't any. How would you recognize an Arahant? Would you see a halo, some kind of golden glow around him or her, or what?

Some monks say they are Arahants, and then you are caught in wondering whether they really are. And sometimes monks who say they are Arahants don't act like Arahants, but what does an Arahant act like? Are we just applying the word *Arahant* to some kind of ethereal image of a saint, some kind of saintly being that you have seen in a picture, some kind of sublime ethereal ideal of human perfection? Or did the Buddha use these terms not for identity or for becoming, but for letting go? So, as with the fetters, you don't *become* a sotāpanna; you let go of the ignorance, the fetters that delude you. So with the first three fetters, letting go of them through understanding them: seeing them as the Buddha knowing the Dhamma rather than as someone trying to get rid of them or be unattached to them.

This is where developing a sense of trust or confidence in awareness is so important. I can still have views and opinions and preferences; that is part of the personality. But it's in a perspective through awareness; I don't go grasping those views and then judging everything through that divisive process of "I'm right, you're wrong." In this dualism the personality makes me separate: my personality is different from yours. Conventions can be very separative. Sectarianism is a problem: Sunnis/Shi'ites, Catholics/ Protestants, Buddhists/Christians, Hindus/Muslims. The separation takes place through ignorance, where you are attached to your way, to your belief, to your convention, to your view, and then that attachment itself. Not that any of those conventions are bad; they are all quite good usually, but the problem is attachment out of ignorance.

So this is to be reflected on. What is attachment to personality view, to conventions, to cultural conditioning? We are culturally conditioned from infancy. I was born into a white, middle-class, Anglican family in Seattle and then all the views and opinions of my parents and all the cultural expectations and rights and wrongs, shoulds and shouldn'ts, come from that. I wasn't born with that. If I had been born in some other place I would be different—different culture, different religion, and that would be the cultural conditioning. The cultural conditioning starts operating from birth, so it's sometimes difficult to get beyond it.

There are so many assumptions and attitudes that are culturally instilled in us when we are still infants and little children, what a girl should be, a boy should be, what good manners are, right and wrong, and expectations of parents of the social class we are born in, and identities with that—often they are assumptions that we never question, never recognize. So I include cultural conditioning within sīlabbata-parāmāsa, and the only way to transcend or get beyond it is awareness. The assumptions, the attitudes that you acquire through osmosis, through just being born and living with your parents and your social group—there is nothing wrong with any of that. Saying that there is one that is better than another, that is cultural arrogance, isn't it?

The British have a long history of cultural arrogance. Going out to save or civilize the rest of the world, to convert them to Christianity, correct them, free them from their barbarian ways, is all cultural arrogance. It is no longer politically correct to think like this, which is good. But to get beyond the whole process, beyond attachment to ideals of democracy and equality and freedom as the Western conditioned mind conceives them, is through awareness. Just recognize this stillpoint, a centered, reflective attention in the present, and then cultivate that. Practice seeing the impermanence of the self-view, the sakkāya-diṭṭhi, the impermanence of cultural conditioning, the arising and ceasing of thoughts, the thinking process.

W E HAVE just three weeks left of the Vassa (rains retreat). The words in this sentence are perceptions of time and change, in the conditioned realm. Vassa is a convention. Autumn doesn't say, "I'm autumn"; we call it that. This is a convention that we use for communicating our cultural attitudes or moral agreements. *Paramattha-sacca,* ultimate reality, is where we get beyond conventions. Conventions are made up and are dependent on other things. Things that are considered good in one conventional form are not considered appropriate in another. We have various biases or prejudices that we get from our culture and the conventions that we have. Living in Europe, we have the old cultural biases of what the French are like, and the Germans, Italians, and so forth.

We have cultural attitudes for perceiving things. We form these various opinions and views. That is why it's easy to have ethnic warfare and racial prejudices, class snobbery, and so forth, because we never question the conventional reality that we have adopted. We just go along with it. We hold various views about our religion, race, and culture and then compare them to somebody else's. On that level we have ideals, say, of democracy, equality, and all that, but we're still very much influenced by the conventional realities that we're conditioned by.

It takes quite a determined effort to get beyond your cultural conditioning. Being American, there was a lot that I just assumed; and I never realized how arrogant I could be until I had to live in another culture. I never saw how American idealism could be another blind spot, how we Americans were shoving our ideas down everybody's throat and saying that we knew what was good for them and how they should run their countries. When you're brought up to think that you're in the most advanced society, that's an assumption. I don't think that I was taught this view in any intentional way. It was assumed. It was an underlying attitude.

It's hard to get beyond these assumptions, these things we pick up. We don't even know we have these attachments until they're reflected in some way, and that's why living in different cultures helps. Living in Thailand helped me to see a lot of these things because the culture was so different. There was the whole attitude that came from living in a Buddhist monastery, where the emphasis was on reflection, mindfulness, and wisdom. I wasn't becoming a kind of ersatz Thai, "going native," as they say, but I was learning to see the subtle attitudes and assumptions that I was conditioned by and that may not be all that easily seen until one finds oneself suffering about something.

One of the problems that we have in meditation is compulsiveness. In our society we are brought up to be very obsessed and compulsive. There are so many shoulds. When you're coming from ideas and ideals, the result is that there are so many "shoulds" in your vocabulary. This idealism has its beauty, so it's not a matter of disregarding it but of recognizing its limitations. This feeling that there is always something we've got to do, that there's something we haven't done and should be doing, that we should be working harder, that we should be practicing more, that we should be more honest, more open, more devout, better natured, and so on. All of that is true. The shoulds are usually right. If things were perfect, then I would be perfect. Everything would be just perfect. I would be ideal and my society would be ideal. Amarāvatī would fit the ideal; we would all be perfect. Then there is nothing more you should do because you've already reached the top. But that's not the way life is.

An idea is something we create, isn't it? You take your ideas from what's best or what's most beautiful, perfect, fair, or just. So the Buddha is pointing to the way life is, which is its changingness. It doesn't stick at the best, does it? You can't hold on to anything. Say, for instance, that you contemplate some flowers, like roses. Sometimes you get a perfect rose just at its peak, absolutely perfect in its form, its color, its fragrance, but you can't keep it that way. It lasts for a brief time before it starts going the other way, and then you just want to get rid of it, throw it out, and get another one.

So with mindfulness we're aware of this changingness. In our meditation we're aware of how our moods and feelings change. When we think of how things *should* be, we get back into ideas and then compare ourselves to what we think good practice is, how many hours we should meditate, how we should do this and that. We can operate from these ideas, which are often very good ideas. But the problem, even if one conforms to all these shoulds, is that there is always something more, always something that could be better. It goes on endlessly. You never get to the root of the problem. You just go on and on to where there's always this feeling that there's something more you *should* be doing. When we reach the end of this, we sometimes give up: "I've had enough of this. To hell with it. I'm just going to enjoy life. I'll disrobe and just go out and have a good time, eat, drink, and make merry until I die." Because one can only be driven so far. You can't sustain it and you reach a point where it doesn't work anymore.

Listening to a should is a fair enough way to think about something. Some people think we shouldn't even think in terms of shoulds. To recognize how things affect us, just notice the feeling that there is something more that I think I have to do. An example of this is a recurring dream that I had when I first went to stay with Luang Por Chah. In 1963 I finished my Master's degree in Berkeley after a year of really compulsive and intense study. I couldn't enjoy anything because every time I went out and tried to enjoy myself I would think, "You've got your exam coming. You've got to pass your Master's degree." I'd go to a party and try to relax, and this voice would say, "You shouldn't be here. You've got to take this exam and you're not ready. You're not good enough for it." So that whole year I couldn't enjoy myself. I just kept driving myself. After I finished my Master's degree I couldn't read a book for about six months. My mind just wouldn't concentrate. I went through Peace Corps training in Hawaii after that, and they wanted me to read all these things and I couldn't. Not even the instructions. I was overloaded. But that left a kind of intensity; the way I would approach anything would be either to think "I can't do it" and give up totally or get into the old compulsive mode.

When I went to stay with Luang Por Chah I kept having this recurring dream as a result of putting a lot of effort into my practice. In the dream, I'd be going into this coffee shop. I'd sit down, order a cup of coffee and a nice pastry, and then the voice would say, "You shouldn't be here. You should be studying for the exam." That would be the recurring theme for this dream which I would have quite often. I'd ask myself, "What's it telling me?" And then my compulsive mind kept thinking, "There's something I'm not doing that I should be doing. I should be practicing more. I should be more mindful. I shouldn't be sleeping so much." I wasn't actually sleeping very much at all. I kept thinking this was a message telling me there is something I'm not doing that I should be doing. I kept trying to think, "What could it be?" I couldn't drive myself any more than I was already doing. I couldn't figure it out. Then one morning after I had this dream, I woke up and I had the answer, and the answer was that there wasn't any examination!

I had just realized that I lived my life as if I were always going to be tested or brought before the authorities and put to the test and that I was never going to be ready or good enough. There would always be more. I could study more. I could read more. I could do more things. I shouldn't be lazy. I shouldn't enjoy life because this would be wasting my time, because the exam is coming and I'm not ready for it. It was a kind of emotional conditioning that I had acquired because the school system in the States is very competitive. You start when you're five years old and you just keep going.

So I had the insight that there wasn't any exam, that I just thought there was, and that I had always lived my life with this attitude that there was going to be a big test that I wasn't prepared for. Maybe my religious background also contributed: you're going to be tested when you die, to see whether you've been good enough to go to heaven, and if not you'll go to hell. There's always this sense that you've got to do something. You're not good enough. I've got too many faults. I've got to get rid of them. I've got to become something that I'm not. The way I am is not good enough.

When I came into monastic life, I brought this tendency into how I practiced, and I could do it for a while but then I realized that if I was going to be a monk that wasn't the purpose of a monk's life. It wasn't meant to be that way. It was just how I was interpreting monasticism from this compulsive viewpoint. So I stopped having the dream once I got the answer to the riddle.

One of the first three fetters we acquire after we're born is sakkāya-diṭṭhi, or "personality view." We're not born with a personality. It's something we acquire. When you're brought up in a very competitive system you compare yourself to others and to ideals. Your value and worth is very much related to what or who is considered the best. And if you don't fit into the category of the best, you sometimes see yourself as not good enough. Even the people whom I used to think of as the best didn't think of themselves in that way. Sometimes we think some people are much happier because we project that onto them. We think they are better off than we are.

When the Buddha emphasized mindfulness as the way, he was pointing to the way things are rather than to the best. In the morning at Wat Pah Pong they'd have these readings from the suttas about what a monk should be, and they were all according to the ideal standard. Wondering how to interpret this, and wanting to live up to such high standards, gave rise to a feeling of "can I really do all that?" One can feel discouraged and despairing because one is looking at life in terms of ideals. But then the teaching of the Buddha isn't based on ideals but on Dhamma, the way things are.

In vipassanā, insight meditation, you're really tuning into impermanence, into tragedy. This isn't a matter of how things should be, but of how they are. All conditioned phenomena are impermanent. It's not that one is saying that all conditioned phenomena should be impermanent. They are. It's a matter of opening to impermanence. It's not trying to project this idea onto

life but of using your intuitive mind to open, to watch, to pay attention. Then you're aware of the changingness.

You're aware of even your own compulsive attitude, "There's something I've got to do." You're aware of that compulsive feeling, attitude, or belief that you're a person with a lot of faults and weaknesses, which is easy to believe as being honest and realistic. Then we think that in order to become an enlightened being we've got to get over these faults, get rid of them in some way, and become an Arahant. This is how the mind works. This way of thinking is often what we read into the scriptures. But with reflective awareness, you notice that such a way of thinking is something you've created in your mind: "I am a person with a lot of faults and weaknesses, and I've got to practice hard in order to overcome them." That's something I'm creating in my mind. I'm creating that attitude. That's not the truth. That which is aware of all this is the awakened state of being. You start to notice the difference between this awareness and what you create by habits based on attachments.

We use this word *Buddho,* the name "Buddha" itself, the one who knows. It's a significant word because it is pointing to a state of attention, of knowing directly, of intuitive awareness, of wisdom. So there's no person. If I say, "I'm Buddha," then that's coming from personality again, from identity. Thinking "I am the Buddha" doesn't work. We have refuge in Buddha: *Buddhaṃ saraṇaṃ gacchāmi.* That's a kind of convention too, but it points to a reality that we can begin to trust in, which is awareness—because the Buddha is Buddho, the one who knows, that which knows, which is awake and aware. It's awakeness. It's not judgmental or critical. The Buddha is not saying, "You should be like this and you shouldn't be like that." It's knowing that all conditioned phenomena are *like this.* Whereas if you're brought up in a religion like Christianity, God tells you what you should be. At least this is the way I was taught: how you should be a good boy and how every time you're bad you hurt God's feelings. If I told a lie, God would be very disappointed in me. This is the kind of moral training a child gets. It's what your parents think, isn't it? It's all mixed up with perceptions of parents and God as a kind of parental figure.

So awakeness, then, is learning to listen and trust in the most simple state of being. It's not jhāna or absorption in anything. It's pure attention. So if you trust in this purity, there is no fault in it. There are no faults in purity, are there? It's perfect. There's no impurity. This is where to trust, in this attentiveness to the present. Once you try to find it, then you start going into doubt. Trust it rather than think about it. Just trust in the immanent act of being awake, attentive in this moment. When I do this, my mind relaxes. I hear the sound of silence. There's no self. There's purity. If I start feeling that I should be doing something, then I'm aware of it. I'm aware of the kamma-vipāka (result of action) of having been through the American education system and having driven myself through this incredibly compulsive way of living life. So the kamma-vipāka arises. In this state of purity, it's not personal. It's not saying, "Ajahn Sumedho is pure now." It's beyond that. You're not talking about it in any kind of personal way. It's a recognition, a realization. It's what you truly are, not a creation. I'm not creating the purity. I'm not creating an ideal of it and then deluding myself with it.

This is where trust comes in, because your personality view is not going to trust awareness. Your personality view is going to say, "There's nothing pure about you. You just had some dirty thoughts. You're really feeling pretty upset and angry about something someone said about you. After all these years, you're still filled with impurities." This is the old inner tyrant. This is the personality view. It's the victim and the victimizer. As the victim it says, "Poor me, I'm so impure," while as the accuser it says, "You're not good enough, you're impure." You can't trust it. Don't take refuge in being a victim or a victimizer. But you can trust in this awakened awareness. And that trust is humbling. It isn't like believing in something. It's learning to relax and be. Trust in the ability simply to be here, open and receptive to whatever is happening now. Even if what's happening is nasty, or whatever the conditions you're experiencing are, that's not a problem if you trust in this purity.

With the Vinaya (discipline), for example, and the idea of trying to keep it pure, the personality view attaches even to this. "Is my Vinaya as pure as theirs?" Then you're just using this convention to increase your sense of personal worth or worthlessness. If you think you're purer than the rest, then that's arrogance, a holier-than-thou attitude. If you think you're impure, then you're going to feel hopeless. You can't do it. Better go and get drunk or something, or at least forget about it for a while. Relax, have a good time. Better than beating yourself up with your ideals of not being pure enough.

Conventions themselves are limited, for their nature is imperfect and changing. Maybe you expect a convention to be perfect. Then maybe after a while you become critical because you see flaws in it. It isn't as good as you thought, or some of it doesn't make sense. But recognize that a convention is like anything else; it is aniccā, dukkha, anattā—impermanent, unsatisfactory, nonself. Theravāda Buddhism is a convention based on morality, on doing good and refraining from evil in action and speech. It's a way of living where we agree to take responsibility for how we live on this planet, in this society. The convention of Theravāda

Buddhism, whether you find it agreeable or not, is an ancient and still useful tradition with a lot of power. It's a viable tradition that still works. It's not a matter of it having to be perfect for us to use it, but of our learning to use it for awakened awareness.

Then we get into the old Buddhist camps of the Mahāyāna, Vajrayāna, and Hīnayāna. We're considered Hīnayāna, the "lesser vehicle." So we could think that means it's probably not as good. Mahāyāna is better, says logic. Lesser vehicle and greater vehicle. Then Vajrayāna, that's the absolute best. You can't get any better than Vajrayāna according to the Tibetans. That's the highest vehicle. So then we start thinking in terms of good, better, best. But all of these are conventions. Whether we call it Mahāyāna, Hīnayāna, or Vajrayāna, they're still just conventions: they're limited, imperfect. Still, they're functional, to be used for mindfulness rather than as some kind of attachment or position that one takes on anything.

These different terms can be very divisive. If we attach to Theravāda and start looking down on every other form of Buddhism, then we think that they're not pure, they're not the original. They may call themselves higher, but they're not the original. We can get arrogant because we've got our own way of justifying our convention. But this is all playing with words. If we look at what is going on with these words, we're just creating Mahāyāna, Hīnayāna, and Vajrayāna in our minds. The refuge is in Buddha, not in these *yānas*. The Buddha knows that every thought is changing and not-self. So trust in that, in the simplicity of that. Because if you don't, then it is going to arouse your old compulsive habits of thinking: "I've got to do more. I've got to develop this. I've got to become a *bodhisattva*. I've got to get the higher practice going." And on and on like that.

When you're caught in that conventional realm and that's all you know, you're easily intimidated and blinded by all the daz-zling positions and attitudes and ideas that people throw at you. So this is where trusting in awareness is not a matter of having the best, or feeling that maybe you should have something better than what you have. That's a creation of your mind, isn't it? When you establish what is adequate, it's not based on what is the best but on what is basic for survival and good health.

In Buddhist monasticism the four requisites are an expression of this. You don't have to have the best food and the best robes; you just have to have what's adequate in terms of survival. Is there any problem with requiring a place to stay or medicine for sickness? It doesn't have to be the very best. In fact, the standard is often established at the lowest point, like rag robes rather than silk robes. Then the Dhamma-Vinaya is respected and taught. These give us a sense of a place where we can live. Standards aren't placed at the very best, but if the Dhamma is taught and the Vinaya is respected, the four requisites are adequate, then that's good enough. So go for it! Go for the practice rather than quibble about the rest. It's better to develop one's awareness rather than going along with one's feelings of criticism or doubt in dealing with the people and the place you are in.

I contemplated this compulsive attitude in myself until I could really see it. It was very insidious, not just a one-off insight. It reminded me of how I approached life in general, full of shoulds, always feeling there was something I should or shouldn't be doing. Just notice and listen to this and learn to relax and trust in the ref-uge. This is very humbling because it doesn't seem like anything. It seems like it's not worth much, this attention in the present. "So what? I want something I should be doing. Tell me what to do next. How many hours should I be sitting? How many hours should I be walking? What should I be developing? Should I do more mettā?" We want something to do and feel very ill at ease when there's nothing to do, nowhere to go. So in monastic life we do offer conventions and structures. We have morning and evening *pūjā* (meditation and devotional practices) and fortnightly recitations and so forth, which gives a conventional form to use in order to do something. Then there's chanting and *piṇḍapāta* (alms round) and all these things that are part of our tradition. This structure is there to help us, like sīla for behavior and structure for the community.

When people go on self-retreat, they let go of the structure and are thrown onto their own. What happens when you're on your own and nobody knows what you're doing? You don't have to look around to see if the senior monk is watching you. You're left to your own devices, so you could sleep all day or you could read novels or go for long walks, or you could really practice hard. There's a whole range of possibilities, and it's left up to you to notice that feeling of what happens when the structure is removed. It's not that one does this in a judgmental way, bringing back the shoulds, such as "I should practice so many hours a day, sit so many hours, walk so many hours, do this and do that, get my practice, get my samādhi together, really get somewhere in my practice." Not that that's wrong, but that may be a very compulsive thing. If you don't live up to it, then what do you feel like? Do you feel guilt ridden if you don't do what you've determined to do? Notice how the mind works and awaken to it.

It's easy if there is a strong leader who tells you to do this and do that and everybody comes, everybody leaves, and everybody marches in step and so forth. This is good training also. But that brings up resistance and rebellion in some people who don't like it. In contrast to this, other people don't like it when someone isn't telling them what to do next, because it leaves them uncertain.

They like the security of everything being controlled and held together by a strong leader. But recognize that this monastic life is for the liberation of the heart. Some strong leaders browbeat you or manipulate you emotionally by saying, "If you really want to please me, you will do this. I won't give you my approval if you don't behave properly," and things like this. I can use my emotional power to try to control and manipulate the situation, but that's not skillful. That's not what we're here for. The onus is on each one of us, isn't it? It's about waking up.

But don't think you have to wake up because Ajahn Sumedho says so. Waking up is just a simple, immanent act of attention: open, relaxed listening, being here and now. It's learning to recognize that, to appreciate that more and more and to trust it. Because you're probably emotionally programmed for the other—either you should or you shouldn't. What we're trying to do here is to provide a situation where you are encouraged to trust and to cultivate this. When we say "cultivate" it's not like having to do anything. It's more learning to relax and trust in being with the flow of life. Because life is like this.

I remember when I first went to Wat Pah Pong, there was such an esprit de corps. We were really there with Luang Por Chah. There were only twenty-two monks, and we were really getting somewhere; we were really a crack troop, top grade, top guns. Then a few years later, I began seeing things that I didn't like and got very critical, thinking it was all falling apart. Then I saw it fall apart, after Luang Por Chah had his stroke. I remember going to Wat Pah Pong a few years after that. At the wat they had an inner monastery where the monks lived, and then in an outer part there was a special kuṭi for Luang Por Chah, which allowed for nursing care and all kinds of things. In addition to this they had an outer sālā (hall) where people came to visit.

You'd go to the outer sālā, and nobody wanted to come to the monastery. All they wanted to do was to see Luang Por Chah, who was ill and couldn't talk or do anything. All the emphasis was on his kuṭi, and no monks wanted to live at the monastery. I remember going there when there were only three monks in this huge monastery—Ajahn Liam and few others—and the place was looking pretty shabby. Usually it was spic and span. The standards had been very high there, sweeping the paths and repairing everything. But suddenly it was like a ghost town with all these empty kuṭis that needed repairing and were dirty and dusty, and the paths not swept and so forth. I remember some people from Bangkok coming to me and saying, "Aah, this place is not good anymore. We want you to come back and be the abbot." They were thinking I should go back and take over. It had changed in a way that they felt it shouldn't have—but now it's back with fifty monks and it's all operating to full capacity.

Things change. So we are open to change. We're not demanding that things change in any way that we want it to or that when it's at a peak that we can keep it that way. That's impossible. But you can be aware when you're at your best or your worst, when you're feeling good, inspired, and enthusiastic or despairing, depressed, and disheartened. This awareness is your refuge. Awareness of the changingness of feelings, of attitudes, of moods: stay with that, because it's a refuge that is indestructible. It's not something that changes. It's a refuge you can trust in. This refuge is not something that you create. It's not a creation. It's not an ideal. It's very practical and very simple but easily overlooked or not noticed. Whenever you're mindful, you're beginning to notice: it's like this.

For instance, when I remind myself that this is pure, this moment, I really make a note of this. This is the path. This is purity. Not anything that I'm creating, just this state of attention. Not attention like *"Achtung!"*—it's more of a relaxed attention. Listening, open, receptive. When you relax into that, it's a natural state, not a created state. It's not dependent on conditions making it that way. It's just that we forget it all the time and get thrown back into the old habits. This is why with mindfulness, we're remembering it more, trusting it more, and cultivating this way of bringing ourselves back into this awareness. Then we get carried away again and come back again. We keep doing that. No matter how recalcitrant, difficult, or wild the emotions or thoughts may be, it's all right. This is the refuge.

We can apply this awareness to everything, such as being personally wounded. When somebody says something that is hurtful, ask the question, "What is it that gets hurt?" If somebody insults me or abuses me in some way and I feel hurt or misunderstood, offended, annoyed, or even angry, what is it that gets angry and annoyed, that gets offended? Is that my refuge—that personality whose feelings get hurt and upset? If I have awareness as a refuge, this never gets upset by anything. You can call it anything you want. But as a person, I can be easily upset. Because the personality, the sakkāya-diṭṭhi, is like that—based on "me" being worthwhile or worthy, being appreciated or not appreciated, being understood properly or misunderstood, being respected or not respected, and all this kind of thing.

My personality is wide open to be hurt, to be offended, to be upset by anything. But personality is not my refuge. If your personality is anything like mine, I wouldn't advise you to take it as a refuge. I wouldn't for a minute want to recommend anyone taking refuge in my personality. But in awareness, yes. Because awareness is pure. If you trust it more and more, even if you're feeling upset, disrespected, and unloved and unappreciated, the

awareness knows that as being anicca, impermanent. It's not judging. It's not making any problems. It's fully accepting the feeling
that "nobody loves me, everybody hates me" as a feeling. And
it goes away naturally. It drops off because its nature is change.

O NE OF THE REFLECTIONS I found helpful for myself is to start where you are, here and now. To be able to recognize the way you are feeling or the state of mind you are in or your body in the present, rather than operating from "Ajahn Sumedho said to listen to the sound of silence and I don't hear anything—what did he mean by the sound of silence?" That is another thought. The main point is not the sound of silence or anything else but realizing the way it is now. So whatever mental state you are in, like wondering what Ajahn Sumedho is talking about—if you are aware that you are thinking that, that is awareness.

Listen to yourself and notice this relationship of sati (mindfulness) to the thought process or the emotional reactions you are experiencing, and then use this expression "they are what they are" or "it is what it is" as a way of looking, not judging. So it is what it is, the suchness. I remember reading about Zen Buddhism where they talk about suchness. I thought, "What is suchness?" because it didn't mean all that much to me at the time. In Pāli they have the word *tathā*. The Buddha referred to himself as the *tathāgatha,* which means suchness, that which is now, rather than "I'm Gotama, the Buddha, born to Queen Māyā and King Suddhodana in Lumbini, and when I was born I took seven steps on seven lotuses." So after his enlightenment there was no Buddha, no Gotama, nothing, nobody, but that which is now, the suchness of that which is present now. So this word *tathatā* has the sense of as-is-ness, suchness.

In Thai "suchness" is *pen yang nun eng*. Ajahn Buddhadāsa—at Suan Mokkh monastery in the south of Thailand—was great. I asked him once what would he want with him if he were isolated on a desert island, and he said just a little note saying *pen yang nun eng:* "this is the way it is," *tathā*. Because this is a reflective thought; it's not a proliferating thought, is it? It's not analyzing, criticizing, figuring out, defining, or anything else, but it is using language to help us to look at something, remind us, because whatever you are experiencing now is what it is, it's an honest statement. People have said, "You know, I experience memories from a previous life," or some kind of unusual psychic experiences, and they want to know what does this really mean, what is the significance of all this—and it is what it is. No matter if it's psychic or coming from another galaxy, or a memory of yesterday or whatever, a mood or a feeling, what we are doing is recognizing it, we are receiving it, and it's the way it is: *tathā*.

This is not a way of pushing anything away, but of receiving it. Because if we have extraordinary experiences then we want to make them into "really fantastic things that are happening to me," and then we get carried away with being interested or fascinated or even frightened by unusual mental experiences. If it is just the same old boring, repetitive thoughts or memories or negative states, it is what it is. So we have this way of reflecting, using this statement "it is what it is"; *tathā* is a word that points to, reminds us, that we are not trying to make anything out of it, dismiss it, deny it, exaggerate it, or proliferate on it. Whatever way you are feeling now, whether you like it or not, whether it is inspired or depressed, right or wrong, sane or crazy, it is what it is in this moment. Now that's an honest statement. You can't beat that.

If you say, "Well, what does it mean, what's the significance in the universal system?" and then you say, "Oh, I think it is..." But then you ask one of the nuns and she says, "No, no, I think it's more like this," so next you ask another monk and he says, "No, no, no, you're wrong, it's not like..." You get all our views and opinions about all these things, what we think it is or its significance or its nonsense or it's real or it's false or it's deluded or it's true or right or wrong. Then we are making more of it, we are adding our own personal view about it. "It is what it is" neither dismisses it nor compounds it. But it is certainly receiving it. It's recognizing that all things come and go, all things arise and cease, all things are born and die—sabbe saṅkhārā aniccā. So this is the Buddha knowing Dhamma.

The statement in the scripture that really inspired me years ago, that really meant a lot to me at the time:

> There is the unborn, uncreated, unformed, unoriginated, therefore there is an escape from the born, created, formed, originated. If it were not for the unborn, uncreated, unformed, unoriginated, there would be no escape from the born, created, formed, originated, but because there is the uncreated, unformed, unborn, unoriginated, there is an escape, there is liberation from the born, the created, the originated (*Udāna* VIII.3).

This puts it in terms of the unborn and the born, the uncreated and the created, the unoriginated and the originated. These are words, yes, but the created, the born, the formed, the originated, these are saṅkhārā, mental formations, aren't they?

What we see, hear, smell, taste, touch, think, feel, the four elements—the earth, fire, water, and wind elements—the thoughts, the memories, the feelings—pleasant, painful, neutral feeling—the physical body, in fact all experience, the whole universe, is the created, the born, the formed, the originated. So that means everything, everything you can think of, imagine, feel, experience…but there is the escape, there is liberation from the born, the created, the originated. There is the unborn. So then reflect on what is the unborn, unformed, uncreated, unoriginated. Is that some kind of metaphysical reality that someday I might understand and we can try to imagine? Try to imagine the unconditioned. You can imagine the conditions of any sort: red, blue, purple, green, white, black, yellow, any form, anything, abstract or clearly defined, big, small, minute, nanotechnology, microscopic, macrocosmic.

One thing goes on to another. The conditioned realm is just like that, one thing goes on to another, and we're trying to sort it all out. What are we doing with our high technology these days? Trying to classify and order phenomena, put them in a computer, on a website. Then it goes on and on and on. It gets more and more refined, but behind all that, ask yourself, at this moment right now, what is the unborn, unconditioned, unformed, unoriginated? Try to imagine it, something that is unborn or uncreated. My mind goes blank. Because it is a negation of the formed, the conditioned, the created. Uncreated, unconditioned, is a negation in terms of English grammar. So imagination is created, is a form, isn't it?

You can imagine forms. You can even imagine abstractions like "uncreated" and "unborn," but isn't that just a kind of intellectual abstraction of the brain? But then why would the Buddha bother with such a statement? He was pointing to the here and now, to awareness here and now. There are statements in the scriptures like "mindfulness is the path to the Deathless"—the Deathless, what is that? Some immortal realm out there, something we can imagine, some kind of immortal nibbāna in outer space? We can imagine a kind of realm but what does "Deathless realm" mean? So you see, the thinking process carries you that far; it can deal with the born, the conditioned, the created, the originated, and that is what science is all about, isn't it? Manipulating the different atoms and so forth.

Science gets more refined, and it is fascinating, interesting, and marvelous in its own way. And it's also terrifying, because, as we manipulate the conditioned realm that we are living in, we lack the wisdom—where do we stop, where are the boundaries? These are the moral dilemmas of today. Where are the moral boundaries now? Having an abortion: when does the fetus, when do the sperm and egg, become a conscious being, when does it become just a medical operation or murder? Where do we fix the boundary in situations like that? Another moral dilemma: unplugging the machines that keep a human body alive even though the brain is dead. A few months ago there was a big deal in America around this. There are opinions and views about all this. But the unborn, this to me seems to be very clearly stated by the Buddha: mindfulness, sati-sampajañña. Appamādo amata-padaṃ: mindfulness—or heedfulness, attentiveness—is the path to the Deathless.

So that is why learning to recognize what mindfulness is, the reality of it, not just trying to define it and then trying to do some-thing—is mindfulness. This is where you have to trust directly in what you are doing, because it is not something I can explain or show you. I am sitting here, mindful, but you might think I'm sitting here with all kinds of wild fantasies going on in my head. I could be... How would you know whether I'm mindful or going mad, so long as I keep an inscrutable expression? So the Buddha used words like anattā, *suññatā* (emptiness) and non-self, nibbāna, nonattachment. These words are all negations. What is nibbāna? It is when you recognize and realize nonattachment. You have to recognize what attachment is before you can realize nonattachment.

There is desire (taṇhā) as an origin. Desire points to this energy in us, the wanting, the longing, that part of our human experience where we want, long for something—for peace, happiness, good food, melodious music, beautiful sights, being a better person, becoming an enlightened Buddha. Or longing to get rid of the pain, the misery, the unfairness, the suffering we experience through this form. So wanting something is desire, is taṇhā; and wanting to get rid of, or not wanting, something is also desire. The four foundations of mindfulness (satipaṭṭhānas) are ways of looking into these things. When we practice vipassanā we are using these four satipaṭṭhānas, which are skillful teachings. But they are pointing always at the way it is.

With *kāyānupassanā satipaṭṭhāna*—the body, investigation of the four elements, this physical body, divide into thirty-two parts: the ways of looking at the body, of investigating, seeing the body not as something personal as if we owned it, but for what it is. It is the way it is: the hair of the head, hair of the body, nails, teeth, and skin. When you take the ten precepts or the higher ordination, this is the mantra I give. The *upajjhāya* (preceptor) says, "Repeat after me: kesā..." they repeat, "Kesā lomā, nakhā, dantā, taco." If you were listening you would think I was giving some secret information, highly classified material, and then I tell you what I have just told them: hair of the head, hair of the body, nails, teeth, and skin. And "Oh," you would like more of a secret mantra, the key to enlightenment, and you're getting just this kind of banal sequence. But it is pointing to the surface, how the appearance—the hair of the head, the hair of the body, nails, teeth, and skin, the appearance—creates our selves, the attraction to these five things. If we look at them in a different way, not in terms of whether our hair is beautiful or not, or the hair of the body, nails, teeth, skin, then we are looking at them just as they are. We are not trying to convince ourselves that they are nasty ugly things, but it is a different way of looking.

It's looking at something "as is" rather than the tendency to want to look at these things in terms of their attractiveness or unattractiveness. So the aim of practice is to realize nibbāna, to be free from delusion. When a monk or nun takes the ordination, this is to realize nibbāna. That is the whole purpose of it, to realize the Deathless. To "realize" is an interesting word because it is about reality, to recognize it. It's not to find it in something you don't have, that you've got to find somewhere else, but it's to recognize or realize. So mindfulness is the way of realization as you witness, as you put yourself in that position of the Buddho, the knowing position, the witnessing position here and now, and patiently bear with the conditions you are experiencing.

What you might be experiencing is "I want to get to nibbāna instantly. I don't want to sit here because I've got pain in my knees and I don't have time to wait patiently." You experience restlessness and desire, so you hold up nibbāna and say, "I want it right now, instant nibbāna." Take a pill and you've got it—that would be very nice. But if you're patient, alert, and embrace the moment with attention, then the mind goes quite empty—it's like a poised attention. The mind rests in a state of poise, waiting with patient receptivity—not trying to find anything or do anything or get rid of anything—but just being in this attitude of poised awareness and openness, listening, fully alert, fully conscious.

Of course things come up because we aren't used to being that way, and then we feel restless. Repressed emotions can start rising up into consciousness; fears and resentments and things like that will come. So don't feel discouraged by what comes up in your consciousness, because it is the way it is. We are putting ourselves into the position of the Buddha knowing the Dhamma rather than "Why do I have to have feelings like this? What is wrong with me that I feel this anger? I've been practicing for years and I still haven't recognized it." Even if such thoughts do arise, that is the way it is. Waiting for this poised attention can even convey this sense that we are expecting something to happen. "When is it going to happen?" You're expecting, anticipating, and then something does happen, and you think, "Oh, I don't like that, that couldn't be it."

Even that expecting, that attitude of waiting for something, can be recognized if you trust your awareness. You recognize the feeling that you're doing this in order to get something: "I'm practicing meditation to get rid of my defilements and realize nibbāna. I'm ignorant and defiled and I practice in order to get rid of all these, so I can become enlightened."

Such reflections reinforce your investigation of the relationship of awareness to your thinking process. If something makes me angry, or if somebody insults or offends me, I think, "How dare you!" But when I look at that feeling of anger—that emotion, that energy of anger—the awareness isn't angry. Awareness never gets angry, but its object can be what we call anger. So by really noticing it, awareness is like the fish in the water. It's the water, it's everywhere. It's not created, not an abstract idea, not something you can create; it's what you can recognize. The reality of awareness is just this. So deliberately investigating it, listen, really listen to yourself. Take an interest in what you are saying—you can say anything, the interest is only in the awareness—and then the thought arises and ceases.

So there was a suggestion the other day about "I am a human being," about investigating the spaces in between the words, to notice the way it is. "I" arises and ceases. I can't sustain "I...I...I..." That's really boring, sustaining the word "I," because it is a creation. That which is aware of "I" is not "I." It has no name, it doesn't say anything, it's anattā: not-self, the unconditioned, the unborn. Before I give the evening reflection I chant the *namo tassa* (Homage to the Buddha) and then "apārutā tesaṃ amatassa dvārā ye sotavantā pamuñcantu saddhaṃ" (*Mahāpadāna Sutta*, Dīgha Nikāya 14), which means "the gates to the Deathless are open"—a pronouncement. After his enlightenment the Buddha said, "The gates to the Deathless are open." Now that's wonderful. That's why I say it, because that really means a lot to me, what the Buddha says—the historical Buddha in the scriptures.

I'm quite willing to take quite seriously what the Buddha said in the past. So the gates to the Deathless are open. What are the gates to the Deathless then? Are they over there? Have they closed, because that was a long time ago, over twenty-five hundred years? Maybe they are not open anymore? "Ye sotavanta pamuñcantu saddha," one who listens; *sota,* is always about the listening, hearing. Trust in this; *pamuñcantu saddhaṃ* is translated generally as faith, trust, paying attention, listening. It's then no longer just some inspired statement in the scripture anymore—you recognize the gate to the Deathless, here and now, the awareness.

Many of you have been practicing very hard, have been on many retreats, and have been at meditation for many years, but what are you doing with that? Is it always trying to attain some-thing? Are you trying to purify yourself, get rid of your defile-ments, get samādhi, attain peaceful states, get rid of your stress problems? What is your purpose for meditating? What is your intention, your aim? Do you think it's a good thing to do, that you make a lot of merit by going on a ten-day retreat, or what is your intention? We might have different intentions at different times. My intention when I first ordained was realizing nibbāna, even when I was a totally confused, messed-up person. When you take the *upasampadā* (higher ordination) the whole aim is liberation, it's a kind of formula. When I say the words "my intention is realizing nibbāna," that's quite a strong direction for me because, on a personal level, I've been through all kinds of experiences during these forty years, experiences of utter despair and blissed-out inspiration. Then there's the boredom, you don't know how boring monastic life can get, and just aversion and criticism, and being criticized and criticizing, and being discon-tented and complaining. In Thailand in the hot season you're just so enervated all the time. "What am I doing here? I can't even get off the floor." Then there are periods when it's all jolly and fun and inspired, and then it changes. The extremes are more interesting, but the dreariness is often where we fail because, as T.S. Eliot said, human beings can't stand very much reality. This intention of realizing nibbāna…that's my intention, and that was made from a rational place, quite deliberately. It wasn't from an inspired moment of just being high—"I want to realize nibbāna." It is a cool, rational statement you make when you are ordained, when you are taking the ordination procedure.

It's a pretty nerve-wracking experience to say all that in the Pāli language, that my intention is to realize nibbāna; but then reflecting on that, that is the point of meditation, of Dhamma. So that's the direction. Then what happens in terms of experience? How much control do I have over that? My health, the way the world changes, monasteries change, teachers die. There are scandals and gossip, disillusionments, and blame and praise. You get honorific titles and you get elevated to a high position, but the higher you get the more people like to shoot at you, so being on a pedestal is not exactly liberation. But then all these things are the conditioned, the born, the created, the originated. The whole experience on a personal level, a physical level, a mental level, is the born, the created, the originated. So more and more this steadiness of awareness increases as you recognize it, and then value it: that's like taking refuge in the Buddha: "Buddhaṃ saraṇaṃ gacchāmi." When I say this, it doesn't mean just reciting Pāli formulas, meaningless formulas, it really means this. When I say, "I take refuge in the Buddha," this awareness is my refuge, now—the Buddho, this sense of awareness, presence. Then over the years just seeing through the illusions I create, the assumptions I've made, the emotional habits that manifest at various times, the reactions to the experience of life when you are being praised or blamed, or successful or failing or everything is going well or everything is falling apart.

Luang Por Chah was very good at getting us to look at the way it is. He had great skill. People wondered about how I could learn from him in the first year or so because we didn't speak the same language, so how could he teach? It was much more intuitive and somehow he understood me well enough to direct my attention to the here and now. So I began to notice how I was making monastic life complicated, and what the suffering was. Is the suffering the heat, the mosquitoes, and the food, or is it my aversion to the heat, the mosquitoes, and the food? So I started contemplating: "What is the suffering? Are mosquitoes the suffering, is the hot weather?" That is the worldly mind: "I'm suffering because it's too hot and the food isn't good. So if I go to a place where there is good weather, no mosquitoes, and good food, I won't suffer."

I'm living here in England, where we have good food, no mosquitoes, and very nice weather. I like English weather, by the way, and I can still create suffering just as easily here as I could in Thailand. "I don't like this food, I don't want mosquitoes, and I don't like hot weather": this is suffering that I create. That's a condition that I create out of ignorance, out of a self-view. I still don't like mosquitoes, but I don't create suffering around that. It's not that I like mosquitoes now because I have meditated for so long. I trust the awareness now more than my personal view about mosquitoes. So I can bear mosquitoes and bad food and heat and cold. Illness I can bear; I can bear disappointment, loss, death of loved ones, being blamed or criticized. These are all bearable if I don't create suffering around them.

Once I developed the awareness of this real refuge I began to deliberately challenge situations where I had been criticized and which used to be unbearable for me because I couldn't take criticism. When people started finding fault with me or blaming me, I used to get very angry or aggressive, or hurt or very offended, and I didn't know how to deal with it. I felt rejected and misunderstood. Whether people's criticisms were accurate or just their own projections didn't matter. I couldn't take any form of criticism, even when it was deserved. I was afraid of it. So I began to see this fear of being blamed, of being rejected, of being criticized. When you live in a community, people will inevitably find fault with you. That's the way society is. I can't expect them to worship me, and I don't want it.

I don't want a community of obsequious sycophants. They like you for a while and then find all kinds of faults with you. "You are a great teacher, Ajahn Sumedho." That's very nice. Then they say, "I've lost faith in you." It's hard to bear, isn't it? As I have confidence in the awareness, I can bear criticism now—rejection and blame—even if it's totally unfair. My refuge is in awareness, not in my self-image or the conditions around me. I can bear it because my refuge is in the Buddha, Dhamma, and Sangha, not in being liked, loved, understood, or appreciated. That's all very nice but it's not a refuge. So this is where we can free ourselves from the suffering of this world while we are still very much living in it and being part of a society.

It's not going away from it, like a hermit, and saying I've had enough of the world, I want nothing more to do with it, with the fickleness of humanity and the ingratitude—I'm fed up, good-bye cruel world. I've felt like that many times, but the awareness is the refuge. You might think that in the Sangha we are all just wonderful people living in compassionate harmony all the time, sharing our conscious experience with one another. This is a good reflection because the refuge is in Sangha, not in this monk or this nun or my best friend, or the monks I really have affinities with, that I get on well with. The Sangha consists of those who practice. It's not a person, not an individual anymore.

CITTĀNUPASSANĀ

Let go of what went before,
Let go of what comes after,
Let go of what's in-between,
And cross over becoming.
With mind completely liberated
You shall come to no more birth and decay.
(*Dhammapada,* v. 348)

WITH *cittānupassanā satipaṭṭhāna*, awareness of mental states as a foundation for mindfulness, the observer is not the observed. As I've been trying to convey during this retreat, mindfulness is just the awareness of whatever you're feeling emotionally, whatever mood you're experiencing right now—the awareness of it, that's mindfulness. When you start analyzing your mood, you're no longer mindful. You're criticizing it, blaming somebody; you're getting involved in it. You may be strongly identified: "This morning I feel like this." The way we think and speak, the language we use, can reinforce our sense of "this mood is mine...I am this, this is me, I'm like this." Mindfulness doesn't have a "me" or "mine" or an "I."

So waking up and observing just what kind of mood you're in, questioning, inquiring. "What is the citta like at this moment?" As I'm doing this, the citta *is* quite peaceful. Just watching, observing my direct experience of this moment. I hear the sound of silence, there's no negative state—it's like this. One of Luang Por Chah's sayings was "know yourself." This was a piece of advice or teaching that he would often give. The Pāli term for mental object is *ārammaṇa*, and in Thai they say, "Roo ahrom yah pen chao ahrom." This translates as "Know the ārammaṇa, the mood or mental state, but don't become the owner of it." So in observing this kind of peaceful state; "I'm very peaceful, I feel very peaceful this morning, and I don't have any problems with negativity right now, and I'm feeling pretty good because I woke up on the right side of the bed—this peace is me, don't you dare upset it!"

Moods sometimes can be very amorphous and unclear. Some moods are very obvious, like when you're angry, upset, or depressed. But most moods are nebulous. You can't really describe them, but they are what they are. They're still ārammaṇa. The mood is easily affected by the existing conditions, whether you're feeling healthy or sick, energetic or tired, whether the sun is shining or it's damp and cold. London on a sunny morning is very different from London on a cold, damp, rainy morning.

The Buddha encouraged us to notice how the conditioned realm is. The conditions are changing because we are sensitive forms, these human bodies and the senses. We're aware of the change; the change affects our consciousness. Change doesn't always mean change for the better, and everything gets better and better, doesn't it? Change also implies things getting worse; being good, pleasant, unpleasant, neutral. What is called *idappaccayatā* in Pāli—when the conditions arise then this is the result. This is reflecting on the realm of conditionality: the body feels tired, it's cold and wet, and you haven't paid your electricity bill, your cat is missing, and you've just lost your job! These conditions are not going to create happiness. But whatever they create, failure or success, loss or happiness, is the way it is.

Awareness of the ārammaṇa is a constant, and it's a refuge. Awareness is like a mirror; it will reflect anything you put in front of it—if you put a beautiful rose, then beauty; if a decaying rat, just that. It doesn't choose. Mirrors don't reject, saying, "I only want beautiful roses and don't bring any dead rats because I don't like smelly, decaying corpses." In the sense realm our experience ranges from the best to the worst, from great pleasure to great pain. So if we're not aware, we become the owner of the object, of the reflection. We like to have beautiful perfect roses reflected, so we try to sustain that. If you try to control everything so that you don't ever have unpleasant things happen, you're going to be terribly disappointed. This realm is this way. It's not a heavenly realm, like I imagine the *deva* (heavenly being) realm where there are only beautiful roses.

Devatās don't get old. They don't get wrinkled and sick. They have ethereal forms. At the very end of life, I think, they get a little battered-looking and then they die. They don't have to go through the long aging process the way we do. I'm just fantasizing. But we're not devatās. We have these bodies, and they're not ethereal forms; they are made of earth, fire, water, wind.

For me the big breakthrough, the big insight, was inquiring into that which is aware of the object—the awareness itself. What I would do is question the conditions that arise—is this awareness? Is that the island you cannot go beyond? The stillpoint, the centeredness, that's the awareness. Exploring this, like the sound of silence, conveys to me this still center. When I cannot notice it and go out into the turning world, I become a person and get caught in my habits, my loves and hates, my likes and dislikes. But if I am centered at this point, it's like the island you cannot go beyond, or the stillpoint of the turning world, the eye of the storm. And then the world revolves around it.

So saṃsāra, the conditioned realm, you get perspective on that; you observe the ārammaṇa. The mood you're in is not the stillpoint, not the center. The mood comes and goes. It changes, revolves; it's happy, sad, elated, depressed, inspired, bored, loving, hateful, and on and on like this. According to the conditions that come together at this point, then the mood is this way. It's so easy to say, "Oh, I'm in a bad mood" or "I'm in a good mood." Our language is like that, so we become the mood, "I feel happy today, everything's fine" or "Today is one of my bad days." That's why I encourage this investigation of thought, so that you're not creating yourself, endlessly reinforcing the sense of a self through your proliferating thoughts.

"I've got to make plans, I'm going to America next month, I've got to reserve the tickets and..."—all this I'm creating. "Oh, I've got to reserve a ticket, I've got to do this, send an email, contact my sister and let the others know when I will be where, people want to see me, make appointments...oh God...so much to do!" This perception, "I'm going to the United States next month," there's nothing wrong with thinking that, but it's in a context. This awareness is what I trust in, and then the dealing with the details of planning a trip to the United States comes from awareness rather than just the sense of "Oh, I've got to go, I've got to make plans" and then that whole way of thinking tends to make me feel I've got so much to do.

I'm still quite capable of thinking that I've much to do, but there's awareness of that as a thought. It no longer has the convincing pressure it had when I didn't know this, when I was heedless. I could get totally exhausted just by thinking about things. I remember watching myself once, thinking of all the responsibilities I had. It was early in the morning and I'd had a good night's sleep, but after thinking of all the things I had to do I felt totally exhausted. Yet I hadn't lifted a finger.

To the conditioned self, all you see is a point, a minute dot, and I'd contemplate, "Does a point have to be just a little dot or can it include everything?" The conventional way of thinking of a point is as a dot, a small little dot—but you can perceive it as a point that includes rather than the dot that excludes everything. If I'm looking at the dot, then I have to exclude everything around that dot. And so if you think of the stillpoint as a tiny little thing, that seems so remote. To try to just live in this dot, this stillpoint, the thinking mind thinks, "That sounds impossible." If you begin to recognize awareness, the stillpoint, is a point that includes— oneness, *ekaggatā,* one-pointedness, unity. So that oneness, or the dot that includes, or the point that includes. Just at this moment you can recognize awareness, it's not excluding anything, it's not dividing anything, it's not judging.

The function of thinking is to separate and divide and compare. So thinking, the function of thinking, is discrimination—comparing one thing with another, judging, evaluating qualities: "this is good and that's bad." If I think, "I am Ajahn Sumedho," it places me as a separate person from you, defines me on the personal level, which excludes you. None of you are "Ajahn Sumedho." So if I'm Ajahn Sumedho that means we're two permanently separate beings. That's the thinking process. And then the unitive one is awareness. "Ajahn Sumedho" then is merely an ārammaṇa.

Words like "unity," "union," "universe," "oneness," or "one-pointedness" *(ekaggatā)*—we have the words, we have the experience of oneness, a mystical experience, and that's intuitive, it's not a thought process. So as soon as you start thinking about it, then you know the oneness is no longer conscious, because you're dividing, you're caught in "I'm here, you're there"—the conventional reality of this moment. The conventions that we create are like this, they're created, man-made.

So investigating, or what in Pāli is called *yoniso manasikāra*. In Thai, as in Pāli, there are a lot of nice words for this, "looking into" and "reflecting upon." Thai is a very psychological language. It's very much about mental states and varying degrees of emotional extremes and so forth. English is, I think, more a language of merchants. But that doesn't matter, because the language isn't the important issue. We use whatever language we have because mindfulness isn't dependent on language. How to use language? Thinking can be so habitual. One just gets caught in conceptual proliferation *(papañca)*. You're thinking of Italy and then pretty soon you're off in Rome, then Naples, and then thinking about Julius Caesar and next Mussolini. The mind just skips around. Then you connect to Hitler, then Churchill, then Roosevelt, then Vietnam, and on it goes. You know, within a few seconds you've been all over the world.

Habit patterns, repetitious thoughts...I used to have incredibly boring, repetitious thoughts. I remember memorizing sonnets of Shakespeare and bombastic Victorian poetry. I thought that if I'm going to think, I want at least to think something intelligent. I grew up in the thirties and forties listening to the radio. So I've got all these thirties and forties pop songs that come up, and some of them are really stupid. Even commercials on the radio when I was a child. Some of those commercials for Pepsi Cola come up out of nowhere. What a plague to have a mind like this. I consider myself an intelligent person, and I've got all these banal and silly things going on in my mind. That's my snobbery really. I'm a bit of a cultural snob at heart. So I looked down on all that nonsense and rubbish. When it comes up, it's not a matter of suppressing it and wiping it out. It's part of the conditioning process when you're growing up, isn't it?

Especially those things that you listened to on the radio or saw on the television when you were a child—the music of that age, the pop culture, the advertising, the attitudes—these are the bases of what we acquire when we're innocent; we haven't been all that fixed yet in our conditioning. As children we just pick up that stuff, and it can stay with us for life.

Awareness doesn't try to change you so you have more intelligent thoughts—it's fine to educate yourself and develop refined tastes, but those pursuits are limiting and divisive. You develop preferences and you get snooty and judgmental—like the old folks of my generation. Some of the music I hear now makes me realize how old I am. "God, it's terrible stuff!" I find myself thinking. It's a conditioning process. The unconditioned then is awareness itself, the being. I used to struggle because I was so caught up in figuring it all out, on the intellectual level and the thinking level. You get caught in "What is it that knows, what is it that knows the object?" And then you want to have some kind of metaphysics or concepts to deal with that. "Is that God? We don't believe in God, we're Buddhists, so we won't use that term—is it the big Self?"

In Advaita they talk about the "self" with a capital S, or Atman. "It must be the big Self, because the little self is the ego, sakkāya-diṭṭhi." So the big Self is looking at the little self, and then you think, "Ah, that's it." But the big Self is still a concept, isn't it? Or God, or ultimate reality, or amata dhamma? These are words, and words are conditions. So long as we depend on words, we are in the dualistic structure of saṃsāra. That's why the pointing, the getting beyond thinking. Not eradicating thinking—we're not making an attack on thought or having aversion to it, but we're putting the thinking thinking process into the ārammaṇa (object) position.

These are skillful means of intentional thinking. We intentionally think something—"I am a human being"—just to investigate that relationship of awareness and thought. You keep pursuing that, contemplating it. It's like holding something and really looking at it; you don't have to analyze it. That's why the content of the thought isn't really important. We're not interested in whether I'm really a human being or only half-human.

For example, if I look at my hand I can see the spaces in between the fingers and the thumb, and the forefinger, the space around the hand, and as I get more reflective, I can see the whole palm of the hand and the fingers together with the space around it all in one glance. This is reflecting. That which is aware has this perspective. It's not analytical, judgmental, saying that my hand is beautiful or ugly, good or bad. What is it that sees the hand? "Well, it's my eyes of course." That's another thought again, isn't it? Seeing is like this. This is a way of using thought for bringing attention to the way it is: "seeing is like this" rather than "my eyes are seeing my hand." So is that the real me that's seeing my hand? It then goes back to trying to figure out everything on that level of thinking. Thinking cannot solve the problem because it's limited. It's a structure, a function, a convention. What isn't a convention is the awareness.

The clues I've been giving, the sound of silence, some of you notice it quite easily, and others are totally bewildered by it! Notice that, the effect of just hearing the phrase "the sound of silence." When I say that, these are words. Is the sound of silence really a sound? People say it's the blood vessels or your nerves, you know, the inner workings of your body create this kind of buzz. We want to define it, want to fix it scientifically. Is it tinnitus? An ear disease? A divine cosmic sound? We're caught in the realm of words, aren't we? We try to figure it out, understand it in terms of analysis or definition. You don't need to do that. It's much easier than that. You don't have to verify and qualify it, have it scientifically proven by scientists. You trust the experience here and now, rather than what some neurologist might say. It doesn't matter what neurologists think. I'm pointing directly at the experience of here and now.

So in this stillness, if I don't notice it, even grasping the term makes me look for something rather than just trusting to be here, relaxed and open. The sense of listening, opening, not listening for something or trying to find something to listen to, but just trusting yourself to listen like this. Patience is also needed, because the mind is restless and we get full of doubt and self-doubt: doubt about practice, about the teacher, about this retreat—thinking will create doubts. So then comes this awareness: if you're caught in a negative state of skepticism or doubt or despair, what is it that knows that? When you say, "I feel despair," what is it that knows despair, that knows this is as the ārammaṇa?

In this kind of questioning, "What is it that knows?" you're not looking for an answer in terms of a Pāli word or an English word or a scientific proof. It's a matter of trusting yourself. You know, this is your life; you're experiencing life from this point. You then might say, "Ajahn Sumedho, am I experiencing it the right way?" You think I might know better than you. You can project omniscience onto me and say, "He can look deep into our souls and know all that's lurking deep down inside, and he probably knows what I'm thinking or what I need." This is still thinking, isn't it? The only one that can know anything at this moment is you. I can make assumptions based on your body language or your expression. I can get clues about what might be going on, but you know the reality of the mood, the memories, the feelings—positive, negative, neutral, whatever. You're not what you think you are; you are somehow incapable and you need me to tell you. Then that's still a thought process, isn't it? Creating yourself as someone who doesn't know and me as someone who knows. That's another creation.

So this sense of trusting, recognizing this awareness, trusting it because it's all we have really, that's the point, that's the liberation, that's the gate to the Deathless. And that's why we say *paccattaṃ veditabbo viññūhi:* to realize this yourself, know it for yourself— and no one can do that or give it to you. The best we can do is to keep pointing. If you keep looking at me pointing, then you'll only see my forefinger. That's the metaphor of the finger pointing at the moon. I point and say, "Look at the moon," and you look at my finger. Then the paññā, the wisdom, comes in. You see the finger is pointing, so you start looking and you see the moon. You don't need to make a big deal about the finger. People suffer from so much self-doubt and disparagement and feelings of inadequacy—the hackneyed term used these days is "lack of self-esteem." It's a habit we get through living in this culture. That's why it's not to be believed in. Don't define yourself or qualify yourself endlessly with adjectives and labels, but wake up to this natural state—that is the refuge.

QUESTIONS ABOUT
REBIRTH AND AWARENESS

THERE'S A NOTE here asking about rebirth. Someone wants to know what the historical Buddha had to say about rebirth, what Ajahn Chah said about it, and whether Buddhists who have a cultural belief in rebirth regard me as lacking faith.

"Rebirth," like "reincarnation," is a term that's used generally referring to having gone through a series of different lives, and then there are various views about whether once you get reincarnated into human form where can you go, become a frog again or something like that. I was teaching a retreat in Australia at the Theosophical Society, where people's views were split. Some held that once you've made it to the human level you can't slide back into a lesser animal one, whereas others insisted that you could. But the truth of the matter is, nobody really knows.

The historical Buddha refers to previous lives in the scriptures and things like this, but for me these things are speculative. Maybe you can remember previous lives, but I have no such memory. So all I can know is from the here and now. We're talking about direct knowing, rather than Buddhist theory, or Buddhist doctrine. When Ajahn Chah taught about rebirth, he did so in the context of paṭiccasamuppāda, or dependent origination. He was talking about the kind of rebirth you can actually witness in daily life; birth is the beginning, death is the ending. How many rebirths have you gone through today, mentally? What is born, dies; what arises, ceases. Rebirth in this sense is actually provable.

In the paṭiccasamuppāda, through desire (taṇhā) comes attachment (upādāna), and then attachment leads to becoming (bhava), becoming leads to rebirth, and rebirth leads to suffering. *Jāti* (birth) is the result of grasping desire. I quite like the idea of reincarnation, and of rebirth, on a theoretical level. I've no bias against it, but it is speculative and it's conceptual. Even if I could remember a previous life or previous lives, they'd still be memories in the present. So we're pointing to the way things are rather than acquiring a sense of "I was…George Washington in a previous life." I once met a psychic woman who read my aura and told me I was Ajahn Chah's grandmother in a previous life, which is rather nice! I don't know how dependable these psychics are.

I was brought up as a Christian to believe that you're born and then you've got this one lifetime to either make it or blow it. I always thought that was pretty dreadful. At least with rebirth, if you blow it in this life you've got another one. You can eventually make it. But we want to get out of the mind-set or fixed view that sees rebirth in terms of "I was so-and-so in a previous life." Questions like "What was I in a previous life?" or "What will I be reborn as?" This is all about "I am." This is the basic delusion of self, that I really was somebody else. I've lived seventy years—am I the same person that existed forty years ago? On a conventional level I've got a birth certificate, legal proof that I was born. My birth certificate has, ironically, my footprint on it. Of course, when I was born my feet were small. Now my feet are bigger than my birth certificate.

Reincarnation, rebirth, is not something that I have strong feelings about. I rather like the idea on the level of theory and possibility. So how do I interpret that and what's the reality of it? Is it just information you get from somebody else? The rebirth that I'm interested in is the rebirth that's happening *now*. The paṭiccasamuppāda starts with ignorance (avijjā), which means not having any understanding of the Four Noble Truths, the three aspects, and the twelve insights. If we do not understand the way things are, everything we do, think, and say comes from delusion. Also, if you explore taṇhā and upādāna (desire and attachment), they lead to *bhava jāti jarā-maraṇa sokāparideva-dukkha-domanassa-upāyāsā* (becoming, birth, aging and death, sorrow, lamentation, pain, grief, and despair).

If one operates from ignorance of the Four Noble Truths, then the result affects the body and mind and everything that we experience. If I start from a self-view, unquestioned, never having investigated the Four Noble Truths, with no insight into the way it is or into Dhamma, then I operate always from "I'm Ajahn Sumedho" and "my life," "when I was born" and "seventy years ago," and what I think and feel, what I've done, my disappointments and the things that have happened and so forth, and I'll have a whole history, a biography of "me and mine." And in any situation, if I'm not aware and I follow the self-view, it always takes me to feeling insecure, something is missing, incomplete, lacking.

In paṭiccasamuppāda, the terms *avijjā-paccayā saṅkhārā, saṅkhāra-paccayā viññāṇaṃ* translate as "ignorance conditions mental formations, mental formations condition sense-consciousness." So mental formations (saṅkhāras) come out of *avijjā*, which are in consciousness, which affect body and mind *(nāmarūpa)*, the six senses *(saḷāyatana),* contact *(phassa)* and feeling *(vedanā).* So we have a consciousness (viññāṇa), body and mind, the six senses and then the contact through the senses, the sense impingement, which results in feeling, which conditions desire, and then desire becomes attachment to that desire, and attachment to the desire is becoming, and then rebirth, which takes us to death, or dukkha. Having explored this paṭiccasamuppāda in terms of avijjā or delusion, if I operate from the position of avijjā, there's always some kind of anxiety—it always leads to some sense of lack, feeling of missing out on something, despair, anguish, fear of death. I see this in myself. Maybe you're different—you've got to find out.

When you have the twelve insights into the Four Noble Truths—the three aspects of each of the four truths—then avijjā is no longer a problem, there is vijjā (right understanding). The important point in paṭiccasamuppāda, as it's formulated, is when there is awareness, since that breaks the chain of events. Say, for example, there is anger: somebody says something that makes me angry, I'm not mindful, I get angry, and then the point where I suddenly realize that I'm angry. If I trust in that awareness of anger by having explored it through the First and Second Noble Truths, then the anger drops away; it ceases at that point: that's *nirodha* (cessation). When there's clinging, it's because of an uninterrupted sequence of phassa, vedanā, taṇhā, and upādāna: there's a sense impingement and then a feeling arises, desire follows from that, and then attachment. So when I started exploring paṭiccasamuppāda, I could catch it only at the attachment. Not at the desire; I couldn't catch the desire at first, but I could suddenly be aware I was attached to something. "I'm suffering, and that means I'm attached to something." So if I was suffering I would ask, "What am I attached to?" I would investigate. What was I attached to? And then by investigating that I began to see attachment to something; I was reborn into a person who was angry with somebody at that moment. You become that way, you become that: being born, grasping anger. One becomes reborn as an angry person.

If I have this insight, I awaken to this whole process—being reborn as an angry person—and I see attachment as the problem. So there's a letting go (the insight into the Second Noble Truth is letting go of desire), a recognizing of desire as desire. If you're attached to it, you're bound to it; you can't see it, you just *are* like this. You're angry and you have no perspective. If you let go of it or just let it be, you have space, you relate to anger as a mental object; and mindfulness is not angry—you begin to notice this. If I use awareness then even if anger arises it's the kamma-vipāka, resultant kamma of my life. So if that particular emotion arises, it is what it is. The more you're aware and trust in awareness, the wider your perspective is on everything. Even with kamma-vipāka anger can still arise, but you don't grasp it. You see it, you know it is anger, and you know it's like fire. You just don't touch it once you know—if you grasp hold of fire it doesn't take a lot of wisdom to recognize and avoid grasping it again. Why be hurt for nothing? Desire's like a fire isn't it? It's hot. If you can explore it, then the grasping of desire is no longer a problem. The grasping is what results in suffering. This is a fire realm: the sun in the sky and the heat in the body. There's the Fire Sermon we chant sometimes. Everything's burning, it says. We're burning right now. These bodies are burning, they've got the fire element, when the fire goes out you're dead, and the body starts decaying.

This is how to use these teachings, like putting rebirth into the context of dependent origination. Then it's not just some kind of Buddhist cultural interpretation or some Buddhist theory, superstition, or whatever. Not many people, even in Buddhist countries, really understand it. It's often cultural. Now this is how Luang Por Chah taught it, like this.

My life has been quite a surprise to me, because, if I just judge myself according to my environment, my parents, my background, social background, I can't figure out how I ever became a Buddhist monk. I was brought up in a Christian family where there was no Buddhist influence. As a child I was attracted to Asian people, although there were none in the Seattle neighborhood where I lived. So why was a little middle-class white boy attracted to them? I could speculate that maybe I was a Chinese monk or something really exciting in a previous life. It wouldn't surprise me if, in the Akashic Records, I had a connection to Buddhism in Asia. Other little boys of my generation did not have the same interests, so why me? It's not important to know, is it? It doesn't make the slightest bit of difference in terms of the here and now and liberation from suffering. It's just fun sometimes to think about such things.

When I met Master Hsuan Hua in the City of Ten Thousand Buddhas in California, he said we were together in a previous life and had some kind of monastic connection. I don't mind, and I wouldn't doubt it. Even with Ajahn Chah there was an affinity there that I couldn't explain. I met many of the great teachers in Thailand before I met him, and they were certainly impressive, but it was only with Ajahn Chah that I felt any great affinity. What was that about? Maybe it's true that I was his grandmother. And I had the same affinity with Master Hsuan Hua. But these are just feelings, intuitions.

I was about twenty-one when I came across Buddhism. I was in the navy and became interested in Buddhism while in Japan. Somebody gave me these books on haiku poetry by R.H. Blythe, a set of four volumes based on the seasons. These books mentioned

Zen. I didn't know what Zen was, so when I returned to San Francisco I looked in a bookstore, and there was this recently published paperback called *Zen Buddhism* by D.T. Suzuki. Something in me knew immediately that this was right. After reading about a paragraph in Suzuki's book, I knew that this was it. I'd go out to Golden Gate Park, sit on the grass, and read. I'd get high, elated—I didn't need drugs.

I couldn't explain it. If you'd asked me what I saw in Buddhism I couldn't have given you a good answer. I've been pursuing that interest for about fifty years now. Certainly it was a powerful connection. Imagine buying a book and, after reading a paragraph, something in you wakes up in an unplanned, unpredictable way. I realized that was the arising of faith; something in me could recognize this. That had to be an intuition, because certainly on the level of self-view, on the level of my conditioned personality, I didn't understand it.

Question: You said something like "without this awareness there wouldn't be anything." Can you explain this again? What did you mean by that?

Well, there'd be no way out of the trap, out of saṃsāra, as I see it. Saṃsāra seems real to the conditioned mind: this body and these emotions are really me. All my emotions say "me, me, what about me, I want to live, I want this, I don't like that." These screaming inner voices of "me and mine" seem very real and convincing. Because we have a physical body that is so sensitive, everything presses in on us. From the time we're born to the time we die, we're in a continuous state of being irritated by sensory impingement. Our experience is one of being irritated for a lifetime.

It's cold or hot, beautiful or ugly, hungry or thirsty, beautiful sounds or cacophonous noises, smells and so forth. This is a sense world, a sense realm, and living in it seems like a hopeless task on that level of self. All you can do is control everything, build a fence around yourself to protect yourself from harsh impingements, and then be very selective about what you let impinge on you. So you become a control freak; you get paranoid and frustrated in this realm of saṃsāra. So you wonder, "What is a way out of that?" The Buddha mentions things like "the gate to the Deathless" and "mindfulness is the path to the Deathless." Is this pointing to some kind of rarefied saṃsāric experience, some refined conscious state, where we can hope to stay as long as possible?

The needs of the physical body, the coarseness of this body, its functions—this is the realm that we live in. We always have to deal with the human body and its pain and unpleasantness. Then you realize that the only possibility is awareness—that's the escape hatch. There is the unconditioned; therefore there is an escape from the conditioned. So then apply that to the here and now, to this moment. Time is an illusion, the past is a memory, the future is a possibility, but now is the knowing. In this knowing position, this Buddho position, escape from the conditioned is possible. We're not getting rid of the conditioned, but we no longer react out of fear and desire to the conditions that are impinging on this form.

So if I trust this awareness. It gives me a perspective on what's impinging on this form, the things that come up in the mind, or the emotional reactions and sensory experiences—pleasurable, painful, whatever. Non-suffering doesn't mean you don't have any more physical pain or discomfort. It means not attaching, not resenting, not wanting something else, but being mindful of the reality of now as it is happening. So we don't create aversion to it; we don't follow our desire for it or try to get something or become someone. When you trust awareness, you have a wider perspective to deal with the kamma-vipāka that arises in the present. The word *vipāka* means "result." After his enlightenment the historical Buddha still had kamma-vipāka. He had to put up with a lot of unpleasant things. He wasn't floating in bliss until the death of his body. He had to deal with difficult issues, threats, blaming, jealousy, and so forth, just like the rest of us. But his relationship to kamma-vipāka was no longer ignorant; he was awakened to it—he could see it in terms of Dhamma. Then there's no more rebirth. So if my relationship to kamma-vipāka is awareness, I'm not creating new kamma with that condition. I'm not following it, not grasping at it, not trying to resist it. You make kamma through trying to suppress things as well as just blindly following.

More and more, one's experience is equanimous, and then joy and compassion come from this emptiness rather than from kammic conditioning. So it's not personal. I can't claim compassion as some kind of personal attainment. Compassion is the result of emptiness. The four brahma-vihāras—*mettā* (loving-kindness), *karuṇā* (compassion), *muditā* (sympathetic joy), and *upekkhā* (equanimity)—come from the empty mind.

Question: Your awareness and my awareness are different. They're not the same awareness, right?

The awareness is exactly the same. But what you're aware of is different! We're one, we're not separate in awareness. If we grasp what we're aware of, then we feel the separation.

Question: I can be aware of my thought or my breath. But to get this knowing position, it's very tricky or subtle, I find. I can be aware that I'm angry but...

Well, that's why you contemplate that. Then the whole sense of "I" falls away. You realize there's no "I" at all. I mean you *know,* because you see through that. But the habitual tendency is to think, "I'm aware," or to ask, "Am I aware, or not aware?" Awareness is perfect and what you're aware of is the Dhamma. When you try to figure it out, then you get caught in the trap of your thoughts, which always go back to "I am" and "me and mine" because thoughts are habits. So you recognize awareness when there's no thought; you notice the spaces between the words, and you have awareness of the present feeling or emotion, exploring them so that you begin to trust your awareness more than what your thoughts or emotions are saying.

It is subtle! It is very precise, too. There is nothing vague about it, once you trust it. It's not a mystical feeling, a kind of vague floating feeling. It's not being spaced out. It's very clear but it does take a kind of determined awareness and investigation to get to the root. This is a paññā or wisdom style teaching. The Four Noble Truths are a wisdom teaching. You're actually developing a discerning ability, and it does not come from the ego at all. I can't claim I'm wise as a person. I can still say very stupid things, and as an inflated ego I might think that I'm a very wise man, but I can see through that. I don't believe that anymore because wisdom isn't conditioned; it isn't something that I can claim through language. It's a natural state of being. If I inflate myself, overestimate myself, my ego—"I'm very wise"—then I start going around acting like a wise person! And then there's always something that's going to happen to make a fool out of me.

COMPOSING the body and mind—one point—there is a reflecting, just opening and observing the state of mind, mood, posture, breath, being the witness, the observer, the knowing. Consciousness in separate form: this consciousness, having been born in a human body, is experienced through this form, from this point here, from this position, from this body. Consciousness knows conditions as conditions, knows the breath, moods, sensations, sensory experiences: these objects can be seen, can be observed in their characteristic of impermanence.

Ajahn Chah used the metaphor of the Hua Lamphong railroad station in Bangkok. The train station is a center from which you can observe all the trains coming and going. You can ride on one of the trains, seeing everything from that particular view, or you can stay in the station and observe the trains coming and going in different directions.

Coming from ignorance, from not understanding the way it is, we identify with conditions and are caught up in their movement. When that happens, we can notice how thinking affects us. My sense of myself as a person, my self-view, goes unquestioned. I always have the sense of being "me." Fear, greed, anger, and confusion arise, conditions change, yet I assume I remain this same person. I'm always Ajahn Sumedho, no matter what I'm doing. It's never questioned, never investigated. By identifying with a concept like that, I take on a kind of permanence. I'm always this person.

It's the same with positions. When I say the word *Ajahn,* this means "teacher"; it's a Thai word taken from the Sanskrit *ācārya.* So I'm an ācārya, an Ajahn, even when I'm asleep in my kuṭi (hut), not teaching anybody. If I identify with "I am an Ajahn" as a kind of continuing permanent identity, then that always gives me the sense of having to be a teacher. If there's the notion that "I am a teacher," then everybody else is somebody I teach. When you get stuck in identification, attached to positions, titles, and identities, it tends to fix you. It does have this effect.

So that's what attachment to perception does; it makes things more than what they really are. When there is awareness, you can see that the teaching and the learning—the teacher and the pupil—are not fixed; they arise according to conditions. Awareness gives us this perspective on the way things are. The notion that Ajahns only teach, that they never learn from anybody else, is limiting. You can be a nuisance if you always come from the teacher's position. You've created an illusion. The actual process is one of learning from each other, isn't it? From the various situations and opportunities that are happening to us.

We are learning and we are teaching each other even though you may not see yourself as a teacher; yet I learn from you and you can learn from me. Fixed identities increase the sense of isolation and loneliness. You tend to act like what you think you are; you get stuck in a position and then you don't know how to relate in any other way. So just observing this actual Ajahn position is dependent on conditions; it's a formality, a convention. In daily life you see changing situations; sometimes this identity is suitable and sometimes not, when it's no longer necessary. In the Sangha some monks say, "I don't want to be an Ajahn. I don't want to be a teacher," because that isolates them in an authority position. Most Western monks and nuns have problems with authority.

I'm in a powerful position right now. So the power of the position, the empowerment from the people around seeing me as Ajahn Sumedho, and my being on this higher platform as a teacher—recognizing that, and knowing how to use power and authority without attaching to it, requires wisdom. There is nothing wrong with power or authority. It's not, "I don't want any authority, or be in any power position, or be a teacher"—that's just going to the opposite extreme, taking an opposite view.

We're reflecting on this centerpoint. For the lifetime of this body each of us has, we are in this center position, the center of the universe, so that life conditions impinge on this form, this body, *the way it is*. The kamma of this human being here—the memories that arise, the cultural and social conditioning that has taken place, the experiences, habits, and so forth—operates because these conditions are that way. They arise and they cease. We remember, so we have memories of our past. Memories of my past are different from yours. The cultural conditioning is different. Our education, social position, ethnic background, experience, age, and gender are different. All these have their effects on consciousness. But the awareness is not any of those things.

It's not Asian or European, male or female, young or old, and it's not a memory. So that's why it's anattā, non-self, because a self, attā, is conditioned through memory. I can remember my past, my life, my mother, my father; I remember where I was born; I remember various experiences. These are all unique to me. Each one of us has our own kamma. So is kamma something you have to believe in to be a Buddhist? I've heard Buddhists say that to be a Buddhist you have to believe in the law of kamma and rebirth. But I've never felt that that was ever an expectation.

The thing that attracted me to Buddhism was that you didn't have to believe in anything. You didn't need to take positions. But these are terms that are used. So what is kamma now, rebirth now? Always bringing attention to the here and now rather than deciding whether you believe in the concepts or not. The concepts are just conditions, words. The word *kamma* sounds exotic; if you instead use "cause and effect," it sounds more Western and scientific. *Kamma* tends to sound like an Asian mystical thing. "It's my kamma" seems like a kind of fatalism, or the reincarnation style. That's a kind of unquestioned belief in past lives: you will be reborn according to the merit or demerit that you have done in this life. So that's how kamma is generally defined, but looking at kamma in the reality of now, it's kamma-vipāka, the result of kamma. The result of having been born seventy years ago—the result of this is old age. If I had never been born, I'd never be seventy years old, obviously.

Death is also in the future. Death of the body is kamma-vipāka, so the result of birth is death. Being born means that what is born is going to end or cease or die. That's on a physical level; the aging process happens because of birth. Or sickness, disease—these are common to all creatures, and we say, "It's my kamma that I have this disease, this disability. I must have done something bad in a previous life and I'm paying for it in this one." This is theoretical and taken from the assumption of a self, a "me," even though I wasn't born "Ajahn Sumedho." In fact my parents had to think of a name for me after I was born. I don't remember being born, coming out and saying, "I'm Robert Jackman." My mother told me I was Robert Jackman. She never told me I was Ajahn Sumedho. That was a later rebirth. So old age is a result of birth.

Sickness is a part of this realm, isn't it? The sense realm, the earth, fire, water, and wind, the way things move and change, the myriad things that affect us, germs and bacteria and so forth. Things you can't even see or recognize are affecting us—the stars in the sky, the position of the sun, the morning light, the temperature of the room, and the people in the room, all these things are affecting us because these are the present conditions, affecting the consciousness that we are experiencing now. So this is the result of kamma then, the vipāka. I found this a very useful way of reflecting. I heard somebody commenting that the tsunami on 26 December 2004 was the kamma of Sri Lanka, Thailand, Indonesia, and India—that this must be their bad kamma. That is all speculative, isn't it? It doesn't really make sense.

The law of kamma even in its more-or-less doctrinal form—in Thailand they do have a way of accepting life because of that sense of kamma. It's not saying, "Why is this happening to me?" but, "It's my kamma." Somehow one is more accepting of life in its various changing phases, rather than resenting the terrible things that have happened. You say, "What did I do?" Or if somebody very nice or innocent is brutalized we say, "It's not fair, what did they do to deserve this?" Whereas at least on a theoretical level kamma is a way of accepting these things we have in our life-span, as our kamma-vipāka—it's like this.

Americans are very idealistic. The American revolution was based on wonderful ideals like democracy, freedom, human rights, ideals of justice, fairness, and equality. These ideals are beautiful. I'm not criticizing them, but attachment to them has its effect on us because then we are always complaining, "It shouldn't be like this." We idealize Buddhism. I've heard Westerners become very inspired by Buddhism. They join a Buddhist society or come here and join this group, and then they become disillusioned

"Buddhists shouldn't be like that," they say. "People here gossip, are opinionated, and they quarrel among themselves. Buddhists shouldn't be like that." And you think, "Yes, that's true, we shouldn't," but this is the way it is.

On the ideal level we should be like Buddha-rūpas. No matter what you do in this room, whether you stand on your head, swear and curse, shout and yell, murder each other, the Buddha-rūpa isn't affected. Buddha-rūpas are ideals; that's an icon, or an ideal form that we create. So it's beautiful and it's a reminder of the equanimity of awareness here and now. But if we compare ourselves to Buddha-rūpas, we are always suffering. This Buddha-rūpa was at Hampstead when I first arrived. It sat in the Hampstead Vihāra, and no doubt it was there years before I arrived, unchanging, unmoved by the events, because it doesn't feel anything, doesn't have to deal with nerves and sight, sound, smell, taste, or touch, and it doesn't have memory. Ideals are insensitive. When you are idealistic you aren't very sensitive anymore. You lose that because you are attached to something that is not alive, that is beautiful but doesn't have any feelings.

So idealistic people can be very cruel, very judgmental, very critical of everything. Idealists are never content because they see that nothing is as good as it should be—I should be more patient, more loving, more sensitive; I should be wise, compassionate, and kind all the time; I should try to be like the Buddha; I shouldn't ever be selfish, shouldn't have these immature reactions, shouldn't be this self-centered, vain person that I am; I'm ashamed of myself; I feel guilty and critical. All this comes from an ideal, so we disparage ourselves endlessly. Guilt is one of the neurotic results, the kamma-vipāka, of our society.

In Western society, we are all quite guilt-ridden due to Judeo-Christian idealism. We suffer a lot from self-disparagement and feelings of guilt. This I trace back to attachment to ideals; it's part of the culture of being born in the United States with its idealistic culture. The ideals are beautiful, but awareness brings us into the present which is not ideal. This present moment, now, is not an ideal; it is what it is. How are you experiencing it now? You can probably think of more ideal situations—a bigger room, maybe: so can we enlarge the shrine room? We could spend our time trying to improve the situation here all the time because we have an ideal of what it should be and then we get annoyed by the fact that it doesn't live up to that. We could spend our ten days here criticizing. So the kamma-vipāka is not what you want, but it is the way it is. This awareness brings us to where we can detach from ideals. Not get rid of them, since ideals inspire us and we need that. But attachment out of ignorance only makes us discontented and critical.

So in the monastic life, the traditional bhikkhu form is not an ideal form. It's based on alms mendicancy, on dependency, on making yourself vulnerable and dependent on the kindness of others. We have to depend on others to offer food, shelter, and something to wear and so forth. But the ideal that I was brought up with was to be independent and self-sufficient. That's the American individual ideal, not to need anybody: "I can do it myself, make my own way in life. I'm not someone who is a beggar and needs things from others. I can take care of myself." That is an ideal. So becoming a bhikkhu, you suddenly find yourself in the "begging" position, and you have your alms bowl. If you try to become the ideal bhikkhu, you are in a trap because you are never going to succeed. But in monastic reflections the emphasis is on developing contentment with what is offered.

We are not saying you have to give us the best: "Only the best, you know, we are high-class beggars." Contentment comes through reflection on the generosity, care, and interest that others extend. Gratitude and contentment are a very strong and stable foundation for practice. We develop this sense of contentment with the material world and what's offered, rather than complaining and wanting better or more. We can have gratitude because this life brings out the generosity of people; so we survive through the goodness and generosity of others.

When I reflect on generosity I feel gratitude. Gratitude is heartfelt, a heart level of experience. If we're contented with little, then we don't spend our lives trying to acquire more, assert ourselves, and prove ourselves as individuals and get our own way. I am culturally conditioned for that, asserting my individuality, my uniqueness, taking care of myself, not humiliating myself by depending on others for things and so forth, and that affects me personally. So I can never be content on that level of self-view. My self-view will never support contentment because it is conditioned for discontentment. Capitalism, the American economy, would fall apart if we were all content. You have to make people continuously discontented so they spend their money.

Modern capitalism is based on making you feel discontented with last year's model. You get the newest improved one, but you are not content with that either because a better one arouses your desire. So the kamma-vipāka of monastic life, from this position, is contentment and gratitude. These provide a very stable base where my life isn't a constant searching or getting caught in the conditions of the mind, which is always critical and discontented. More and more I have this space, time, stability, to be with the flow of life as it happens to this form.

CONSCIOUSNESS

Where do water, earth, fire, and wind
have no footing?
Where are long and short,
coarse and fine,
fair and foul,
name and form
brought to an end?
Consciousness which is
non-manifestative,
limitless, not becoming anything at all:
Here water, earth, fire, and wind
have no footing.
Here long and short,
coarse and fine,
fair and foul,
name and form,
are all brought to an end.
With the cessation of consciousness
each is here brought to an end.
(*Kevaddha Sutta,* Dīgha Nikāya 11)

CONSCIOUSNESS is a subject that has become quite important these days. We are all experiencing consciousness; we want to understand it and define it. Some people say that they equate consciousness with thinking or memory. I have heard scientists and psychologists say that animals don't have consciousness, because they don't think or remember. This seems ridiculous. But in terms of this moment, right now, *this* is consciousness. We are just listening—pure consciousness before you start thinking. Just make a note of this: consciousness is like *this*. I am listening, I am with this present moment, being present, being here and now. Taking the word "consciousness" and making a mental note: "Consciousness is like *this*." It's where thought, feeling, and emotion arise. When we are unconscious we don't feel, we don't think. Consciousness, then, is like the field that allows thought, memory, emotion, and feeling to appear and disappear.

Consciousness is not personal. To become personal you have to make a claim to it: "I am a conscious person." But there's just awareness, this entrance into noting the present, and at this moment consciousness is like *this*. Then one can notice the sound of silence, the sense of just sustaining, being able to rest in a natural state of consciousness that is nonpersonal and unattached. Noting this is like informing or educating oneself about the way it is. When we are born, consciousness within this separate form starts operating. A newborn baby is conscious, yet it doesn't have a concept of itself being male or female or anything like that. Those are conditions that one acquires after birth.

This is a conscious realm. We may think of a universal consciousness, and consciousness as it is used in the five khandhas: rūpa (form), vedanā (feeling), saññā (perception), saṅkhārā (mental formations), and viññāṇa (sense-consciousness). But there is also this consciousness which is unattached, unlimited. In two places in the Tipiṭaka, there is reference to *viññāṇaṃ anidassanaṃ anantaṃ sabbato pabhaṃ*—a mouthful of words that point to this state of natural consciousness, this reality. I find it very useful to clearly note "consciousness is like *this*." If I start thinking about it, then I want to define it: "Is there an immortal consciousness?" Or we want to make it into a metaphysical doctrine, or deny it by saying, "Consciousness is aniccā, dukkha, anattā." We want to pin it down or define it either as impermanent and not-self, or raise it up as something we hold to as a metaphysical position. But we are not interested in proclaiming metaphysical doctrines, or in limiting ourselves to an interpretation that we may have acquired through this tradition. We are trying to explore it in terms of experience. This is Luang Por Chah's *pen paccattaṃ:* it's something that you realize for yourself. So what I am saying now is an exploration. I'm not trying to convince you or convert you to my viewpoint.

Consciousness is like *this*. Right now there is definitely consciousness. There is alertness and awareness. Then conditions arise and cease. If you just sustain and rest in consciousness, unattached, not trying to do anything, find anything, or become anything, but just relax and trust, then things arise. Suddenly you may be aware of a physical feeling, a memory, or an emotion. So that memory or sensation becomes conscious, then it ceases. Consciousness is like a vehicle; it's the way things are.

Is consciousness something to do with the brain? We tend to think of it as some kind of mental state that depends on the brain. The attitude of Western scientists is that consciousness is in the brain. But the more you explore it with sati-sampajañña and sati-paññā, the more you see that the brain, the nervous system, and the whole psychophysical formation arises in consciousness and is imbued with consciousness. That is why we can be aware of the body and reflect on the four postures—sitting, standing, walking, and lying down. Being aware of sitting as you experience it now, you are not limited to something that is in the brain. The body is in consciousness; you are aware of the whole body in the experience of sitting.

That consciousness is not personal. It's not consciousness in my head or in yours. Each of us has our own conscious experience going on. But is this consciousness the thing that unites us? Is it our "oneness"? I'm just questioning; there are different ways of looking at it. When we let go of the differences—"I am Ajahn Sumedho and you are this other person"—when we let go of these identities and attachments, consciousness is still functioning. It's pure; it has no quality of being personal, no condition of being male or female. You can't put a quality into it, but it is like *this*. When we begin to recognize that consciousness is that which binds us together and is our common ground, then we see that this is universal. When we spread mettā to a billion Chinese over in China, maybe it's not just sentimentality and nice thoughts, maybe there is power there. I don't know, I am questioning. I am not going to limit myself to a particular viewpoint that my cultural background has conditioned me to accept, because most of that is pretty flawed. I do not find my cultural conditioning very dependable.

Sometimes Theravāda comes across as annihilationism. You get into this "no soul, no God, no self" fixation, this attachment to a view. Or is the Buddha's teaching there to be investigated and explored? We are not trying to confirm somebody's view about the Pāli canon, but using the Pāli canon to explore our own experience. It's a different way of looking at it. If you investigate this a lot, you begin to really see the difference between pure

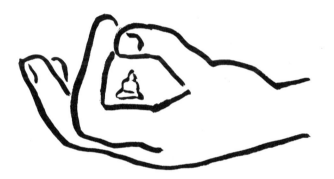

consciousness and when self arises. It's not hazy or fuzzy—"Is there self now?"—that kind of thing; it's a clear knowing.

So then the self arises. I start thinking about myself, my feelings, my memories, my past, my fears and desires, and the whole world arises around "Ajahn Sumedho." It takes off into orbit— my views, my feelings, and my opinions. I can get caught into that world, that view of me that arises in consciousness. But if I know that, then my refuge is no longer in being a person, I'm not taking refuge in being a personality, or in my views and opinions. Then I can let go, so the world of Ajahn Sumedho ends. What remains when the world ends is the *anidassana viññāṇa*—this primal, nondiscriminative consciousness; it's still operating. It doesn't mean Ajahn Sumedho dies and the world ends, or that I'm *un*conscious.

I remember somebody getting very frightened by this talk about the end of the world. "Buddhists are just practicing medi- tation to see the end of the world. They really want to destroy the world. They hate the world and they want to see it end"—this kind of panic reaction. To us the world is seen in physical terms— this planet, the world of continents and oceans, north pole and south pole. But in Buddha-Dhamma the world is something we create in consciousness. That's why we can be living in different worlds. The world of Ajahn Sumedho is not going to be same as the world you create, but that world arises and ceases, and that which is aware of the world's arising and ceasing transcends the world. It's *lokuttara* (transcendental) rather than *lokiya* (worldly).

When we are born into a physical birth, we have conscious- ness within this form. This point of consciousness starts oper- ating, and then, of course, we acquire our sense of self through our mothers and fathers and cultural background. So we acquire different values, our sense of self as a person, and that's based not on Dhamma but on avijjā—on views, opinions, and preferences that cultures have. That's why there can be endless problems with different cultural attitudes. Living in a multicultural community like this, it's easy to misunderstand each other, because we're conditioned in different ways of looking at ourselves and the world around us. So remember that cultural conditioning comes out of avijjā (ignorance) of Dhamma. What we are doing now is informing consciousness with paññā, which is a universal wisdom rather than some cultural philosophy.

Buddha-Dhamma, when you look at it, is not a cultural teaching. It's not about Indian culture or civilization; it's about the natural laws that we live with, the arising and ceasing of phenomena; it's about the way things are. The Dhamma teachings are pointing to the way things are—that aren't bound by cultural limitations. We talk about aniccā, dukkha, anattā. That's not Indian philosophy or culture; these are things to be realized. You are not operating from some basic belief system that is cultural. The Buddha's emphasis is on waking up, on paying attention, rather than on grasping some doctrinal position that you start with. This is why many of us can relate to it, because we're not trying to become Indians or convert to some religious doctrine that came out of India. The Buddha awakened to the way it is, to the natural law. So when we are exploring consciousness, teachings such as the five khandhas are skillful or expedient means to explore and examine our experience. The teachings are not saying, "You have got to believe in the five khandhas and believe that there is no self. You cannot believe in God anymore. To be a Buddhist you have to believe that there is no God." There are Buddhists who have this mentality. They want to make doctrinal positions about being Buddhist. But to me the Buddha's teaching is not based on a doctrine, but on this encouragement to awaken. You are starting from here and now, from awakened attention, rather than from trying to prove that the Buddha actually lived. Somebody might say, "Maybe there was never any Buddha; maybe it was just a myth." But it doesn't matter, because we don't need to prove that Gotama Buddha actually lived; that's not the issue, is it? We are not trying to prove historical facts, but to recognize that what we are actually experiencing now is like *this*.

When we allow ourselves just to rest in conscious awareness, this is a natural state; it's not a created one. It's not a refined conditioning that we are after, not just bliss and tranquillity, because this world, this conscious realm that we are a part of, includes the coarse and the refined. This is not just a refined realm that we are experiencing, not a *deva-loka* (divine realm) or *brahma-loka* (highest heavenly realm). This is a realm where we run the gamut from the coarse to the refined. We have got to deal with the realities of a physical body, which is quite a coarse condition. In deva realms, beings do not have physical bodies; they have ethereal ones. We would all like ethereal bodies, wouldn't we? They're made out of ether rather than all these slimy things that go on inside our bodies—bones, pus, and blood, all of these yucky conditions that we have to live with. To defecate every day—devatās don't have to do things like that. Sometimes we like to create this illusion that we are devatās. We don't like these functions; we like privacy. We don't want people to notice, because of the coarseness of the physical conditions that we are living with. But consciousness includes the gradations from the coarse to the most refined.

Another thing to notice is the compulsive sense of having to do something, having to get or attain something, having to get rid of your defilements. When you're trusting in your "real home," then you can have perspective on this conditioning of the emotions. We come from very competitive goal-oriented societies. We are very much programmed always to feel that there is something that we have to do or have to get. We are always lacking something and we have got to find out what it is. Or we have to get rid of something: our weaknesses, faults, and bad habits. Notice that this is just an attitude that arises and ceases. It's the competitive world, the world of a self.

We can always see ourselves in terms of what's wrong with us as persons. There are always so many flaws and inadequacies. There is no perfect personality that I have ever noticed. Personality is all over the place. Some of it is all right and some of it is really wacky. There is no personality that you can take refuge in. You are never going to make yourself into a perfect personality. So when you judge yourself, you find so many problems, inadequacies, flaws, and weaknesses. Maybe you are comparing yourself to some ideal person, some unselfish and superlative personality. That which is aware of personality is not personal. You can be aware of the personal as a mental object. These personality conditions arise and cease. You find yourself suddenly feeling very insecure or acting very childish because the conditions for that personality have arisen.

When my parents were alive I went to stay with them for about three weeks, because they were really sick. I was abbot of Amarāvatī, a fifty-five-year-old Ajahn Sumedho, and I went home and lived in the same little house with my mother and father. It brought up all kinds of childish emotions—because the conditions were there for that. You were born through your parents. Mothers and fathers bring up your memories, your connections of infancy onward. So a lot of the conditions that arise in families are conditions for feeling like a child again, even when you're a fifty-five-year-old Buddhist monk and abbot of a monastery. My mother and father could easily revert back and see me as a child. Rationally they could see I was a middle-aged man, but they would still sometimes act like I was their child. Then you feel this rebelliousness and adolescent resentment about being treated like a child. So don't be surprised at some of the emotional states that arise. Throughout your life, as you get old, kamma ripens and then these conditions appear in consciousness. Don't despair if you find yourself at fifty years old feeling very childish. Just be aware of that for what it is. It is what it is. The conditions for that particular emotion are present, so then it becomes conscious. Your refuge is in this awareness rather than in trying to make yourself into an ideal man or woman—mature, responsible, capable, successful, "normal," and all the rest—those are ideals.

Here I am not looked at as a child. I'm the oldest person here! You may see me in terms of a father figure, because an old man like me brings out the sense of authority. I'm an authority figure, a patriarch, a father figure, a male figure—a grandfatherly figure to some of you. It's interesting just to see this state when the conditions are there. Rationally you can say, "He's not my father!" but emotionally you may feel like that, acting toward me like I'm a father, because it's an emotional habit. When the conditions for that kind of male authority figure are present, then this is what you are feeling—it's like *this*. There's nothing wrong with it, just notice it's the way it is. Trust your refuge in this awareness, not in some idea that you shouldn't project fatherly images onto me, or that you shouldn't feel disempowered by a male authority figure and things like this. If you feel disempowered by me, then just recognize it as a condition that has arisen, rather than blaming me or blaming yourself, because then you are back into the world you are creating—your personal world, and believing in that as your reality.

I used to get really angry when women would get bossy. When any woman would show any kind of bossiness, I would just feel this rage. I wondered why I would get so upset or enraged by somebody's tone of voice or bossy attitude. I could see that, it was like when I was a boy, trying to get my way against my mother. If that's not been fully resolved yet, then when the conditions for that rage are present this is what will arise. It's through awareness of it that you resolve it. When you understand it and see what it is, you can resolve it or let it go. Then you are not stuck with the same old reactions all the time.

Our refuge then is in awareness, not in trying to sustain refined experiences in consciousness, because you can't do that. You can maybe learn, through developing a skill, to increase your experience of refinement, but inevitably you have to allow coarseness to manifest, to be a part of your conscious experience. Resting in this conscious awareness is referred to as "coming home" or "our real home." It's a place to rest, like a home. In your home you are no longer a foreigner or an alien. You begin to recognize it through a sense of relief in being home at last, in not being a stranger, a wanderer out in the wilderness. The world of Ajahn Sumedho can arise, and then it's like I'm not at home anymore, because Ajahn Sumedho is an alien, a stranger! He never feels quite at home anywhere. Am I American now? Am I British or am I Thai? Where do I feel at home as Ajahn Sumedho? I don't even know what nationality I am anymore, or where I feel most at home. I feel more at home here than in America because I've lived here for so long. In Thailand I feel at home because it's the paradise for Buddhist monks and they treat you so well; but still you have to get visas and you're always a Phra Farang. Here in England, no matter how many years I have been here, I am still, to most people, an American. When I go back to America I don't know what I am: "You don't look like an American anymore. You've got a funny accent. We don't know where you are from!" That's the world that is created. When it drops away, what's left is our real home.

THINKING AND HABITS

A QUESTION has been asked: How does the reflecting mind differ from the thinking mind that we identify with? We are conditioned to think, to use logic and reason—thinking becomes habitual. Mindfulness does not operate out of habit but through awareness; otherwise it is ignorance. *Avijjā, viññāṇa,* and *papañca* are the Pāli terms. Avijjā is ignorance, viññāṇa is consciousness, and papañca is conceptual proliferation. So this is the momentum of habits. When we are caught in papañca, we wander around unquestioningly in the momentum of thoughts that are stimulated by memories or impingements. In Marcel Proust's masterpiece, *Remembrance of Things Past,* we read how a taste of a piece of cake and tea can set off a chain of remembered events. So that is papañca. And then we use thought to reason things out—logic. Thought is very useful; thinking is a good tool, I have found.

We are educated to think and to acquire knowledge from books and from lectures. This is the information age, an age of computers and websites and everything. There is a plethora of information at your fingertips. I just ask my secretary a question, "Do you know if ____?" and he looks it up on the website and gives me all the details. You don't even have to go to the library anymore.

We are educated to think like that. So reason and logic have a certain value in the worldly life, but papañca is often what takes us to depression, anxiety, or worry. Some habits of the mind, like thinking of the future: What's going to happen to me? To modify the Beatles song: "Will you still feed me, will you still need me, when I'm seventy-four?" Or regret, guilt, remorse, about things you have said or done in the past. So you can see how the ego is built around this idea of "me and mine," and around time and the past and future. This is a trap. One gets caught into it, and it always leads to dukkha. Avijjā, ignorance, is suffering.

Suffering is not the pain in your knees. It's the aversion to the pain, because this realm is like this. Pain is a part of the experience—physical pain and disease, old age, sickness, death, loss of what is loved, grief, sorrow, despair, anguish—and this is not depressing. I mean, these are all variable experiences. We learn from this as humans, and in a human lifetime we have to experience the loss of loved ones, separation. We have this monastic reflection: "All that is mine, beloved and pleasing, will become otherwise, will become separated from me." In monasticism we have ways of reflecting on these events. It can be quite depressing when you think about it on a personal level: all that is mine, beloved and pleasing, will become otherwise, will become separated from me. If I think about that, proliferate on that, I might as well just kill myself right now, get it over with. But then in terms of Dhamma, we are looking, knowing the world as the world. This is what being born is all about.

Being born in a mortal, sensitive form in a sense realm on planet Earth with its earth, fire, water, and wind elements; being conscious, being sensitive—these are endurable and bearable, but what we can't bear is our own ignorance. So I've watched myself many times. When I first went to live with Ajahn Chah I couldn't understand the language, and then he'd give desanās (Dhamma talks) in the Isahn dialect of Northeast Thailand for sometimes up to five hours in the evening. And I'd say, "Well, I don't see any point in me coming to these. I'm being reasonable, because I don't understand the language and I just suffer a lot—the pain in those legs—and it's just a miserable experience." And he'd say, "You still have to come." He was being unreasonable, I felt.

So then I was sitting there in the polite posture with one leg folded in front…when you listen to a desanā, you have to sit like this according to Thai etiquette. For someone who has never sat in that posture before it's pretty excruciating after about three minutes, and for five hours! My mind would say, "I can't stand this, I've had enough, it's not fair, I'm leaving, I can't take it," and then I found out that I could. The mind was screaming away, but by watching, observing, I found I had quite an ability to bear pain, physical discomfort, disease, loss, broken heart, disappointment, disillusionment, criticism, and blame, where on a personal level I'd think that I just couldn't bear it, that I'd be shattered and destroyed. But before there was a lot of fear and anxiety about losing what I wanted, or things not going my way. I was worried and anxious about almost everything. On that level of conceptual proliferation, papañca, it just goes on like that, and my mind says, "I can't stand it, I've had enough, I'm fed up."

When you say, "I'm fed up," sometimes you say it with great force. I knew one monk who, whenever he said he was fed up, would say it in way that just pierced my heart. Sometimes I would say to myself, "I'm fed up," but when I saw I could bear it, I recognized that I couldn't trust this papañca. The rational mind, the critical mind, as I've been saying many times, the inner critic, the superego, the tyrant, the "jackal" as they call it in Nonviolent Communication training, is always criticizing me. So no matter how good or how careful I try to be, the jackal is always saying, "You know..." People could praise me, "You are a great teacher, your talk was so wonderful" and all that, but the inner jackal would say, "You know it's not true." So I realized that even if I could attain all the titles and accolades, it wouldn't make much difference because the inner jackal would still go on. So how could I trust such a thing? Is that trustworthy, the inner jackal? Is that something I should give attention to and believe in, or is it just a habit of papañca?

By reflecting on these forces—this self-critic, this very righteous know-it-all authority inside me, the big judge, the inner tyrant—I no longer gave them any further reinforcement. It's like noting something and reflecting on it. Now, when you reflect on this very rational critical force, it may seem intelligent. And if you were brought up in a family that tends to be critical—where you could never express praise or affirmation of someone's goodness because that would inflate his or her ego—honesty always meant admitting your faults. So if you were praised too much, or thought too well of yourself, you were conceited; and having an inflated ego, a big head, was a danger. English culture is very much like that, isn't it? Boasting or bragging or telling anybody how good you are is really despised. But every English person is willing to tell you about his or her faults. This is a cultural problem.

In Thailand, for example, they often think of all the good things they have done. Ajahn Chah told me to reflect on my own goodness, to think of all the good things; and I found that quite difficult. I could write pages about my faults, but I couldn't get very much going when I tried thinking of my goodness. Yet on reflection I can say I'm a good person, and I love the good. I don't have strong criminal tendencies or love to torture, steal, lie, and insult. I'm not a psychopath. I've never had any criminal tendencies. I've never enjoyed harming other things, never got any pleasure out of cruelty or intentional harming. I then began to see that basically I'm very good. Otherwise why would I be a monk all these years? Buddhist monasticism is not the place to be bad. It's not a lifestyle where you can get a full range of evil actions.

So reflecting, using thought for reflection, like taking just the First Noble Truth, dukkha (suffering). So you think dukkha, First Noble Truth—that is a thought. But you are taking a thought and then reflecting on dukkha. This is not through the intellect, like trying to find the perfect English definition for dukkha, as many monks try to do, endlessly. Searching for the perfect English equivalent for the Pāli word *dukkha,* I'm tired of that. I'm no longer interested on that level because it doesn't matter. "Suffering": good enough. It gets the point across. So then you look at that. What does that really mean in terms of what is happening to me now? I began to notice there is anxiety, self-consciousness, worry about what other people think of me, worry about making a mistake, doing something wrong, the mind would say, "I can't stand any more of this, I've had enough, I'm going to leave." That is starting to look at a lot of this conceptual proliferation, the inner tyrant that says, "You shouldn't have thoughts like that. That thought was bad and you shouldn't think negative thoughts."

I could see that getting caught in these habits led me to suffer from anxiety, worry, and self-consciousness. I've had quite a good life, I don't have a lot to complain about. I wasn't born in poverty, to cruel parents, or in an inhumane society, and I wasn't persecuted, deprived, or abused. In spite of all that, the suffering was unbearable. So by the time I was thirty I felt like a burnt-out case. I felt weary. The worldly life had no promise for me. I could, if I wanted to, get a good job and do all the right things according to my parents' wishes, but there was no interest, nothing in me that moved me toward that kind of ambition.

The life that I was born into bored me. I couldn't bear to live the kind of life my parents lived because it was boring to me, just to spend my life making money and having a family. It certainly was not tantalizing to me. This world-weariness is called *nibbidā* in Pāli. This isn't depression or self-pity; it's weariness. Even at thirty I had seen enough of the world, had enough experience. And so the only thing left was to become a monk. So then the door of opportunity opened and I became a Buddhist monk.

In the monastic life in Thailand with Ajahn Chah, the Buddhist meditation was about developing this reflective capacity but not just "me thinking about myself." It gave me this perspective, these tools that I've been sharing with you, how to use the Four Noble Truths. And so my reflective mind began to notice the anger. I used to feel anger and then somebody would say, "You are angry," and I would say, "No I'm not." I could be in the midst of anger and never know it or admit it—I was that blind. Or I didn't know how to admit…I didn't know how I felt about anything. So people would say, "How do you feel about this?" and I didn't know. I didn't know what I felt about anything, because I had operated in a different way. Rather than through being sensitive or admitting what I was feeling, I was always trying to become something, to live up to standards, or operating habitually. So I had to really observe feeling when I became a monk staying with Ajahn Chah.

I had to observe the restlessness, anger, and resentment about having to sit for five hours listening to Luang Por Chah rattling on and everybody having a good time. He was very charming and entertaining, and people were mesmerized and laughing. He had a good sense of humor and I would sit there angry and furious. Reflecting on that fury, I began to notice this little boy, this little immature child saying, "I'm going to run away. I'm going to really hurt you, Luang Por Chah, because I am leaving." And then I started reflecting on that—I remember doing that to my mother. When she didn't give me what I wanted, I used to say, "I'm going to go," hoping that she'd say, "Oh, don't go, I'll do anything you want." I was listening to these voices, because there was nothing else to do. Monastic life isn't exciting or adventurous. It's a simplification, so you're just basically living the routine life of a Buddhist monk. You chant, you can't even sing; but the chanting was boring. I used to like Italian opera, so my mind was off thinking of arias, emotional fortes, and whatnot.

Still, I was very interested in developing this reflective way of living, and the life there freed me from having to make a living and getting caught up in a foolish society that I was already disillusioned with. At least I was with like-minded people and with a very good, very wise teacher. I was really very fortunate. Then living in relationship with the other monks and the laypeople was very prescribed according to Vinaya, the monastic discipline, and Thai cultural tradition. So I just adapted. I could be critical of all that, but then I decided that wasn't what I was interested in, on that conventional level. Instead I learned what the cause of suffering is and how to liberate myself from that. That's the main thrust. The intention is to realize nibbāna and not make a big deal about the world around you.

The monastic environment is moral. There is a strong sense of morality and nonviolence and of living with good people and a wise teacher. There was the Dhamma and the Vinaya. So I decided I wasn't going to spend my time complaining about it.

The Vinaya has all these little rules, and personally I don't like rules at all. I don't like these fussy little things and I used to feel such aversion when they started reading the Vinaya: "I'm going to fall asleep." And they read the Vinaya every morning—this was before I understood Thai—for maybe half an hour. Sometimes a monk who loved reading commentaries on the Vinaya would get so absorbed he'd go on for an hour and everybody would fall asleep. We'd all be asleep and he wouldn't even notice. I'd sit there and fulminate: "This is a waste of time. The monks aren't even paying attention. What a stupid thing to be doing."

Then I would reflect on my state of mind, my critical mind, my resentment. That was what I was interested in, not in trying to set the monastery right but just learning from the experiences I was having. I began to see that really I could bear all that. What I couldn't bear was this grumbling, complaining, critical *me* that kept whining, "This is a waste of time, this is stupid, you don't have to do it like this." That was the First Noble Truth, the duk-kha. I wasn't there to try to arrange life according to my wishes. I had deliberately put myself in that situation, under somebody else; I knew I needed to be under a teacher. I needed to learn how to obey, how to follow a form. I had been too much the free spirit doing everything to manipulate life and get my own way. I was good at that. And I could have done that easily as a Buddhist monk—at some monasteries, a big guy like me can intimidate, come on strong, and they offered all kinds of cushy monasteries to stay in. Instead I chose this place in Ubon, a remote part of Thailand, that was considered the Paris Island of Buddhist monasteries. Parris Island is a Marine training camp in the United States.

I learned a lot just from watching myself. As I began to understand Thai, I'd hear Luang Por Chah use this phrase *Poo roo* (the knowing one) a lot. I had the Western mind-set that nibbāna and liberation meant just getting rid of everything. That was my cultural habit and the easiest way for me to interpret Pāli scripture. It even says in paṭiccasamuppāda (dependent origination) on the nirodha side of it, where your consciousness ceases, and everything ceases, and that sounds like total annihilation. That was how my logical mind worked when I tried to understand the Pāli teachings from a Western perspective. Luang Por Chah would use Pāli terms like *kāmasukhallikānuyoga* and *attakilamathānuyoga*. I looked up these Pāli words and also *majjhimā paṭipadā*, the middle way. They come from the Buddha's first sermon, the *Dhammacakka Sutta,* a teaching on the Four Noble Truths, which we chanted and had to memorize.

Kāmasukhallikānuyoga is a sort of eternalism of happiness, or a belief in heaven or something on that level, where you are feeling happy forever; attakilamathānuyoga is annihilationism—everything just ceases into a void of nothingness and oblivion. Now these are logical sequences of the thinking mind, like heaven or a kind of eternal heavenly experience. I was brought up Christian to think I had a separate soul and that if I did what God wanted then, when I died, I would go as a separate soul to live forever with Jesus up in heaven. That's the Christian model I had. In that model, if you failed at your attempts and you didn't please God, you got sent to the opposite, to hell, where you experienced unmitigated misery forever. That's pretty severe, a very threatening situation, isn't it? And yet intuitively I couldn't really go along with that. Something in me couldn't believe in that. So I tended more toward annihilationism. I liked the idea of oblivion, of disappearing, of vanishing. I just wanted to be invisible and disappear. That was more appealing than the other. So then the majjhimā paṭipadā, the middle way: what is that? That is a kind of compromise between the two. Then I began, through meditation, through reflection, to recognize mindfulness as transcending thoughts. Using the gap between the words, the self-questioning style—who am I? who is letting go? who is the Buddho? what is it that knows? And asking myself questions where the mind stops thinking. When you ask yourself a question, for a moment, there is no thought. For example, the question "who am I?" might be answered with "Sumedho." I knew that already, so I wasn't interested in that as an answer, so who *am* I? It's nonplussing. The thinking mind stops. And just reflecting on the gaps between thoughts gave me insight into the space around things in my mind.

I started reflecting on space, just my visual space. For example, in the monastery I would be sitting together with the other monks and I'd say here's Ajahn So-and-so and there's Ajahn So-and-so, and I'd get to see them all through their names and through my memories of them as people: he's like this and he's like that. Then I started to reflect on the spaces between the monks, as a practice of exploring instead of just going along. I'd notice the spaces between the monks who were doing evening pūjā. This is a different way of looking at something, reflecting on space rather than going along with the convention of this monk's name is this and he's like this and so forth. This is a way of experimenting, investigating reality, noticing the way it is—using space as a reference rather than obsessing about forms, names, and personal reactions.

I then began to notice that after reflecting on space I felt spacious. Space has no boundaries so it's different than "I like this monk, I don't like that one; this is a good monk, that one is not; I'm senior to this one, that one is senior to me; this monk eats silently, that one makes too much noise." When you are living together you really irritate each other a lot, so this was a way of investigating, here and now, in our ordinary monastic life with

Ajahn Chah. I was reflecting on experience rather than whining about it, ignoring it, judging it, or rationalizing it. I was taking the Buddha's teachings and then applying them to the moment. I never saw the Buddha's teachings as theoretical or as ideals about how things should be. I saw them as pointing to something as ordinary as dukkha, its causes, its cessation, and the way of non-suffering. So this is all about here and now. It's not about me trying to become enlightened in the future.

As for my notion of practicing hard so I would become enlightened, I changed that to the question "What is enlightenment?" Because it is a theory, isn't it? When Kondañña understood the *Dhammacakka Sutta,* the world shook and maybe earthquakes were expected. Or is enlightenment our true nature? Is it simply mindfulness? And "enlightenment" is sometimes compared to a blinding flash, so bright you can't see afterward. That kind of light is too much for the eyes, but if you get the right light then you can see everything properly. What I was interested in was not being blinded by light but being able to see clearly, to know in clarity, not to be caught in endless doubt, in skeptical problems I created through habitual thinking and conceptual proliferation. So that is about here and now.

The Buddha is always pointing to the here and now; *sandiṭṭhiko* (apparent here and now), *akāliko* (timeless), *ehipassiko* (encouraging investigation), *opanayiko* (leading inwards), *paccattaṃ veditabbo viññūhi* (to be experienced individually by the wise), the Dhamma teachings, what Dhamma is. In monastic life you attach to a lot of things and you suffer from that. My habit of attaching was strong. I could quite easily give up all the worldly stuff, but I found I was getting obsessed with all kinds of silly things in monastic life. I was suffering because I always was wanting or idealizing something: wanting monasteries to be different, not wanting certain monks to be the way they are, or just thinking that it was all a waste of time. So it brought up arrogance, conceit, opinions, views, and obsessions. The sensual delights were very limited at Wat Pah Pong; we were strictly celibate, of course, and we had only one meal a day. Here we have chocolate every day, so this is a luxury hotel by comparison.

One of the things that the Buddha allowed in the Vinaya is sugar in the evenings. I was never that keen on sweets, but suddenly I was obsessed about sugar. So I went on a fast. Ajahn Chah gave me permission to fast for a week. Then in the middle of the fast he gave me a bag of sugar. I took it back to my kuṭi, and I couldn't help myself. I took one taste and it tasted so fantastic that I ate the whole bag. I couldn't stop, just totally gave in, and then spent time meditating about how I was going to get more. Then I thought that this was ridiculous, because my critical mind was looking down on this stupid and despicable behavior. Then you don't want anyone to find out that you are spending the whole hour thinking about how you are going to get the sugar. But I began to see that all the sense pleasures that I had as a layperson were a kind of energy fix on what was sensually pleasurable, and so sugar was happiness. So I just observed this mad, driven obsession, rather than trying to suppress it because I didn't like it; this is what was happening. The suffering around being obsessed about something you know is ridiculous, and you know that eating sugar is not very good for you, yet it doesn't make the slightest bit of difference. So you keep observing this instead of trying to control it. You do not try to get rid of this obsession for sweets, but you see it in terms of the First Noble Truth.

Once the thinking process starts, the possibility, the anticipation and so forth, it keeps going. Getting to understand how your mind works—the space between the thoughts, the silence, the sound of silence—stops the thinking process. So this is reflecting on non-thinking. I do not proliferate about non-thinking, but I think and observe in the stillness; and I see that stillness is like this. Now those are thoughts, but it's a reflective thinking. It's not a rational sequence, and it's not habitual thinking. And then I ask myself questions in this stillness: Is there any self? Can I find a self in this? And so just by asking myself these questions, I listen, and in this stillness of the sound of silence there is certainly awareness, intelligence, consciousness, but I can't find any self in it. And that is intuitive awareness. I really can't find any self. So then I notice how I create myself by thinking about myself, about what I like and don't like, and how I get into my critical judgmental phase with my views and opinions. I can become a very strong personality, fed up easily, and quick to move into conceit or self-disparagement and on.

All these habits come about through conceptual proliferation, papañca. But then, being able to recognize the difference between awareness and consciousness, and ignorance and consciousness. My consciousness is affected by all these proliferating thoughts connected to "me and mine": I don't like this or approve of that; I don't want to do this and don't see the point; you shouldn't have said that; I like this monk but not that one. This is all avijjā–paccayā saṅkhārā (ignorance conditions mental formations). The conscious experience is one of suffering, because the self isn't peaceful, is not real, and changes according to conditions. Depending on whether you are praised, appreciated, and liked or you are criticized, despised, and rejected, the proliferations are different, but the awareness is the same. So just by reflecting on the way it is, you see what the refuge is. You can't trust the other. I can't trust my proliferating habits; they lie all the time. The inner tyrant, the jackal, just says the same bloody thing over and over. Now there is no way that I am going to appease the jackal. No matter how good I am it will never say, "You are really good, Sumedho." It will always say, "You think you are so good, don't you, but you are not." So you can't win on that level, there is no way out, because it is a habit; it doesn't have any life of its own. That is all it knows how to do. It doesn't know how to praise or appreciate anything or reflect; it just knows how to make life miserable. So will you trust that? I won't.

So the refuge is in the Buddha, in this awareness. Through investigation I trust it. I've tested it out and explored it for many years to make sure. The experiences of my life are part of this way of learning, because the experiences change and things happen in unexpected or even unwanted ways. The refuge remains the same, whereas conditions are dependent on other conditions that you have no control over. So I leave you to your Buddho.

FORM AND CONVENTION

WE ARE USING the structures of the ten-day retreat for awareness: the eight precepts, the morning and evening pūjā, the mealtime. Daily life, conventions, structures, routines, and schedules can become obsessive and compulsive when you get addicted or bound by them, so we need to know how to use them for awareness. In daily life in a monastery you have certain structures and reference points for reflection: morning chanting, salutation to the Buddha, Dhamma, and Sangha, ceremonies, chanting in Pāli or in English. These are not meant to be attachments; they are points of reference. It's like the tip of your nose for ānāpānasati, the posture, the sound of silence, the four foundations of mindfulness, the Four Noble Truths. These are all conventions and forms. So how do we use them for awakening, for developing? You can start with "all you have to do is be mindful; mindfulness is the path to the Deathless." That's true, that's it. But then, after you have stopped that, you can go right back into heedlessness.

Structures and conventions can be fetters. By being attached to them we feel guilty; we feel bound, intimidated, or committed. It has to be like this otherwise we don't feel right. These are ways of recognizing the way we hold a convention. The grasping is the problem, not the convention. Conventions are neutral, or they may be moral or renunciant conventions. The first five of the eight precepts—not harming, not stealing, and so forth—are more like moral conventions. The other three precepts are not eating food in the afternoon; not dancing, singing, or dressing up (these are known as the "renunciant precepts" since there is nothing immoral about dancing, singing, dressing in beautiful clothes, enjoying shows, playing sports), not sleeping on high or luxurious beds. Buddhism isn't a puritanical, sour-grapes type of teaching; it's about restraint and renunciation. And renunciation isn't done from some kind of negative condemnation of beauty and pleasure. It has to come from your own resolve to simplify life.

Problems of stress arise because modern society is complicated and offers many options and choices. You have to make so many decisions. Going shopping in Tesco is really stressful. You have to figure out which soap powder or salad dressing you want. So many options for food—what shall we have for dinner tonight?—so many kinds of entertainment and distraction. So renunciation is not a negative put-down or a puritanical rejection of the pleasures of life. It's a way of simplifying the options. The boundaries are not vast, so that our attention can be aimed more at practice and developing awareness, sustaining, and observing the monkey-mind. In Thailand they call it the monkey-mind because monkeys, they are restless creatures, they swing from tree to tree, grab a banana, then they see another banana, drop the one they are holding and reach for the next one. That sounds like my mind. So what I have been pointing to is very simple, the ultimate simplicity.

You can't get more simple than mindfulness because it is not anything you can create. It is just a matter of paying attention and being present, it's not a complicated technique or a complexity.

It's so simple, but we are conditioned for complexity, so we tend to make things complex all the time, complicate everything. One of the translations of the word *saṅkhāra* is "compounded." I quite like that because in the conditioning of the mind nothing is just what it is; you put something else onto it. You are sitting and observing and then a negative thought arises in your mind, and you think, "That's bad." That's a compounding. The act of judging it, putting the label "bad" onto it, makes it more than what it is. We go back into the saṃsāric world, the complicated world we create. Whereas mindfulness is just aware of its presences and its absences. It is not concerned with whether they are good or bad. It is not looking at them from that critical position.

So "bad" is a criticism, or "that's good," "that's right," and "that's wrong." And then it goes into "I'm good," "I'm bad," "I shouldn't feel like this," "I shouldn't have these thoughts or desires," "I should be more compassionate and patient." So you see, it gets increasingly more complicated with judgments, criticisms, and a sense of self that is identified with these different conditions. It gets even more complicated. If you have a bad thought you think, "I am bad, I am a bad person, I'm not very good...." "These thoughts arise because people are inconsiderate and they don't respect me. And because of their lack of sensitivity and understanding, I have these bad thoughts," so it gets increasingly more complicated.

Getting to simplicity, then you can't make simplicity but you can idealize simplicity, the simple life, the pure life, the natural way. Just being with the flow, the oneness, the wholeness, love, these are ideas and ideals that we have. Just like the peace people, the peace organizations, "we want peace," or the animal rights people, or the ones who are trying to murder abortionists, or people who experiment with animals... That is ideal; respect the rights of animals, not intentionally take the life of anything. Then the condemnation, the pointing, the condemning, and acting on that, creates evil kamma. You start acting on your aversion to scientists who experiment on animals and really perpetuating the very thing you are condemning. So the awareness doesn't condemn and doesn't approve. Its function is discernment, knowing.

So knowing, "the breath is like this, the inhalation is like this." "Is that a good inhalation or a bad inhalation?" "Which is better, inhaling or exhaling?" Off we go into the saṃsāric complexities and stress, whereas if we are just aware of inhalation as it is, that is very simple. The body inhales whether you are aware of it or not. You're not trying to make yourself inhale in a perfect way but just trusting yourself to be aware, develop that attention and sustained awareness around this natural sensation and physical activity of breathing. Experiencing the body sitting, standing, walking, and lying down. Awareness—cittānupassanā practice—awareness of the state of mind, is not judging it, just recognizing how the mood is. So this is like reflecting on the way it is, the Buddha knowing the Dhamma, this catch-all phrase. All conditions are impermanent: sabbe saṅkhārā aniccā. This is a reflective thought. It is not a projection onto life. You don't go around quoting "all conditions are impermanent" from some attachment to the idea.

Reflection helps us to notice, to observe, to be with change rather than just holding on to the view that everything is impermanent. So noticing this retreat: you don't have to decide what you are going to eat, and you don't have to go shopping and all that. Notice the simplicity of life when you come here and just fit into its conventional form. You are not occupied with a lot of choices or decisions, so you can observe your reaction to the restraint of the eight precepts, to the noble silence, and to the schedule. We are not requiring that you like everything or that everything agree with you or suit your temperament. We are not trying to make everything comfortable for you. We need to recognize our resistances and reactions to the conventions: "This is the way we do it and it has to be done like this. So just shut up and watch your mind. Don't make a problem, don't rock the boat."—that is the tyrannical approach.

Then the opposite reaction: "I just want to be free and follow my heart. I feel suffocated by these restrictions. I don't feel like I'm myself. I feel false and unreal. I need to feel free to live my life, to follow my heart," and so forth. So this is the reflectiveness. These are reactions—since this isn't a prison camp or anything like that, we choose to come here. The agreement is to live within this structure; the point is not conformity or institutionalizing but encouraging awareness. In my first few years in Thailand I remember feeling very suffocated by the monastic life, the strict Vinaya and all that. I had this sense of being suffocated and smothered and had strong resistance to it. Yet I also made an incredible effort to conform, to get approval through conformity: stiff upper lip, just conform, and you'll get a lot of praise. People said, "Oh, that American monk, he's really good, he is really strict," and things like that. I quite liked being praised, obeying everything, and being very good. I got social approval, and I quite liked that.

Inwardly there was also the other side, rebelliousness and resistance. With Ajahn Chah we had to eat from our alms bowls, and I didn't like the food very much because it was totally different. In the Northeast they eat sticky rice, and Ajahn Chah would mix all the food together. People would deliberately prepare all these different soups and curries, and then the monks would mix them up in these big basins, so you would get this sloppy mess ladled into your bowl. In Northeast Thai cooking they use these little green chilies. I soon found that the big red chilies are not dangerous but the little green ones are, and when you get one of those you feel like you are on fire. Some of the monks would pour everything together. They'd serve you coffee or Pepsi-Cola and pour that into the alms bowl with the curries. My mind would think, "Ah, this is unbearable," and I'd get into being very critical and think, "This is stupid. You should just eat your food. You don't have to make it into something repulsive." I'd get very indignant and righteous.

Then I'd start thinking, "But I should be able to do that too," and I'd start criticizing myself. So once I just became so enraged by this that I stood up, took my alms bowl, and left the sālā, and dumped the contents outside the door. I wasn't always a paragon of patience. But fortunately Ajahn Chah's approach was to cultivate awareness, so I began to learn how to use the conventions for awareness and restraint, rather than seeing them as a suppressing convention that suffocated me. I was able to see my resistance and feeling of suffocation as something I created onto the present. Ultimately, it was a good situation. I couldn't be in a better place on the planet, I felt. Where else could you live with a wise teacher and generous laypeople who would support a foreigner toward enlightenment? Everything was going for me, I was living with very trustworthy and very good monks, in a society which was very devout. So when I started to appreciate the goodness of the life, a sense of contentment arose, a feeling of being content and grateful for the opportunity, for the occasion that was given to me.

So reflecting on the use of form and conventions…sometimes in monasteries we suspend morning and evening chanting or go off to our kuṭis and practice by ourselves. This is not a judgment—"it has to be like this otherwise you are not a real monk"—but a different structure. When there is no structure, what happens? When you are by yourself in a little kuṭi with no senior monks watching you, nobody around but yourself, what do you do? This is interesting because one can become very institutionalized, very conformist to structure, such that when the structure is gone, you don't know what to do. That is important to recognize: the dependency on structure, on convention, and the feeling of confusion that comes when the conventions are not there anymore. When it's up to you, up to you following your heart, what is it like?

I used to impose a structure when I was alone. "Self-discipline" I called it. I'd make the structures so that I would discipline myself and not be lazy and just waste my time. But the inner listening, just being aware, is the whole point. I began to see attachment to ideals, structures, conventions—even attachment to the view of following your heart and freedom, for that's another convention, isn't it? "Just be aware, that's all, that's it." So Ajahn Chah would say, "That's true, but not right; that's right, but not true"—a very interesting reflection. What did he mean? If it's true, it's right; if it's right, it's true. True is right and right is true, said my thinking mind. "True but not right, right but not true"? I had to start reflecting on what I understand by "right" and "true." To me it was like truth is right and being right is the truth. You should be right, and you shouldn't be wrong. This is true. Then reflecting on it, listening to this in myself—this thinking mind, the habitual thought patterns, this dualistic right/wrong, true/false—what is the awareness of that?

I can be a very righteous person and judgmental; judgments are not alien to my personality at all. But when I listen to judgments, when I listen to myself making them—deciding what's right and wrong in my peremptory style of thinking—I see it isn't peaceful and it doesn't lead to peace. It leads to increasing criticism either about myself or about the world around me. It is divisive, because if I am right and you don't agree with me, then you are wrong. And then you can get into thinking, "Well, we are all right in our own way." So on the level of thinking you just can't win, without expanding into incredible intolerance or very narrow-minded fundamentalism. So listening, seeing that, observing this thinking mind that creates the words "right" and "wrong" and holds a position. And then the stillness that comes from awareness is peace itself.

Mindfulness, when you recognize it and cultivate the stillness, is not a matter of judging in any way. It doesn't need any approval or disapproval, true or false, right or wrong. It is what it is, the stillpoint, the center of the turning world. So it is a matter of recognition, realization, and what the Third Noble Truth is all about: the cessation of suffering, the nirodha. Theravāda Buddhism, especially the vipassanā teachings in the West, sometimes makes me wonder how often people ever realize stillness or cessation. These people often go to other things like Zen, or Dzogchen in the Tibetan tradition. The big deal now in vipassanā circles in America is going to a Dzogchen retreat. I don't know that much about Dzogchen, but it is about spaciousness and the Deathless, or the unconditioned, recognizing that. When you ask people who have done vipassanā, they say, "Well, we note everything, we note this and we note that," and it is so busy that they never seem to get to the realization where they aren't noting anything: where they aren't labeling or trying to notice every subtle movement, every flicker, every change that is happening in the conditioning of the mind, recognizing the infinite space or the stillness behind all these changing conditions. Somehow this paradigm of the Four Noble Truths is very seldom practiced.

There are also many *abhidhamma* (analytical) style meditations which use stages a lot—the seven stages of purity and levels of enlightenment—formulas like this. Luang Por Chah used the Four Noble Truths as a way of reflecting on the daily life of a monastery. The Third and Fourth Noble Truths are like Dzogchen really, for this is where this realization takes place. It is no longer intellectual or identifying subtlety and minutiae or mental changes. It is cultivating the awareness behind any kind of change whether it is coarse or subtle, and that is ultimate simplicity. When you get into all the subtleties of mental conditioning, there is no end to it. It is just ongoing, because that is the nature of the conditioned realm, proliferating, changing, moving, coarse and subtle. The body is quite coarse, so it is more obvious. With the breath, you are getting a little more subtle, and if you concentrate on the breath, the breath becomes increasingly refined. Sometimes it disappears, as though you are not breathing at all, very tranquil.

I used to aim for that, levels of concentration where the breath would disappear. I thought that was an attainment. But then I began to notice that all my efforts at meditation were for wanting this refined state, this tranquillity. And then I would feel frustrated and annoyed with the coarseness of life, because in the monastery you have to do quite a lot of coarse work. The work wasn't with computers; it wasn't so refined. It was sweeping the ground, cleaning, drawing water from wells, and doing very menial chores. I wanted the refined states because I liked them. I liked sensory deprivation where all the coarser impingements and activities are gone and you are just learning to be with increasing subtleties and refined mental states, and you become peaceful, very tranquillized.

Then a dog barks or the clock chimes. I used to get really frantic over that. In Thai monasteries they love these chiming clocks in the sālā, so people would donate these really fancy clocks, some with mother-of-pearl inlay, and they were not very synchronized, so you would get all this chiming. "I can't practice here, I've got to go back to my kuṭi. This is so irritating, and why do they allow these clocks anyway?" I would get into one of my indignant phases: "I don't like this. They shouldn't allow it." And I'd observe that. It wasn't so nice and peaceful, always being indignant, critical, and upset, and then trying to arrange life so that there were no noisy clocks and everything was under control so I could really practice. Then usually some obsession of the mind would come up. Once I was in an ideal place for three months, where everything was perfect except my mind. Here I was, "Now I can really..." and then some kind of obsession would start creeping up into consciousness, and I kept trying to suppress it by concentrating even more. I wanted to get rid of those obsessive thoughts or doubts, squeeze them out. But when you are alone all day and night, with nothing to do, you just get tired of squeezing out and controlling everything.

So Luang Por Chah's emphasis on awareness was very wise because in the daily monastic life at Wat Pah Pong—putting on your robes, going on the alms round, cleaning your alms bowl, doing chores, sweeping the ground, making your robes, morning and evening pūjā, listening to a monk rattle on about Vinaya with everybody falling asleep, the mosquitoes and the heat—everything was included. You began to get the idea that he wasn't into trying to create perfect situations. It was about being aware, using awareness, developing awareness. Whatever was happening, one could learn from it: from refinement, from coarseness, from the body, from emotional habits, and from the thinking mind.

A N ATTITUDE of conviviality is an attempt to encourage you to open to the holy life as beautiful and enjoyable, rather than just shut down. But sometimes we see meditation as a way not of opening but of shutting ourselves off from things. Remember, words are limited, so when we say "shut down" these are only words which convey some meaning to you in whatever way you grasp them.

In any religious tradition there is a lot of confusion because what is said at times seems to be contradictory: at one moment you are being told to shut down, close your eyes, and concentrate your mind on the breath; and then you are asked to open up with mettā for all sentient beings. This is just to point out the limitation of words and conventions. When we grasp conventions, we bind ourselves to particular views. Teachers might even encourage this by the way we interpret the scriptures. But remember to bring back the awareness that each of us as individuals experiences, which is the center of the universe.

When you see yourself in personal terms as someone who needs to get something or get rid of something, you limit yourself to being someone who has to get something you don't yet have or get rid of something you shouldn't have. So we reflect on this and learn to be the witness, Buddho—that which is awake and aware, which listens to and knows personality views and emotional states without taking them personally.

It's that rather than operating from the position that "I'm meditating" or "I must get something that I don't yet have, I've got to attain certain states of concentration in order to reach the advanced meditation practices." It's not that this belief is wrong, but it limits you to being someone who has to get or attain something that you feel you don't yet have. Alternatively, you can go into the purification mode: "I'm a sinner and I need to purify myself. I've got to get rid of my bad thoughts and habits, my childish emotions and desires, and my greed, hatred, and delusion." But in this case you're assuming that you are somebody who has these negative qualities. That's why this awareness, this awakeness, is the essence of the Buddhist teaching. *Buddho* simply means awakened awareness.

What I encourage is a moving toward simplicity, rather than complexity. We're already complicated personalities. Our cultural and social conditioning is usually very complicated. We're educated and literate, which means that we know a lot and have much experience. This means that we are no longer simple. We've lost the simplicity that we had as children and have become rather complicated characters. The monastic form is a move toward simplicity. At times it may look complicated, but the whole thrust of the Dhamma-Vinaya is toward simplifying everything rather than complicating it.

What is most simple is to wake up—"Buddha" means "awake," it's as simple as that. The most profound teaching is the phrase "wake up." Hearing this, one then asks, "What am I supposed to do next?" We complicate it again because we're not used to being really awake and fully present. We're used to thinking about things and analyzing them, trying to get something or get rid of something; achieving and attaining. In the scriptures there are occasions where a person is enlightened by just a word or something very simple.

One tends to think that people in the past had more pāramī (perfections) and a greater ability to awaken and be fully liberated than us. We see ourselves through complicated memories and perceptions. My personality is very complicated: it has likes and dislikes, it feels happy and sad, and it changes at the snap of a finger. If I hear somebody say something irritating, that can trigger anger in a moment. When the conditions arise, consequent states come to be—anger, happiness, elation. But with sati-sampajañña we're learning to sustain an awareness that transcends these emotions.

If we couldn't do this there would be no hope, no point in even trying to be Buddhist monks or nuns, or anything else at all. We'd be helpless victims of our habits and stay trapped in repetitive patterns. The way out is awakeness, attention. Conviviality is goodwill, happiness, brightness, welcoming, opening. When I'm convivial, I'm open. When I'm in a bad mood then I'm not, and my mind says, "Leave me alone, don't bother me."

It is easy to hold strong views about meditation, Theravāda Buddhism, or whatever convention we are using. People have very strong views and when they hold to any religious convention they tend to form very strong opinions around it. In Theravāda circles you have strong views such as: "We're the original teaching, the pure teaching; you've got to do this in order to get that; saṃsāra and nibbāna are polar opposites," and so it goes on. These are just some of the viewpoints and ideas that we get from holding to a tradition. But in awakened consciousness there's no convention. Instead, consciousness perceives phenomena in terms of Dhamma—the natural way. It's not created or dependent upon conditions supporting it. If you hold to a view then you are bound and limited by that very thing that you are grasping.

In awakened awareness there's no grasping. It's a simple, immanent act of being here, being patient. It takes trust, especially trust in yourself. No one can make you do it or magically do it for you. Trusting this moment is therefore very important. I am by nature a questioner, a doubter or skeptic. I tend to disbelieve and be suspicious. This is an unpleasant condition to live with, because I would love to rest in a belief that I am fully committed to.

In contrast, the skeptical approach is a real challenge. One has to use it to learn to trust, not in views or doctrines, but in the simple ability that each of us has to be aware. Awareness includes concentration. When you do concentration practices or put your attention on one thing, you shut out everything else. With samatha practice you choose an object and then sustain your attention on it. But awareness is broad, like a floodlight; it's wide open and includes everything, whatever it may be.

Learning to trust in this awareness is an act of faith, but it is also very much aligned with wisdom. It's something that you have to experiment with and get a feeling for. No matter how well I might describe or expound on this particular subject, it is still something that you have to know for yourself. Doubt is one of our main problems, because we don't trust ourselves. Many of us strongly believe that we are defined by the limitations of our past, our memories, our personality; we're thoroughly convinced of that. But we can't trust that. I can't trust my personality; it will say anything! Nor can I trust my emotions; they flicker around and change constantly. Depending on whether the sun's out or it's raining, whether things are going well or falling apart, my emotions react accordingly. What I trust is my awareness. It is something for you to find out for yourself. Don't trust what I say. Anything I describe now is just an encouragement for you to trust.

This inclusive awareness is very simple and totally natural. The mind stops and you are just open and receptive. Even if you're tense and uptight, just open to it by accepting it and allowing it to be as it is. Tension, despair, pain—just allow your experience to be exactly as it is rather than try to get rid of it. If you conceive of this openness as a happy state, then you create a mental impression of it as something you might not be feeling and would like to feel. Being in a pleasant state of mind is not a prerequisite for inclusive awareness. One can be in the pits of hell and misery and yet still open to the experience of being aware, and thus allow even the most upsetting states to be just what they are.

I've found this to be a real challenge, for there are so many mental and emotional states that I don't like at all. I've spent my life trying to get rid of them. From childhood onward one develops the habit of trying to get rid of unpleasant mental states by distracting one's attention, doing anything to get away from them. In one's life one develops so many ways of distracting oneself from feelings such as despair, unhappiness, depression, and fear that one no longer even does so consciously—it becomes habitual to distract oneself from painful experience. The encouragement now is to begin to notice it, even to notice the way one distracts oneself. It's a matter of opening to the way it is, not the way you think it should be or the way you think it is. It's a state of not really knowing anything in particular.

In this awareness it's not that you know anything. You're just allowing things to be what they are. You don't have to perceive them with thoughts or words, or analyze them; you're just allowing the experience to be, just the way it is. It's more a case of developing an intuitive sense, what I call intuitive awareness. When you begin to trust in this awareness you can relax a bit. If you're trying to control the mind then you're back in your habit of trying to hold on to some things and get rid of others, rather than just allowing things to be what they are.

With intuitive awareness we are taking our refuge in awakeness, which is expansive, unlimited. Thought and mental conception create boundaries. The body is a boundary; emotional habits are boundaries; language is a boundary; words expressing feelings are also boundaries. Joy, sorrow, and neutrality are all conditioned and dependent upon other conditions. Through awakening we begin to recognize what transcends all of this. If what I'm saying sounds like rubbish, be aware of that. Open to the fact that you don't like what I'm saying. It's like this. It's not that you have to like it: you're starting from the way it is rather than having to figure out what I'm trying to say.

The thought of parting has a certain effect on consciousness. Whatever is happening for you now is that way, it is what it is. Separation and the idea of separation is like *this*. It's a matter of recognizing what it is and not judging what you see. As soon as you add to it in any way, it becomes more than what it is; it becomes personal, emotional, complicated. This sense realm in which we live, this planet Earth, is like this. One's whole life is an endless procession of meeting and separating. We get so used to it that we hardly notice it or reflect on it. Sadness is the natural response to being separated from what one likes, from people one loves. But the awareness of that sadness is not itself sad. The emotion we feel is sadness, but when the emotion is held in awareness then the awareness itself is not sad. The same is true when being present with thinking of something that gives rise to excitement or joy. The awareness is not excited; it holds the excitement. Awareness embraces the feeling of excitement or sadness but it does not get excited or sad. So it's a matter of learning to trust in that awareness rather than just endlessly struggling with whatever feelings might be arising.

Have you ever noticed that even when you're in a state of complete confusion there's something that does not get lost? There's an awareness of the confusion. If you are not clear about this, it is easy to attach to the state of being confused and wind yourself up even more, creating even more complications. If you trust yourself to open to the confusion, you will begin to find a way of liberating yourself from being caught in the conditioned realm, endlessly being propelled into emotional habits arising out of fear and desire.

Desire is natural to this realm. So why shouldn't we have desire? What's wrong with desire anyway? We struggle to get rid of all our desires. Trying to purify our minds and conquering desire becomes a personal challenge, doesn't it? But can you do it? I can't. I can suppress desires sometimes and convince myself that I don't have any, but I can't sustain it. When you contemplate the way things are, you see that this realm is like this—what is attractive and beautiful one desires to move toward and grasp; what is ugly and repulsive gives rise to the impulse to withdraw from. That's just the way it is; it's not some kind of personal flaw. In that movement of attraction and aversion there is an awareness that embraces both of them. You can be aware of being attracted to things and aware of being repelled.

This awareness is subtle and simple. But if no one ever points it out, we don't learn to trust in it, and so we will relate to meditation from the mind state of achieving and attaining. It is very easy to go back into this dualistic struggle: trying to get and trying to get rid of. Right and wrong, good and bad—we're very easily intimidated by righteous feelings. When we're dealing with religion it's so easy to get righteous. In one way we're right—we should let go of desire and we should take on responsibility for our lives and keep the precepts, and we should strive on with diligence. This is right, this is good.

Some might accuse me of teaching a path where it doesn't matter how you behave, that you can do anything and just watch it: you could rob a bank and still be mindful of your actions; you could experiment with alcohol and drugs, or see how mindful and aware you are when hallucinating on mushrooms. If I did teach that, the door would be wide open, wouldn't it? But I'm not promoting that viewpoint. I'm not actually saying you should disregard the precepts. But you can see how, if you're caught in a righteous view, you might assume that I'm promoting the opposite—saying that people shouldn't act in the way their righteous viewpoint encourages.

The precepts are a vehicle that simplifies our lives and limits our behavior. If we don't have boundaries we tend to get lost. If we have no way of knowing limitations, then we follow any impulse or idea that we might feel inclined to in the moment. So Vinaya and sīla is always a form of restriction. It's a vehicle; its purpose is to aid reflection. But if you grasp it you become someone who obeys all the rules without reflecting on what you're doing. This is the other extreme from the complete hedonistic way: you become institutionalized into the monastic form, keeping the party line and obeying all the rules, being a good monk or nun, feeling that that is what you are supposed to do—but you're not really open to it and aware of what you're doing. The doubting mind, the thinking mind, the righteous mind, the suspicious mind will always question.

Some of you are probably thinking, "Well, I'm not ready for that yet. What you're teaching is for advanced students. I just need to learn how to be a good monk and a good nun." This is fine, learn how to be a good monk or nun, but also connect with just being aware. The thing is not to try complicating yourself even more by adopting another role, but to learn to observe how the restrictions of this form bring into the open one's resistance, indulgence, attachment, and aversion, to see that all of these reactions are like this. In this way you're going beyond the dualistic structures of thought and conditioned phenomena. Your refuge is in the Deathless, the unconditioned—in Dhamma itself rather than someone else's view about Dhamma.

Over the years I've developed this awareness so that now I experience consciousness as very expanded. There's a huge spaciousness that I can rest in. The conditions that I'm experiencing both physically and emotionally are reflected in that spaciousness; they're held and supported in it, allowed to be. If I had not developed this awareness then it would be difficult, because I'm always struggling with my feelings. Sometimes the Sangha will be going well, and people will say that they love Amarāvatī and want to remain monks and nuns all their lives and that they believe Theravāda Buddhism is the only way. Then all of a sudden they change to saying that they're fed up with this joint and want to convert to some other religion. Then one can feel dejected and think one has to convince them that joining some other religion is not the way, getting into one's righteous Buddhist mood about how "right" one is. One can get into thinking that we've got everything here and that it's wonderful and that people should be grateful.

One can say, "Don't be selfish, don't be stupid." Emotionally we are like that. If we're emotionally attached to the way we do things, we feel threatened by anyone who questions it. I've found that whenever I get upset by someone criticizing Theravāda Buddhism, our Sangha, or the way we do things, it is due to my personality and its tendency to attach and identify with these things. You can't trust that at all. But you can trust awareness. As you begin to recognize it and know it, you can rest more in being aware and listening to the sound of silence. As you sustain awareness in this way, consciousness can expand and become infinite. When this occurs you are just present in a conscious moment and you lose the sense of being a self—being a person, this body. It just drops away and can no longer sustain itself.

It is not possible for emotional habits to sustain themselves, because, being impermanent, their nature is to arise and cease. You then begin to recognize the value of this expansiveness, which some people call emptiness. Whatever you choose to name it doesn't really matter, so long as you can recognize it. It's a natural state, it's not created—I don't create this emptiness. It's not that I have to go through a whole process of concentrating my mind on something in order to be able to do this and then, having done so, hold my mind there in order to block out everything else. When I was into concentration practices I was always feeling frustrated because just when I'd be getting somewhere someone would slam the door. That type of practice is all about trying to shut out, control, and limit everything. It can be skillful to do that kind of practice, but if you hold on to it then you are limited by it; you can't take life as it comes and instead you start controlling everything. The result of that type of practice is that you believe life has to be a certain way: "I have to be at this place, live with these people, not with those others, and I need these structures and conditions in order to get my samādhi." So then you are bound to that way of structuring your life.

You see monks going all over the place trying to find the perfect monastery where they can get their samādhi together. But in this expansive awareness everything belongs, so it doesn't demand certain conditions in which it may be cultivated. Intuitive awareness allows you to accept life as a flow, rather than being endlessly frustrated when life seems difficult or unpleasant.

Coming into the temple this evening was very nice indeed. The stillness of the place is fantastic. This is the best place in the whole world! That's only an opinion, you know, not a pronouncement. I find the stillness and silence in this place to be palpable as soon as you come in. But then, can I spend the rest of my life sitting in here? Stillness is here in the heart. The stillness is about being present; it's not dependent on a temple or a place. Trusting in your awareness, you begin to notice that even in the midst of places like London and Bangkok, in confusing or acrimonious situations, you can always recognize this stillness once you value and appreciate it. It does take determination to be able to do this. Much of the time it doesn't seem like anything and having goal-oriented practices seems more attractive: "I want something to do, something to sink my teeth into!" We're conditioned always to be doing something rather than just trusting and opening to the present. We can even make *this* into a big deal: "I've got to open to the present all of the time!" Then we just grasp the idea of it, which is not what I mean.

Conviviality is an attitude of openness and being at ease with life: at ease with being alive and breathing, at ease with being present with what is arising in consciousness. If you grasp the idea "I should be convivial," then you've missed the point— what I'm saying is merely an encouragement toward trusting, relaxing, and letting go. Enjoy life here, open to it rather than endlessly trying to perfect it, which can bind us to a critical attitude toward the place. Open to the aversion, let aversion be what it is. I'm not asking you not to be averse to it, but to open to that aversion or restlessness, or whatever positive or negative feelings you have.

CONSCIOUSNESS is what we are all experiencing right now—it is the bonding experience that we all have right at this moment. Consciousness is about the realm of form. We experience consciousness through form. When we contemplate the four elements *(dhātu)*—earth, water, fire, and wind—plus space and consciousness, this is a totality of experience in terms of an individual human being.

The physical condition of a body and the physical realm in which we live are combinations of these four elements, combined with space and consciousness. We can contemplate the four elements as a way of understanding our body not as a personal identity or as something belonging to us. Space and consciousness have no boundaries; they're infinite. Consciousness, then, is what we're using in meditation in order to contemplate the way things are.

We get very confused because consciousness is not something we can get hold of in the way that we can see earth, water, fire, and wind, or conditions of the mind like emotions. Because we are conscious we can actually be aware of thoughts, emotions, and the body as they exist and manifest at the present moment. Sometimes we think of consciousness in a very limited way, just as something that arises through contact via the eye, ear, nose, and so forth—just in terms of sensory consciousness. In this case consciousness is very much limited to perceiving through the senses. But it is possible to begin to recognize consciousness that is not attached to the senses, which is what I point to when I refer to the sound of silence. When you begin to notice that sound, there is a consciousness that is unattached. As you sustain awareness with the sound of silence, you find you can begin to reflect and get perspective on your thoughts, emotions, feelings, sense activity, and experience, which all arise in consciousness in the present.

It is important to recognize that this is something really wonderful that we can do. The whole point of the samaṇa's (renunciant) life, really, is aimed at this kind of realization. Of course, obstructions come with our commitment to the delusions that we create: our strong sense of being a separate self, our identification with the body as who we are, and our emotional habits, thoughts, and feelings by which we create ourselves and derive our sense of having a personality which we tend to identify with and which we allow to push us around. This is why I encourage you to rest and relax into this awareness that comes when you recognize the sound of silence. Just rest in this state of openness and receptivity. Don't attach to the idea of it. You can attach to the idea of the sound of silence and of attaining something with it, and keep creating some false illusions around it.

That's not it—it's not a matter of trying to make anything out of it, but of fully opening to this present moment in a way that is unattached. This recognition of nonattachment is something you know through your awareness rather than through a description. All one can say about it is something like "don't attach to anything" and "let go of everything." But then people do attach and say, "We shouldn't be attached to anything"—and so they attach to the idea of nonattachment. We are so committed to thinking and trying to figure everything out in terms of ideas, theories, techniques, the party line, the Theravāda approach…and we bind ourselves to these conditions, even though the teaching is about letting go or nonattachment. This is why I really encourage you to *observe* attachment.

Trust yourself in this awareness. And rather than holding to the view that you shouldn't be attached, recognize that attachment is like *this*. In the early days I used to practice attaching to things intentionally, just so I would know what attachment is like, rather than having some idea that I shouldn't be attached to anything and then in some desperate way always trying to be detached—which would have been self-deception, so long as the basic delusion that gave rise to the attachment had not been penetrated. Thinking, "I'm someone who is attached and shouldn't be" is an attachment, isn't it? "I am a monk who has all these attachments, these hang-ups, and they're obstructions and I shouldn't be attached to them. I've got to get rid of them, let go of them." You end up fooling yourself and are endlessly disappointed, because you can't do it that way—it doesn't work. This is why I emphasize this pure state of consciousness. Now don't just take it for granted. Don't try to figure it out or think about it very much: learn to just *do it*. Contact this resonating sound or vibration, learn to stay with it for a count of five, or practice so that you get used to it and appreciate it. If you really cultivate it, it gives you this state where you begin to be conscious without being attached, so that the conditions that arise in consciousness may be seen in the perspective of arising and ceasing.

When we let go and just abide in pure, unattached consciousness, that is also the experience of love—unconditioned love. Pure consciousness accepts everything. It is not a divisive function; it doesn't have preferences of any sort. It accepts everything and every condition for what it is—the bad, the good, the demons, anything. So when you begin to trust in it, *mettā bhāvanā* (loving-kindness practice) comes alive. Rather than just spreading good thoughts and altruistic ideas, it becomes very practical and very real. For what do we mean by "love?"

To many people, love is the ultimate attachment: when you love somebody you want to possess them. Often what passes for love in modern consciousness is a very strong attachment to another person, thing, or creature. But if you really want to apply this word to that which accepts, then you have mettā—love that is unattached, which has no preferences, which accepts everything and sees everything as belonging.

When you begin to trust in the awareness, the conscious moment that is infinite, then everything belongs in it. From the perspective of this conscious being, whatever arises in consciousness is accepted and welcomed, whether it's through the senses from the outside or from inside—the emotional and physical conditions which become conscious in this present moment. This sense of love, acceptance, and nonjudgment accepts everything that you are thinking, feeling, and experiencing; it allows everything to be what it is. When we don't allow things to be as they are, then we are trying to get something that we don't have or get rid of something that we don't want. So in terms of purifying the mind, consciousness is already pure. You don't need to purify it; you don't have to do anything.

You begin to not identify by not holding on to the conventional view of yourself as being this person, this way, this condition, this body. These views begin to drop away; they are not the way things really are. In meditation, if you trust in awareness then certain things come into consciousness: worries, resentments, self-consciousness, memories, bright ideas, or whatever. Our relationship to them is accepting, embracing, allowing. In action and speech we accept both the good, which we act on when we can, and the bad, which we don't—uncritically. That to me is what love is; it's not critical. That applies most to what arises in my consciousness, my own kamma, emotions, feelings, and memories. Behind it all is the sound of silence. It's like this enormous, vast, infinite space that allows things to be what they are, because everything belongs. The nature of conditions is to arise and cease. That is the way it is. So we don't demand that they are otherwise or complain because we'd like to hold on to the good stuff and annihilate the bad. Our true nature is pure. When we begin to realize and fully trust and appreciate this, we see that this is real. It's not theoretical, abstract, or an idea—it's reality.

Consciousness is very real. It's not something you create. This is consciousness right now. That you are conscious is a fact; it's just the way it is. The conditions that we might be experiencing may be different. One person may be happy, another sad, confused, tired, depressed, worried about the future, regretting the past, and so on. Who knows all of the various conditions that are going on in all of us at this moment? Only you know what is occurring in your particular experience now. Whatever it is—good or bad, whether you want it or not—it's the way it is. So then your relationship to it may be through purity of being rather than through identifying with the conditioned. You can never purify the conditioned. You can't make yourself a "pure person." That's not where purity is. Purifying yourself as a person is a hopeless task, like trying to polish a brick to make it into a mirror. It's demanding the impossible, which means you will fail and be disappointed. This is where the awakened state is the original purity. In other words, you have always been pure. You have never ever for one moment been impure. Even if you're a serial killer, the worst demon in the universe, you're still pure because that purity is impossible to destroy. The problem lies not in becoming impure but in the attachment to the illusion that we create in our mind: the demon is so attached to being a demon that he forgets his original purity, this presence here and now.

ENDING

O N THE LAST evening of a retreat we notice the sense of
ending. Tomorrow at this time you'll be back in your
homes with your families. So now we can reflect on
how different it was in the beginning when the retreat began,
and how it is now when it's coming to an end. Reflecting on
the way it is, on the beginning and ending, does not mean we
are making anything out of that, other than just recognizing our
perceptions—morning and evening pūjā, coming together and
separating. This is a way of integrating the Dhamma into daily
life—the way it is. So at the end the mind starts to think about
what I have to do when I go home. At the beginning you are
thinking, "Will I be able to stand ten days of this?" So that which
is aware is awareness. It reflects on the flow of our lives, the coming together, the separating, the beginning, the ending, in this
most ordinary way that it happens, getting up in the morning,
going to bed in the evening.

What this does is keep reminding you to be the knowing, be
the awareness, rather than seeing yourself as always limited to your
emotions and thoughts and the conditions that you experience.
So you begin to have more confidence, more certainty in the
refuge of the Buddha, rather than being endlessly bound in your

habitual thoughts and emotions and never really noticing life, but just reacting to it, being caught in the reactions you have to experience.

When I had my first powerful insight into cessation I was a sāmaṇera in Nong Khai and I had an insight into this Third Noble Truth. The emotional reaction was that I threw myself on the floor and started crying, "I can't do it," and yet at the same time I was watching this, almost like I was out of my body, although it wasn't as extreme as that might sound. There was a watching of this creature crying, "I can't do it," and yet this knowing, recognizing that this was just a habit. This is not a real person, this is not really me and mine. Now if you had happened to come in at that time what would you have thought? "Ajahn Sumedho is really in a terrible state, he's having a breakdown." But actually I wasn't. It was a real insight, a powerful experience. So that is where we often make our judgments—on how things look, the reactions. That is where we can get it wrong, even with ourselves. It is so easy to think, "I can't do it, it is really me thinking I can't do it," when with insight, it isn't coming from emotion, it isn't coming from the personality.

Whatever insights you have had during this retreat, recognize the special conditions that a retreat offers. It is a special situation, and it is important to make that fully conscious. This is so you are not connecting your insights with the retreat situation: "In order to have insight, I need controlled conditions and special situations." You don't really. That is the danger, always depending on retreats or extreme situations and then feeling you can't be mindful in daily life. Don't believe such thoughts. Start from where you are. If you go home and get all confused and think, "I can't practice," just trust yourself to be aware that that is a thought—"I can't practice in daily life, just too many responsibilities, too much..."

Then stop. Who is thinking that? What is that? That is a thought, isn't it?—I create myself as somebody who can't do it. With that awareness you begin to catch these moments, begin to awaken; to not convince yourself that you can do it in daily life, because that is the same thing. Just have the confidence to be aware of how you create yourself. Like falling down on the floor and crying "I can't do it"—that was witnessed at the time, not believed. Have this position of the Buddha listening to the Dhamma, so when the inner tyrant starts nagging and abusing, you listen to it, recognize it.

That which listens to your self-criticisms and self-judgments, that is your refuge, that awareness, not the know-it-all critic, the jackal, the tyrant. This is very important, otherwise we persecute ourselves endlessly. This very self-disparaging critical tendency of the intellect, all the shoulds and shouldn'ts... On the emotional level, be aware of what you are really feeling. The tyrant will be passing judgment on you and react with, "Why do I have to feel jealousy, you shouldn't be jealous, you are a bad person, because jealousy is disgusting," and there is this critic coming down heavily on you, telling you that jealousy is bad. If jealousy is an emotion you are having at the time, then what does that feel like as a physical experience that is not a judgment? Your rational mind will pass judgment and tell you that you shouldn't have this emotion, but don't believe that.

When you have some emotion, it is the way it is, but a skillful relationship to the emotion is one of reflecting on it, receiving it for what it is, arising, ceasing, anattā, not-self. This is a very skillful way to resolve kamma because there is in most of us an inner war of the rational mind judging the emotional experience, and then we get confused. We often feel the rational mind is the intelligent one, that it knows all about how we should feel and what we should do and what we should believe in and what is right and wrong. The emotional reality isn't that way. Fear, anxiety, worry, despair, jealousy, envy, unworthiness, self-disparagement, anger, resentment, indignation, grief, greed, sexual desire, lust—all these aren't rational or sensible, but they are part of what being human is about. Our emotional world is like this. It is not reasonable or rational. But it is sensitive. And so our relationship to sensitivity is not judgmental or denigrating or resisting, but receiving. So this is where the intuitive awareness is the refuge. And this is what we all need to learn.

Sometimes we wonder why we are the way we are. We are brought up in a society which is competitive, comparing yourself, "He's better than I am" or "I'm better than you are" and that kind of thing. This is the result of comparing ourselves with standards, principles, and with each other. I remember as a teenager especially, the opinion of others was so important, you became obsessed with how you looked and whether people liked you. You developed a sense of envy for those who seemed to have it all, and you looked down on those who just don't fit anywhere, the ones that everybody ignores or makes fun of. That's a crime. As I remember my teenage years, they were horrible. I felt it was a dreadful experience. This then is what we learn from them, about the way we are. We may not be the way we want, but the way we are—that is obvious. We learn this from the physical body: from the way the body is, whether it is tall or short, male or female, light or dark, beautiful or plain, big nose or little nose, blue eyes or brown eyes, healthy or sick, strong or weak.

"Why couldn't I be born strong, healthy, handsome, intelligent, have the best of everything, have the best equipment to start life with?" But you learn from the way you are. So I found in living this life, in meditation, it is a waste of time to envy others, to wish we were like somebody else. That's useless. So whatever way you are—there is no standard or ideal way you should be—I encourage you to see that the path, the way to liberation, is through awareness. Not through trying to make yourself fit into some ideal or trying to become like somebody else, or feel that you have to prove yourself in our competitive society, or feel that you can't do it. But if you do compare or judge yourself like this, then observe *that*. Be aware of this sense of "I'm better than you" or "I'm inferior" or even "we're just the same."

Also acknowledge the centerpoint of the turning world. Whatever impinges on you, whether you are sitting, standing, walking, lying down, tired or rested, happy or sad, succeeding or failing—whatever way the world goes or changes—there is still the centerpoint, there is still the point of knowing. Buddho is this centerpoint and knows the Dhamma. It is through this reflecting and remembering, because it is so easy to fall back into old patterns and habits. Even though they are bad habits and we know they are not good for us, we are still used to them. So we can find ourselves falling back into ways of thinking and acting that we know are harmful, but it is easy to do it because we are used to thinking like that or acting like that. That is why on that level we can feel a sense of despair and hopelessness with ourselves.

We think we would like to get out of these traps of the mind, and we try and then we fail, and then we make judgments. But that sense of "I shouldn't feel like this, shouldn't have these habits. I've got to get rid of this, got to become like that"—that whole process can be witnessed. So with the Second Noble Truth, we can have insight into desire and attachment—into kāma-taṇhā (sensual desire), bhava-taṇhā (desire for becoming), and vibhava-taṇhā (wanting to get rid of) of the Second Noble Truth—and with that insight we have this sense of letting go. The insight into letting go—and again, I repeat, letting go is not resisting or getting rid of but *letting it be what it is*. So this is where the Four Noble Truths are helpful. Referring to them gives you a formula or a structure, not as something to grasp but as a reminder to yourself, because the tendency is to forget and to get caught up in the old patterns, or to feel despair about your meditation or believe that you can only really meditate under ideal conditions or special situations.

I've traveled a lot in the past twenty years, all over the world. When you are traveling you have to wait in line to go through customs and immigration, wait in line for your baggage—a lot of waiting. So I've developed this into meditation practice. When I first started traveling I could see that when I got into a line, like waiting for them to check my passport, there was something in me that just wanted to get through, get this over with, get inside the departure lounge, and then I'd feel impatient and wonder whether I got in the right line or not, because the one that looked longer is now shorter and somebody in front is holding up my line. So a kind of resentment and restlessness would develop. It could be quite a miserable situation because the main thing was to get through and meet the people who had invited me.

I began to reflect on this restlessness and impatience. I started regarding being in line as a meditation, and I watched. Now I can observe these tendencies of mine such as disliking the bureaucracy of immigration or wanting to get out of a plane as soon as possible to meet people. I quite like the whole process, going to Heathrow airport, and just seeing what happens. Now that I'm old and well known, they upgrade me. But this is just one example of how to take something that is a necessity like traveling, such as waiting for your bag to appear on the carousel, and contemplating it. Only one time in all these years has my bag ever been the first one to surface and that was at Shannon airport.

So I would get the trolley and move to the carousel, it would start, and as the bags would start popping up. I would contemplate the moment when I saw my bag for the first time. There was a kind of happiness in that, a kind of relief, because there was always the thought that maybe they didn't put it on the plane or they sent it off somewhere else, and would it really appear? So just noticing that relief, quite a happy moment, when you spot your bag on the carousel.

It's like that, as you gain confidence in awareness, in this connected awareness. That is the easiest way, by noticing awareness and using it as a reference point, by learning to sustain attention and to recognize it everywhere you go. At first I could observe it when things were quiet and still. It was difficult in noisy places or traffic jams, in airport lines, in meetings and conferences, and when talking to somebody, listening to music, or whatever. But then you begin to recognize that awareness underlies everything all the time.

What I found is that this reference point is very practical and useful because it is always available. It does take determination to keep noticing it until you recognize it wherever you are—whatever is happening, whatever your state of mind or however your body feels, here and now—and then developing that. I would use mala beads, and then think *Buddho,* and listen to the sound of silence, enter the silence, the stillness. I'd do maybe five or six beads and just for that time sustain that stillness, that sound of silence, not trying to do all 108 beads. You are not trying to be perfect, but you are acting in a way that develops stillness, like counting to five. I listen to the sound of silence and count "one, two, three, four, five." So this is a skillful means, or upāya, to become more confident in sustaining awareness.

You can use it with the breath also, or when doing walking meditation. Determine to walk from this point to that point in stillness; the awareness is then all-embracing. The sound of silence isn't a sound that blots out anything or hides anything. It actually allows everything to be what it is. So even with the chanting, when I do the pūjā, when I'm chanting *namo tassa bhagavato,* I'm in the stillness. Before I'd developed that I'd be wandering all over the place. I'd be chanting *namo tassa bhagavato arahato* fast, because the chanting itself was also a habit. After learning it, you memorize it, and then you didn't have to think about it. You chanted but you'd be thinking about something else or wanting to get the chanting over with so you could sit. Being in this stillness also allows the words themselves to permeate consciousness, so that *namo tassa bhagavato* is no longer a perfunctory chant. You register this as a beautiful thing, to be able to think, "Homage to the blessed, noble, perfectly, enlightened one, *bhagavato ara-hato sammā-sambuddhassa.*" These are beautiful thoughts, beautiful concepts, and they are in the stillness of the mind rather than just sounds you are making while you are thinking of something else.

These are ways that I've developed to integrate awareness into the flow of life, wherever I am. And then I can see, I can be aware of, the subtleties of feeling and mental experience because there is this incredible space, this infinity of awareness. You can then feel the subtle movement of restlessness or the arising of something. You have a way of beginning to tune into the energies of the body more, just the subtle energies of your own body, and your assumptions and attitudes. It's a way to get beyond cultural conditioning. We acquire so much of it in early childhood, whole cultural attitudes and assumptions that are part of the conditioning process. Where can one get beyond one's cultural conditioning? In this stillness, in this silence, which is not cultural and not conditioned by anything, yet is fully conscious and intelligent. It is not a dull, stupid state. I don't go into a trance or disappear into a void. I am fully present. There is this sense of presence, consciousness, and then this discerning, like the Buddha's Dhamma, the wisdom faculty begins to not just think "all conditions are impermanent" but knows that.

A condition, whether it is subtle or coarse, mental or physical, sensual, emotional, intellectual, personal or impersonal, good or bad, one has a relationship to it of knowing it rather than becoming or judging or resisting or fighting. In the context of daily life, we have a sense of responsibility for living in the society. The usual advice "Do good and refrain from doing bad," is the commonsense approach. It doesn't mean that the bad isn't Dhamma, or that anything bad is you, but it is what it is. The trust is in this intuition, so that your response to specific events and contingencies that arise comes from awareness and compassion, and spontaneity. This way one can respond to the specific events or the daily routine, it is not just based on idealism anymore, or a kind of clutching through moral precepts in a personal way.

In the Noble Eightfold Path, right speech, right action, and right livelihood come from right view. This means that with right view you can respond appropriately to the contingencies and the routine of daily life, family life, working life, monastic life, or whatever life you are living. You begin to integrate it into your life as you live it. Don't put Buddha-Dhamma on a pillar on a shrine and worship it there. A shrine, like a Buddha-rūpa in a temple, is merely for reminding, for reflection, not for your projections. I was involved in the process of having the Buddha-rūpa in this temple cast and was quite interested in the process. In Thailand casting is still done in the ancient way, and so I was involved in the whole process. It was fascinating to watch—they do it beautifully. There is a ceremony at the end to inaugurate the image. During the process the mold is placed in the ground and then molten bronze is poured into it. In Thailand women will take quite valuable gold necklaces or bracelets and put them in this pot where all the gold melts, which is very moving to see, or they give you gold to put in, and it melts and you pour it into the top of the head of the Buddha-rūpa. Some laypeople from England also contributed their old wedding bands.

This is an old custom, but it is quite beautiful to see. For this Buddha-rūpa, first they made a small model in wax and then asked you if something should be different—the robes, the mouth, the nose, anything like that. If you said that the nose should be a little bigger or the mouth a little different, they were quite willing to change it. Then it was brought here and put on the shrine in the temple. I had this sense, when I sat in front of it, that it was judging me in some way, this enormous golden Buddha. At first I felt like it was criticizing me because I can never be as good as I imagine I should be, even after all these years. Then I read in the scriptures about this monk and the Buddha would say, "foolish monk," and I always imagine this refers to me.

I noticed my reaction. Why do I have to look at this Buddha-rūpa that way? Actually what the Buddha-rūpa is doing is blessing me all the time. When I sit in front of it now, the centerpoint in the temple, the Buddha is always blessing me—once I changed the way I looked at it. Now that is a reflection. It is just a bronze image and so forth, but we have a choice about how we look at things. We are not condemned to respond always in the same way to situations. The Buddha is a blessing, the Buddha is blessing us, and this awareness then is a blessing. When you trust in awareness, your life is a blessing rather than a disaster or a curse. So you begin to change from the self-conscious, self-critical, fear-ridden, anxiety-ridden, worried individual to someone who is blessed by life just by being conscious and aware. Then everything is within a state of blessedness.

It is worth remembering this because it is so easy to fall back into the self-conscious, self-disparaging fears and anxieties, the habit patterns of the conditioned world. This awareness gives me this sense of being blessed. Even the body, the way I am. It is no longer a critical mind making value judgments, moral judgments about me as a person, but it is a blessing. This is where the devotional side develops, because the personality is conditioned to be critical, self-conscious, and threatened. Awareness transcends that. It is no longer the way that I choose to experience consciousness through misery, suffering, and ignorance. So the awakening or the ability to awaken, what we have been doing here, paying attention, observing, witnessing, this is a blessed state of being, a natural state, in which even the defects or the sickness or the disabilities or the tragedies or the complications of life are no longer the obsessions that we obsess our consciousness with anymore. So that we aren't ruining our lives with regret, guilt, fear, grief, hatred, delusion, as we would if we had no insight.

TOWARD THE FUTURE

THIS IS THE LAST day the mind can start to think about the future. So just reflect on the results of having been here for the past ten days, not in a critical way in terms of good, bad, or whatever but as the way it is. This moment here and now, the formal meditation retreat, the eight precepts, the three refuges, the meditation, the schedule we have been following, what you have been hearing from me, what has been affecting you. At this moment there is the result, just this recognition, the way it is—a listening, an observing, not a statement about how good, bad, peaceful, or confused you are. These are value judgments again, some kind of conceived opinion or value judgment rather than just being the receiver, the way it is.

Reflecting on time, the future, the unknown: you go home today, tomorrow you go to work, but these things haven't happened yet. This is not a memory, this is possibility, an expectation, an anticipation. But these are mental states we create in the here and now. Expectation or anticipation is like this. You may be dreading tomorrow or you may have hopes. In terms of this moment here and now, tomorrow is the unknown. So there is a knowing, a knowing of not-knowing. Or knowing a mental state like anticipating or expecting or assuming that tomorrow will be something or other. So these projections into the future are all mental formations we create in the present.

The past is a memory, so the memories of this retreat are just memories. Memories come and go, very ephemeral when you notice memory. Remembering is a condition that arises and ceases. It has no core or substance. So the past is a memory. We remember the past, the human mind is like this. We have retentive memory so we can remember things that have happened many years ago. Some people lose their memories: they are still conscious, but all the security that comes through believing and depending on memories is gone. Resting and being present is liberation—here and now. It is not about memory or the past or future. I have gained a lot of insight through contemplating time. Here and now, what is yesterday? A memory. So I'm just pointing to the way it is. I'm not denying or judging anything I remember about yesterday. I'm not making anything out of it. I'm just recognizing memory in terms of Dhamma.

Exploring this in terms of relating to other people: I'll be returning to a branch monastery at Chithurst—but what is Chithurst right now? It is a memory, isn't it? A perception. I remember "Chithurst." I have a long history with Chithurst, many memories about moving there and about the derelict house and all the things that have happened over twenty-five years. But in terms of this moment, the reality of this moment, Chithurst and my memories about it are just that, memories. When you explore memories, you stop believing in them so strongly and you no longer live in their world, assuming all kinds of things from just remembering. Paññā in this sense is being aware of the way it is, rather than holding views, opinions, and emotional reactions to memories. Or, applying this to people: like where is your mother right now?

That term "mother" is a memory that arises. I remember
when my mother died thirteen or fourteen years ago. When the
perception of mother comes up I have memories of her and her
death. Even if your mother is still alive, in this moment when
you're remembering your mother, is she in London or in Edin-
burgh? In this moment that is a perception, a memory. In terms
of the relative moment, that is a perception, that is not mother,
that's a memory. So we are investigating the way it is, the five
khandhas. We live in a world of illusion, remembering things
and thinking we know people because we have memories of
them. In the reality of this moment, what we remember of them
is an ephemeral condition of the mind that arises and ceases in
the present. So if we have unpleasant memories or unfortunate
experiences with somebody, and then we hear the name of
this person, the memory starts—"difficult, impossible, stubborn,
can't get along with that person." What you are looking at is
a memory of that person, *not* that person. You remember that
person as stubborn and difficult, but that is a memory that arises
in the present.

You then anticipate meeting this person: "Oh, we're going to
meet tomorrow. It's going to be difficult." This anticipation is in
the present. I have to have a meeting tomorrow and I know there
is going to be trouble, and so I am anticipating difficulties. That
is the way it is—anticipation, expectation, hope, dreading, and all
that—not dismissing it but putting it in the context of Dhamma,
establishing a sense of pure presence, paccuppanna-dhamma, here
and now. When you actually meet the person, you are with the
person, one to one. And if you trust in awareness in the present,
then you are not seeing the person through memory. If I form an
opinion about you and then meet you, I tend to have this opinion and my reaction to you is from a memory. So I am looking

at you through a distortion rather than receiving you as you are in the present.

When I go back to my kuṭi and remember somebody, that is not a person, is it? It is a memory. So this way of reflecting helps to break down the illusion that people are permanently what we think. If we see through this, then we can relate to others through mindfulness rather than reactivity, prejudice, biases, assumptions. The five khandhas—rūpa, vedanā, saññā, saṅkhārā, viññāṇa—are a very skillful means that the Buddha uses, an upāya, for investigation. Sometimes they are called five "heaps." I rather like that term. A heap of rūpa (form), a heap of vedanā (feeling). A heap isn't even organized, is it? It's not nicely arranged in an efficient way like on your computer. When you think of a heap you think of a heap of this and a heap of that, a pile of something, so in this way it is like the world of infinite variety. What is in a heap can be all kinds of things, how big the heap is and all the different things that can be in one heap... One just gets lost if one gets thrown into the heap, so if you spend your life trying to sort out each heap, you just get confused, it's hopeless.

It's like counting the sand grains in the Ganges River, trying to sort everything out on that level of the differences, the varieties, the subtlety, the coarseness, the microscopic, the macroscopic. The human individual is just incapable of handling that, only a God can do that. The Buddha used the handful of leaves as another metaphor. He is not handing us heaps and heaps of Dhamma. We would be overwhelmed, smothered under the heap; just a handful of saṅkhāras. The five khandhas, five leaves— we can manage that. And if you reflect, you know that the five categories are ways of dividing up what you see, different ways of looking at the same thing. "All saṅkhārās are impermanent" is a reflection, so all the five khandhas in nature are impermanent in terms of the present moment.

The six *āyatanas* (sense bases) are another way of looking at the senses: what we see, hear, smell, taste, touch, think. So we are seeing the Dhamma, the Buddha's teachings, as skillful means to investigate experience in the present: the infinite variety of feelings, perceptions, and thoughts; the four elements of earth, fire, water, and wind; permutations and variations on all the sankhāras. As a human individual we can't do all this, it is just too much to bear, so we are specializing in one little aspect of an aspect. The point of Dhamma, of awareness in the present, is not getting involved in sorting out all the sankhāras, comparing them and judging them and lining them up, filing them away—that's like counting all the sand grains in the Ganges. Now, if you have ever been to the Ganges, you know there is so much sand that even a cubic inch of it would be impossible to manage. Trying to count all those grains would be pointless, a waste of your life. "How many sand grains are in that river?" Ridiculous. We don't need to know that. We don't need to know everything about everything.

Knowing the way it is in terms of Dhamma—so this sabbe sankhārā aniccā, all conditions are impermanent—simplifies it. Or the five khandhas, the six āyatanas, these are just ways of reflecting on this moment by pointing to the body, to the sensitivity through feelings, perceptions, mental formations, and consciousness. Consciousness, viññāṇa, is the most interesting one of the whole lot because we experience it through ignorance, through avijjā. Consciousness then is through perceiving, through attachment, through memory, through identity with the other four khandhas. We are conscious through rūpa, vedanā, saññā, sankhāra. Usually we are conscious through attachment, so we tend to see things through memory, habit, through attachment to the body.

We just assume without question that we *are* our bodies: "I am this body and everything about it, its age, gender, height, size, color, appearance, is all me." We never look into this. This is avijjā, ignorance. We operate from this unquestioned conditioning that "this body is me." With vipassanā we investigate what the body is, right at this moment, rather than forming opinions or adopting views. "Well, the Buddha said the body is not self, so I believe that it is not self." That is imposing an idea on the moment. "The Buddha said it was true and I believe it: this body is not mine." But then you are not really investigating, not really seeing. You are grasping Buddhist ideas, and that is not liberating.

Investigation, yoniso manasikāra, is observing the way it is. That is why in *kāyānupassanā satipaṭṭhāna,* contemplation of the body, we bring the body into consciousness, being aware of it as an experience here and now: the postures of sitting, standing, walking, and lying down; the breath; heat and cold; pleasurable, painful, and neutral sensations. I remember when I first started with this practice it was much easier for me to go over to the library and look at a book on human anatomy with color pictures and diagrams showing the muscles, nerves, organs, liver, spleen. It was much easier. I was conditioned to look in books. But we want to realize that the liver and the spleen, the skeleton, the blood, the heart, the brain, are *in here,* something going on right now.

Education makes one depend on charts and graphs and illustrations, to see reality by looking at something out there rather than trusting in the awareness of this physical body as like this. Those pictures in the anatomy book, what are they pointing to? Something that I am experiencing now. So, trying to objectify my liver at this moment, I assume it's there. But its not on that level that we are working, to feel each organ in terms of the words that we have for them like "liver," "pancreas," "intestine," and so forth, but to use awareness as a means of reflecting on the reality of the limitation of this human form, this body, as we experience it in the present—experience it through being conscious of it now. So use the four postures and the breath to tune in to your body and observe it in a totally different way, this is my body, or even from a position of vanity. This is what we call sati-sampajañña, this attention in the present is an intuitive awareness that includes everything. The body is like *this* at this moment. Using the Pāli word *rūpa* for the body is a way of remembering. This Pāli word brings my attention to the body as I experience it now: the pressure of sitting here, the way the thumb of my right hand is touching, slightly grasping, the fourth finger on the left.

So what is it that is aware of the body as experience right now? Can my body see itself, can my right hand see my left hand, or what is it that is aware? At this moment I can be aware of the right hand, the left hand, and both together, or the whole body or a part of the body. Consciousness embraces the whole of this body, and if we recognize that, then we begin to notice the different physical conditions, feelings. So this consciousness, it's viññāṇa. When we are born, we are conscious through a form. At the birth of a baby, it is separate; the umbilical cord is cut. It is a separate form that is conscious. We don't create this consciousness. It is not an artificial experience, it is natural. Consciousness isn't self. We might want to say "my consciousness," but that is memory again. Consciousness is like this; then intuitive awareness puts us in the position of recognizing that consciousness is knowing. It has this measureless, immeasurable sense. It has no boundary. In this moment if you are just aware then consciousness is operating, you are not binding the experience to a particular form.

This is where it is important to recognize pure awareness, consciousness, and paññā, wisdom, discerning the way it is. After we are born the conditioning process starts, and we operate from habits and from ignorance, avijjā. Vipassanā meditation is using consciousness with wisdom. This is what the Buddha was pointing to. This is the reality of consciousness. We are all conscious, and that consciousness is not personal, not "my consciousness" or uniquely "mine," unless I think that and grasp that kind of illusion. But this is a conscious universe, isn't it?

The universe is one, the whole universe is conscious, and this is the reality of consciousness. It includes everything. But we are coming out of ignorance, our experience of consciousness is restricted to memory and conditioning. So we see ourselves as separate and confined to the particular habits and perceptions that we acquired after being born.

This retreat is about breaking out of that illusion. It is like informing consciousness with paññā, wisdom. Luang Por Chah used the word *obrom,* which means to inform, to teach the way it is through awareness and wisdom—so that we do not operate from the conditioned thinking and perception we have acquired through avijjā. If we do not understand things as they are, if we are not awake, we create illusions and then believe in them. And this means there is always something missing, something wrong, something lacking, something amiss, and we take that personally. We can see how there is something wrong with ourselves or wrong with the world. "Why can't we live in harmony and do away with war?" We have these ideals. "Wouldn't it be nice if...?" Wouldn't it be nice if everything were nice. But on the conditioned level, how can you demand everything be nice because niceness is dependent on conditions. To feel nice, you have to have certain conditions for that feeling.

So the saṅkhāras, saṃsāra, the conditioned realm is like this. It is basically an irritation, having a human body. We are born into a form that is going to be irritated until it dies. I hope this doesn't depress you. How long can you sit in comfort without feeling hungry or thirsty, or how much of our life is spent trying to reduce irritation? This arises from being limited to having this physical body. How can you control life so that only nice things impinge on it, because inevitably we have to deal with not-nice things too? Conditions are what they are, but they have that range of pleasure to pain, that whole range from the best to the worst in terms of the quality that we experience in the present. So when you reflect in this way, it is not worth trying to make everything nice all the time because inevitably you will fail. It is like trying to do something totally impossible, so why do it? Awakening and reflecting is the way of liberation—seeing things as they are, informing consciousness through wisdom, through paññā, rather than merely being a helpless victim of your conditioning.

NOT LOOKING FOR ANSWERS,
NOT ASKING FOR FAVORS

I USED TO HATE feeling confused. I loved having a sense of certainty and mental clarity. Whenever I felt confused by anything, I'd try to find some kind of clear answer, to get rid of the emotional state of confusion. I'd distract myself from it or try to get somebody else to give me the answer. I wanted authorities and Ajahns, the big guys, to come and say, "That's right, that's wrong, that's good, that's bad." I wanted to be clear and needed somebody, an authority figure that I trusted and respected, to straighten me out.

Sometimes we think that good teachers, meditation retreats, the precepts, the refuges, or a wonderful Sangha are going to make us really happy and solve all our problems. We reach out for help, hoping this thing or that will do it for us. It's like wanting God to come and help us out of our mess. And then when He doesn't come and solve our problems, we don't believe in God anymore. "I asked Him to help and He didn't." This is a childlike way of looking at life. We get ourselves into trouble and expect mommy and daddy to come and save the day, to clean up the mess we've made.

Years ago, I became very confused when I found out that one of our American Buddhist nuns had left our community and become a born-again Christian. I had just said to another nun, "She's really wonderful. She's so wise, so purehearted. She'll be a great inspiration to you in your nun's life." I was really embarrassed and confused when I heard the news. I thought, "How could she fall for it?" I remember asking my teacher, Ajahn Chah, "How could she do that?" He looked at me with a mischievous smile and said, "Maybe she's right." He made me look at what I was doing—feeling defensive and paranoid, wanting a clear explanation, wanting to understand, wanting him to tell me that she'd betrayed the Buddhist religion. So I started looking at the confusion. When I began to embrace it and totally accept it, it dropped away. Through acknowledging the emotional confusion, it ceased being a problem; it seemed to dissolve into thin air. I became aware of how much I resisted confusion as an experience.

In meditation, we can notice these difficult states of mind: not knowing what to do next or feeling confused about our practice, ourselves, or life. In our practice we do not try to get rid of these mind states but simply acknowledge what they feel like: this is uncertainty and insecurity; this is grief and anguish; this is depression, worry, and anxiety; this is fear, aversion, guilt, remorse. We might try to make the case that if we were healthy normal people we wouldn't have these emotions. But the idea of a normal person is a fantasy of the mind. Do you know any really normal people? I don't.

The Buddha spoke instead of one who listens, who pays attention, who is awake, who is attentive here and now, whose mind is open and receptive and trusts in the present moment and in oneself. This is his encouragement to us. Our attitude toward meditation need not be one of striving to get rid of our defilements, our *kilesas,* our faults, in order to become something better. It should be one of opening up, paying attention to life, experiencing the here and now, and trusting in our ability to receive life as experience. We don't have to do anything with it. We don't have to straighten out all the crooked parts, solve every problem, justify everything, or make everything better. After all, there will always be something wrong when we're living in the conditioned realm: something wrong with me, with the people I live with, with the monastery, with the retreat center, with the country. Conditions are always changing; we will never find any permanent perfection. We may experience a peak moment when everything is wonderful and just the way we want it, but we can't sustain the conditions of that moment. We can't live at the peak point of inhalation; we have to exhale.

The same applies to all the good things of life—happy times, loving relationships, success, good fortune. These things are certainly enjoyable and not to be despised, but we shouldn't put our faith in something that is in the process of changing. Once it reaches a peak, it can only go in the other direction. We're asked not to take refuge in wealth, other people, countries or political systems, relationships, nice houses or good retreat centers. Instead, we're asked to take refuge in our own ability to be awake, to pay attention to life no matter what the conditions might be in the present moment. The simple willingness to acknowledge things for what they are—as changing conditions—liberates us from being caught in the power of attachment, in struggling with the emotions or thoughts that we're experiencing.

Notice how difficult it is when you're trying to resist things, trying to get rid of bad thoughts, emotional states, or pain. What is the result of resisting? When I try to get rid of what I don't like in my mind, I become obsessed by it. What about you? Think of somebody you really can't stand, someone who really hurts your feelings. The very conditions of feeling angry and resentful actually obsess our minds with that particular person. We make a big deal out of it, pushing, pushing, pushing. The more we push, the more obsessed we become.

Try this out in your meditation. Notice what you don't like, don't want, hate, or are frightened of. When you resist these things, you're actually empowering them, giving them tremendous influence and power over your conscious experience. But when you welcome them and open up to the flow of life in both its good and bad aspects, what happens? I know from my experience that when I'm accepting and welcoming of conditioned experience, things drop away from me. They come in and they go away. We're actually opening the door, letting in all the fear, anxiety, worry, resentment, anger, and grief. This doesn't mean that we have to approve of or like what's happening.

It's not about making moral judgments. It's simply about acknowledging the presence of whatever we're experiencing in a welcoming way—not trying to get rid of it by resisting it, holding on to it, or identifying with it. When we're totally accepting of something as it exists in the present, then we can begin to recognize the cessation of those conditions.

The freedom from suffering that the Buddha talked about isn't in itself an end to pain and stress. Instead it's a matter of creating a choice. I can either get caught up in the pain that comes to me, attach to it, and be overwhelmed, or I can embrace it with acceptance and understanding, not add more suffering to the existing pain, the unfair experiences, the criticisms or the misery that I face. Even after his enlightenment, the Buddha experienced all kinds of horrendous things. His cousin tried to murder him, people tried to frame him, blame him, and criticize him. He experienced severe physical illness. But the Buddha didn't create suffering around those experiences. His response was never one of anger, resentment, hatred, or blame, but one of acknowledgment.

This has been a really valuable thing for me to know. It's taught me not to ask for favors in life or to hope that if I meditate a lot I can avoid unpleasant experiences. "God, I've been a monk for thirty-three years. Please reward me for being a good boy." I've tried that and it doesn't work. To accept life without making pleas is very liberating, because I no longer feel a need to control or manipulate conditions for my own benefit. I don't need to worry or feel anxious about my future. There's a sense of trust and confidence, a fearlessness that comes through learning to trust, to relax, to open to life, and to investigate experience rather than to resist or be frightened by it. If you're willing to learn from the suffering in life, you'll discover the unshakability of your own mind.

APPENDIX

The talks in this book were given on the following dates.

GLOSSARY

THE FOLLOWING WORDS are mostly Pāli, the language of the Theravāda Buddhist scriptures (Tipiṭaka). They are brief translations for quick reference, rather than exhaustive or refined definitions.

Abhidhamma: Analytical doctrine of the Buddhist Pāli canon.

Ajahn: (Thai) Teacher; from the Pāli *ācariya:* in the Amarāvatī community, a bhikkhu or *sīladharā* who has completed ten rains retreats *(vassa).*

Akāliko: Timeless.

Amata: Deathless.

Anāgāmi: "Non-returner," the third stage on the path to nibbāna.

Ānāpānasati: Mindfulness of breathing.

Anattā: Literally, "not-self, no-self, non-self," i.e., impersonal, without individual essence; neither a person nor belonging to a person. One of the three characteristics of conditioned phenomena.

Aniccā: Transient, impermanent, unstable, having the nature to arise and pass away. One of the three characteristics of conditioned phenomena.

Arahant: A fully enlightened person; according to the Pāli canon, the fourth stage on the path.

Ārammaṇa: Mental objects; in Thai usage, also mood, emotion.

Ariya: Noble.

Asubha: Non-beautiful. *Asubha-kammaṭṭhāna* is a practice that involves contemplating the various unattractive parts of the body.

Attā: Literally, "self," i.e., the ego, personality.

Attakilamathānuyoga: Self-mortification, self-torture.

Avijjā: Ignorance, not-knowing, delusion.

Avijjā-paccayā saṅkhārā: Ignorance as a condition for mental formations.

Bhava: Becoming.

Bhāvanā: Meditation or mental cultivation.

Bhikkhu: A fully ordained Buddhist monk.

Bodhisattva: (Sanskrit) Literally, "one who is intent on full enlightenment." Enlightenment is delayed so that all the virtues *(pāramī)* are developed and innumerable sentient beings are saved, as taught in the Mahāyāna school.

Brahmā: A being in the highest heavenly realms.

Brahma-loka: Highest heavenly realms.

Buddha-rūpa: Statue of the Buddha.

Buddho: The awakened one, the one who knows, the knowing.

Chao Khun: (Thai) Ecclesiastic title from the king of Thailand.

Citta: Mind or heart.

Cittānupassanā: Mindfulness of the mind or mood.

Dantā: Teeth.

Desanā: A talk on the teachings of the Buddha.

Deva, devatā: Heavenly being, angel.

Devadūta: Literally, "heavenly messenger." There are four such messengers: old age, sickness, death, and a renunciant.

Deva-loka: Heavenly realm.

Dhamma: The teaching of the Buddha as contained in the scriptures; not dogmatic in character, but more like a raft or vehicle to convey the disciple to deliverance. Also the truth and reality toward which that teaching points; that which is beyond words, concepts, or intellectual understanding.

Dhamma-Vinaya: The teachings and monastic discipline.

Dhutaṅga: Special renunciant observances, ascetic practices.

Dosa: Hatred.

Dukkha: Literally, "hard to bear." Dis-ease, discontent, or suffering, anguish, conflict, unsatisfactoriness. One of the three characteristics of conditioned phenomena.

Dzogchen: Natural Great Perfection, the highest teaching of Tibetan Buddhism.

Ehipassiko: Encouraging investigation, inviting to come and see.

Ekaggatā: One-pointedness, singleness, unification.

Farang: (Thai) Foreigner, Westerner.

Hīnayāna: Literally, "lesser vehicle." A term coined by Mahāyāna Buddhists for a group of earlier Buddhist schools. One of the three major Buddhist traditions: see *Theravāda*.

Idappaccayatā: The law of conditionality: "because of this, that arises."

Jāti: Birth.

Jhāna: Meditative absorptions; deep states of rapture, joy, and one-pointedness.

Kāmarāga-carita: A lustful, greedy temperament.

Kāmasukhallikānuyoga: Sensual indulgence.

Kāma-taṇhā: Sensual desire.

Kamma: Action or cause which is created by habitual impulses, volitions, intentions. In popular usage it often includes the result or effect of the action, although the proper term for this is *vipāka*.

Kamma-vipāka: The "effect" or result or fruition of kamma.

Karuṇā: Compassion.

Kāyānupassanā: Mindfulness of the body.

Kesā: Hair of the head.

Khandha: Group, aggregate, heap—the term the Buddha used to refer to each of the five components of human psycho-physical existence (form, feelings, perceptions, mental formations, sense consciousness).

Kilesa: Defilements; unwholesome qualities that cloud the mind.

Kuṭi: Hut; typical abode of a forest bhikkhu.

Lobha: Greed.

Lokavidū: "Knower of the world." An epithet of the Buddha.

Lomā: Hair of the body.

Luang Por: (Thai) Literally, "revered father." Title of respect and affection for an elder monk and teacher.

Magga: Path.

Mahāyāna: One of the three major Buddhist traditions. It lays particular emphasis on altruism, compassion, and realization of "emptiness" as essentials for full awakening.

Majjhimā paṭipadā: The Middle Way.

Mettā: "Loving-kindness," one of the Sublime Abidings.

Moha: Delusion.

Muditā: Sympathetic joy, rejoicing in others' success.

Nakhā: Nails.

Nibbāna: Literally, "extinguishing of a fire." Freedom from attachments, quenching, coolness. The basis for the enlightened vision of things as they are.

Nibbidā: Disenchantment, world-weariness, turning away.

Nirodha: Cessation.

Opanayiko: Leading inward or onward, applicable.

Paccattaṃ veditabbo viññūhi: To be realized for yourself.

Paccuppanna-dhamma: What has arisen just now, present-moment phenomena.

Pāli: The ancient Indian language of the Theravāda Pāli canon, akin to Sanskrit. The collection of texts preserved by the Theravāda school and, by extension, the language in which those texts are composed.

Paññā: Discriminative wisdom, discernment.

Papañca: Mental proliferation, conceptual proliferation, complication.

Paramattha-dhamma: Ultimate reality.

Paramattha-sacca: Ultimate truth.

Pāramī: "Perfection." The ten perfections in Theravāda Buddhism for realizing Buddhahood are giving, morality, renunciation, wisdom, energy, patience, truthfulness, determination, loving-kindness, and equanimity.

Pariyatti: Study, from a conceptual point of view, particularly of the Buddhist scriptures.

Paṭiccasamuppāda: "Dependent origination." It explains the way psychophysical phenomena come into being in dependence on one another.

Paṭipadā: "Way, path"; putting the teachings into practice.

Paṭipatti: The practice.

Paṭivedha: The realization of the Dhamma.

Pen paccattaṃ: (Thai) Something that you realize for yourself.

Phra: (Thai) Venerable; a monk. Respectful title.

Piṇḍapāta: Alms food; or the alms round on which the food is received.

Pūjā: A devotional offering, chanting, bowing, etc.

Rūpa: Form or matter. The physical elements that make up the body, i.e., earth, water, fire, and wind (solidity, cohesion, temperature, and motion or vibration).

Sakadāgāmī: Once-returner.

Sakkāya-diṭṭhi: Personality view. Self-view.

Sālā: A hall, usually where the monastics eat their food and other ceremonies are held.

Samādhi: Meditative concentration, collectedness.

Samaṇa: Renunciant, contemplative (term for ordained monks or nuns).

Samatha: Calm.

Sammā: right. From the Noble Eightfold Path: *sammā-diṭṭhi:* right understanding; *sammā-saṅkappo:* right intention; *sammā-vācā:* right speech; *sammā-kammanto:* right action; *sammā-ājīvo:* right livelihood; *sammā-vāyāmo:* right effort; *sammā-sati:* right mindfulness; *sammā-samādhi:* right concentration.

Saṃsāra-vaṭṭa: The circle of birth and death.

Samudaya: Origin.

Saṃyojana: Literally, "fetters"; the ten obstacles to liberation.

Sandiṭṭhiko: Apparent here and now.

Sangha: The community of those who practice the Buddha's way. More specifically, those who have formally committed themselves to the lifestyle of a mendicant monk or nun.

Saṅkhārā: Mental formations. Conditioned phenomena in general.

Saññā: Perception.

Sati: Mindfulness, awareness.

Sati-paññā: Literally, "mindfulness and wisdom."

Satipaṭṭhāna: The four foundations of mindfulness (body, feelings, mind, mental phenomena).

Sati-sampajañña: Literally, "mindfulness and clear understanding." Also intuitive awareness, apperception.

Sīla: Moral virtue, also used to refer to the precepts of moral conduct.

Sīlabbata-parāmāsa: Attachment to rites and rituals, clinging to precepts and practices.

Sīladharā: "One who upholds virtue," a term used for Buddhist nuns ordained by Ajahn Sumedho.

Soka-parideva-dukkha-domanassupāyāsā: Literally, "sorrow, lamentation, pain, grief, and despair."

Sotāpanna: Literally, "stream enterer"; a person that is definitely on the path to nibbāna.

Sotāpatti: stream entry.

Sutta: Discourse of the Buddha or one of his disciples.

Suññatā: Literally, "emptiness"—see *anattā*.

Taco: Skin.

Taṇhā: Craving.

Tathā: Such, thus.

Tathāgata: Term for the Buddha. "One thus come/gone."

Tathatā: Suchness, thusness.

Theravāda: Literally, "Teaching of the Elders"; the name of the oldest form of the Buddha's teachings, the texts of which are written in the Pāli language.

Tipiṭaka: Literally, "Three baskets"—the Pāli Canon or the scriptures of the Theravāda school.

Upādāna: Grasping, clinging, attachment.

Upajjhāya: A preceptor who presides at the ordination ceremony.

Upasampadā: Higher ordination—to become a Bhikkhu. "Acceptance" into the Bhikkhu-Sangha.

Upāya: Skillful means. Using different resources to realize the teachings of the Buddha.

Upekkhā: Equanimity.

Vajrayāna: A Buddhist school that makes extensive use of symbols and mantras to convey teachings. Associated with Tibet primarily.

Vedanā: Feelings or sensations, of pleasure, pain, or neutrality.

Vibhava-taṇhā: Desire for not-being, for annihilation. Wanting to get rid of.

Vicikicchā: Doubt.

Vinaya: The monastic discipline, or the scriptural collection of its rules and commentaries on them.

Viññāṇa: Sense consciousness, cognizance.

Vipassanā: Insight meditation, "looking into things."

Viveka: Literally, "detachment" or "solitude."

Wat: (Thai) Monastery or temple.

Yāna: Literally, "vehicle." A Buddhist tradition or school.

Yoniso manasikāra: Wise reflection, "going to the roots."

INDEX

M
magga (path), 119, 342
Mahāpadhāna Sutta, 42, 221
Mahārāhulovāda Sutta, 55
Mahāyāna Buddhism, 186, 187, 205, 342
Majjhima Nikāya, 9–10
majjhimā paṭipadā (the middle way), 128, 342
Malaysia, 115
memory, 63, 115–16, 249–50, 267, 321–24
  anattā and, 87
  consciousness and, 263–64
  emotions and, 143
  mental states and, 236
  rebirth and, 214, 237–38
  the sound of silence and, 164
  suffering and, 145, 173–74
mental formations (saṅkhārā), 68, 122, 181, 283, 345
mental objects (ārammaṇa), 68, 182, 228–30, 339
mental states, awareness of, 227–36
merit, 222
metaphysics, 82, 257
mettā (loving-kindness) practice, 50–51, 102, 166, 207
  consciousness and, 258
  described, 104, 342
  rebirth and, 245
Michaël, Salim, 7
mind
  anattā and, 79–81, 83–84
  body contemplation and, 103
  dedication of offerings and, 64, 69–70
  emotions and, 134–36
  habits of the, 267–80
  identity and, 92, 97
  intuitive awareness and, 45
  mental states and, 231
  mindfulness of the (cittānupas-sanā), 4, 110, 227–36, 284, 340
  "monkey," 106, 282
  opinions and, 183–85

  the present moment and, 29, 34–35, 37, 43–44
  the sound of silence and, 163–66, 169–70
  suffering and, 156, 171–73, 176–77, 182
  trusting your intuition and, 109, 110
mindfulness, 8, 196–98, 200, 210.
  See also sati-paññā (mindfulness and wisdom); sati-sampajañña (mindfulness and clear understanding)
  anattā and, 73, 79, 85
  body contemplation and, 21, 106
  of the breath, 24–25
  conventions and, 282–83, 288
  dedication of offerings and, 65
  described, 116
  emotions and, 140–42
  four foundations of, 218
  Four Noble Truths and, 129
  intuitive awareness and, 47–48, 59
  mental states and, 227–36
  of the mind (cittānupassanā), 4, 110, 227–36, 284, 340
  opinions and, 185
  the present moment and, 37–38, 40–41
  rebirth and, 244
  the sound of silence and, 167–68
  suffering and, 175, 180
  taking refuge in awareness and, 213–24, 217–19
  trusting your intuition and, 112–13
miracle, of instruction, xi
Monet, Claude, x
monkey mind, 106, 282
morality, 217, 273, 283, 319, 334
  anattā and, 81
  emotions and, 135
  identity and, 94
  taking things personally and, 195, 203, 204
Mormons, 186–87
Muslims, 192

ABOUT THE AUTHOR

AJAHN SUMEDHO was born in Seattle, Washington, in 1934. After serving four years in the U.S. Navy as a medic, he completed a BA in Far Eastern Studies and a MA in South Asian Studies.

In 1966 he went to Thailand to practice meditation at Wat Mahathat in Bangkok. Not long afterward he went forth as a novice monk in a remote part of the country, Nong Khai, and a year of solitary practice followed; he received full ordination in 1967.

Although fruitful, the solitary practice showed him the need for a teacher who could more actively guide him. A fortuitous encounter with a visiting monk led him to Ubon Province, to practice with Venerable Ajahn Chah. He formally became a student of Venerable Ajahn Chah and remained under his close guidance for ten years. In 1975 Ajahn Sumedho established Wat Pah Nanachat, the International Forest Monastery, also in Ubon Province, where Westerners could be trained in English.

In 1977 he accompanied Ajahn Chah to England and took up residence at the Hampstead Vihāra with three other monks.

Ajahn Sumedho has ordained more than a hundred aspirants

of many nationalities and has established monasteries in England, as well as branch monasteries overseas. He is currently resident as senior incumbent at Amarāvatī Buddhist Monastery in Hertfordshire, England.

In the Buddha's Words
An Anthology of Discourses from the Pali Canon
Edited and introduced by Bhikkhu Bodhi
Foreword by the Dalai Lama

"Any amount of study or practice that helps to deepen wisdom and assist us to emerge from layers of delusion is precious. This book could contribute to this enterprise more than almost anything else in print."—Andrew Olendzki, Executive Director of the Barre Center of Buddhist Studies, in *Buddhadharma: The Practitioner's Quarterly*

The Mind and the Way
Buddhist Reflections on Life
Ajahn Sumedo

"Sumedho presents Buddhism as a way rather than a religion. A graduate of the University of California-Berkeley, a Navy fighter pilot, and a Peace Corps volunteer, the author spent ten years as a contemplative forest monk before establishing the first forest monastery in England. His book deals with the nature of suffering, and the release from it by living a virtuous life awakening the mind to the impermanence of all things. Sumedho uses traditional insight meditation practices to open the heart and mind to the path of truth; he promotes a life of nonattachment, enriched with loving kindness; a simple life of nonexcess, profound goodness, cooperation rather than competition, and the mind that transcends but does not abandon the world. The keyword is balance. With its humorous observations upon his early days in Thailand, Sumedho's work is acutely practical and easy to read."—*Library Journal*

About Wisdom Publications

Wisdom Publications is the leading publisher of classic and contemporary Buddhist books and practical works on mindfulness. To learn more about us or to explore our other books, please visit our website at wisdompubs.org or contact us at the address below.

Wisdom Publications
199 Elm Street
Somerville, MA 02144 USA

We are a 501(c)(3) organization, and donations in support of our mission are tax deductible.

Wisdom Publications is affiliated with the Foundation for the Preservation of the Mahayana Tradition (FPMT).